REA's Test Prep Books Are The Best!

(a sample of the hundreds of letters REA receives each year)

" I studied this guide exclusively and passed the [CLEP Introductory Sociology] test with 12 points to spare. "
Student, Dallas, TX

" This book was right on target with what was on the [CLEP Introductory Sociology] test. I highly advise studying it before you take the exam. "
Student, Washington, DC

" Your book was such a better value and was so much more complete than anything your competition has produced — and I have them all! "
Teacher, Virginia Beach, VA

" Compared to the other books that my fellow students had, your book was the most useful in helping me get a great score. "
Student, North Hollywood, CA

" Your book was responsible for my success on the exam, which helped me get into the college of my choice... I will look for REA the next time I need help. "
Student, Chesterfield, MO

" Just a short note to say thanks for the great support your book gave me in helping me pass the test... I'm on my way to a B.S. degree because of you! "
Student, Orlando, FL

(more on next page)

(continued from front page)

" I just wanted to thank you for helping me get a great score
on the AP U.S. History exam... Thank you for making great test preps! "
Student, Los Angeles, CA

" Your *Fundamentals of Engineering Exam* book was the absolute best
preparation I could have had for the exam, and it is one of the major
reasons I did so well and passed the FE on my first try. "
Student, Sweetwater, TN

" I used your book to prepare for the test and found that the advice and the
sample tests were highly relevant... Without using any other material, I earned
very high scores and will be going to the graduate school of my choice. "
Student, New Orleans, LA

" What I found in your book was a wealth of information sufficient to shore up
my basic skills in math and verbal... The section on analytical ability was
excellent. The practice tests were challenging and the answer explanations most
helpful. It certainly is the *Best Test Prep for the GRE!* "
Student, Pullman, WA

" I really appreciate the help from your excellent book. Please keep up
the great work. "
Student, Albuquerque, NM

" I am writing to thank you for your test preparation... your book helped me
immeasurably and I have nothing but praise for your *GRE* preparation."
Student, Benton Harbor, MI

(more on front page)

THE BEST TEST PREPARATION FOR THE

CLEP

Introduction to Educational Psychology

Raymond E. Webster, Ph.D.
Professor of Psychology
East Carolina University
Greenville, North Carolina

Research & Education Association
Visit our website at
www.rea.com

Research & Education Association
61 Ethel Road West
Piscataway, New Jersey 08854
E-mail: info@rea.com

The Best Test Preparation for the
CLEP INTRODUCTION TO
EDUCATIONAL PSYCHOLOGY EXAM

Published 2011

Printed in the United States of America

Library of Congress Control Number 2005933128

ISBN-13: 978-0-7386-0093-2
ISBN-10: 0-7386-0093-8

About the Author

Raymond E. Webster, Ph.D., is a professor of psychology at East Carolina University, where he has taught since 1983 and served as Director of Graduate Studies in School Psychology for 14 years. Dr. Webster is a licensed psychologist with specialties in School and Clinical Psychology, a nationally certified school psychologist, and a licensed school psychologist in North Carolina. In addition to his teaching duties, he has been in private practice for 22 years and served as a consultant to 15 school districts and a number of Child Protective Service agencies in North Carolina. His clinical and research areas have focused on the learning and intellectual characteristics of learning-disabled children and the effects of emotional, physical, and sexual abuse on children. He regularly teaches courses in Educational Psychology, Learning, and Psychological Testing.

Dr. Webster received his Ph.D. in Educational Psychology from the University of Connecticut, an M.S. degree in Clinical Psychology from Purdue University, and an M.A. in School Psychology from Rhode Island College. He is the author of numerous publications, including books, psychological tests, book chapters and monographs, and articles in professional scholarly journals. Dr. Webster has also made many presentations at professional psychology and education meetings. He has been active in the martial arts for over 30 years and holds the rank of fourth degree black belt in Gojo Shorin karate.

About Research & Education Association

Founded in 1959, Research & Education Association (REA) is dedicated to publishing the finest and most effective educational materials–including software, study guides, and test preps–for students in middle school, high school, college, graduate school, and beyond.

REA's test preparation series includes books and software for all academic levels in almost all disciplines. REA publishes test preps for students who have not yet entered high school, as well as high school students preparing to enter college. Students from countries around the world seeking to attend college in the United States will find the assistance they need in REA's publications. For college students seeking advanced degrees, REA publishes test preps for many major graduate school admission examinations in a wide variety of disciplines, including engineering, law, and medicine. Students at every level, in every field, with every ambition can find what they are looking for among REA's publications.

REA's series presents tests that accurately depict the official exams in both degree of difficulty and types of questions. REA's practice tests are always based upon the most recently administered exams, and include every type of question that can be expected on the actual exams.

REA's publications and educational materials are highly regarded and continually receive an unprecedented amount of praise from professionals, instructors, librarians, parents, and students. Our authors are as diverse as the subject matter represented in the books we publish. They are well known in their respective disciplines and serve on the faculties of prestigious colleges and universities throughout the United States and Canada.

We invite you to visit us at *www.rea.com* to find out how "REA is making the world smarter."

Acknowledgments

In addition to our author, we would like to thank Larry B. Kling, Vice President, Editorial, for his overall guidance, which brought this publication to completion; Pam Weston, Vice President, Publishing, for setting the quality standards for production integrity and managing the publication to completion; Diane Goldschmidt, Associate Editor, for editorial contributions.

We also extend our thanks to Jody Berman, developmental editor, Barbara McGowran, copy editor, and Karen Brown, proofreader, for their contributions. Kathy Caratozzolo of Caragraphics typeset the manuscript, our cover was designed by Christine Saul, and Terry Casey of INKandLINE prepared our index.

CONTENTS

CLEP INTRODUCTION TO EDUCATIONAL PSYCHOLOGY
Independent Study Schedule

The following study schedule allows for thorough preparation for the CLEP Introduction to Educational Psychology. Although it is designed for four weeks, it can be reduced to a two-week course by collapsing each two-week period into one. Be sure to set aside enough time—at least two hours each day—to study. But no matter which study schedule works best for you, the more time you spend studying, the more prepared and relaxed you will feel on the day of the exam.

Week	Activity
1	Read and study the Introduction section of this book, which will introduce you to the CLEP Introduction to Educational Psychology exam. Then take Practice Test 1 to determine your strengths and weaknesses. Assess your results by using our raw score conversion table. You can then determine the areas in which you need to strengthen your skills.
2 & 3	Carefully read and study the Educational Psychology Review included in Chapters 1 through 9 of this book.
4	Take Practice Test 2 and carefully review the explanations for all incorrect answers. If there are any types of questions or particular subjects that seem difficult to you, review those subjects by studying again the appropriate sections of the Educational Psychology Review.

Note: If you care to, and time allows, retake Practice Tests 1 and 2. This will help strengthen the areas in which your performance may still be lagging and build your overall confidence.

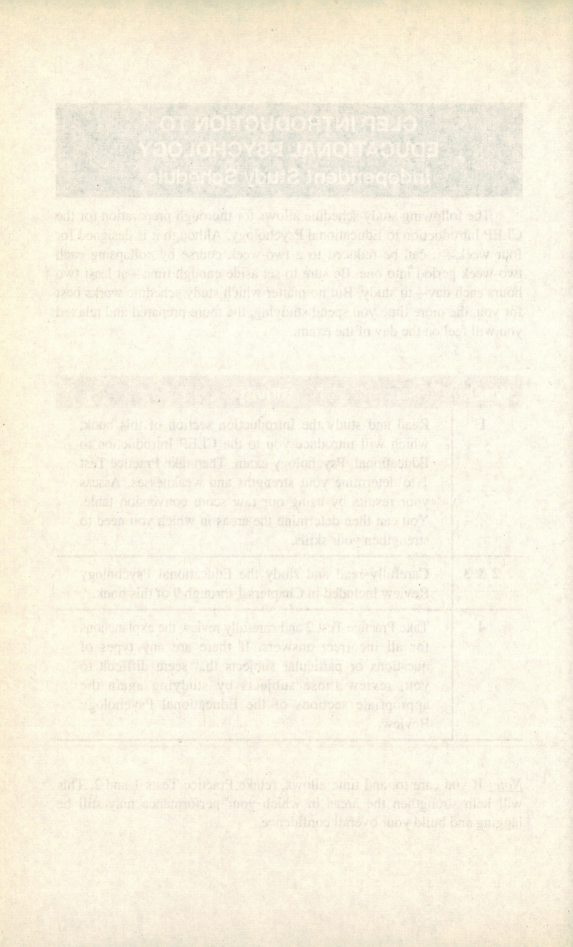

▼

Passing the
CLEP Introduction to
Educational Psychology
Exam

PASSING THE CLEP INTRODUCTION TO EDUCATIONAL PSYCHOLOGY EXAM

ABOUT THIS BOOK

This book provides you with complete preparation for the CLEP Introduction to Educational Psychology exam. Inside you will find a concise review of the subject matter, as well as tips and strategies for test-taking. We also give you two practice tests, all based on the official CLEP Introduction to Educational Psychology exam. Our practice tests contain every type of question that you can expect to encounter on the actual exam. Following each practice test you will find an answer key with detailed explanations designed to help you more completely understand the test material.

All CLEP exams are computer-based. As you can see, the practice tests in our book are presented as paper-and-pencil exams. The content and format of the actual CLEP subject exam are faithfully mirrored. We detail the format and content of the CLEP Introduction to Educational Psychology on pages xvii–xviii.

ABOUT THE EXAM

Who takes the CLEP Introduction to Educational Psychology and what is it used for?

CLEP (College-Level Examination Program) examinations are typically taken by people who have acquired knowledge outside the classroom and wish to bypass certain college courses and earn college credit. The CLEP is designed to reward students for learning—no matter where or how that knowledge was acquired. The CLEP is the most widely accepted credit-by-examination program in the country, with more than 2,900 colleges and universities granting credit for satisfactory scores on CLEP exams.

Although most CLEP examinees are adults returning to college, many graduating high school seniors, enrolled college students, military personnel, and international students also take the exams to earn college credit or to demonstrate their ability to perform at the college level. There are no prerequisites, such as age or educational status, for taking CLEP examinations. However, because policies on granting credits vary among colleges, you should contact the particular institution from which you wish to receive CLEP credit.

There are two categories of CLEP examinations:

1. **CLEP General Examinations**, which are five separate tests that cover material usually taken as requirements during the first two years of college. CLEP General Examinations are available for College Composition and College Composition Modular, Humanities, Mathematics, Natural Sciences, and Social Sciences and History.

2. **CLEP Subject Examinations**, which include material usually covered in an undergraduate course with a similar title. For a complete list of the subject examinations offered, visit the College Board website.

Who administers the exam?

The CLEP tests are developed by the College Board, administered by Educational Testing Service (ETS), and involve the assistance of educators throughout the United States. The test development process is designed and implemented to ensure that the content and difficulty level of the test are appropriate.

When and where is the exam given?

The CLEP Introduction to Educational Psychology is administered each month throughout the year at more than 1,300 test centers in the United States and can be arranged for candidates abroad on request. To find the test center nearest you and to register for the exam, you should obtain a copy of the free booklets *CLEP Colleges* and *CLEP Information for Candidates and Registration Form*. They are available at most colleges where CLEP credit is granted, or by contacting:

CLEP Services
P.O. Box 6600
Princeton, NJ 08541-6600
Phone: (800) 257-9558 (8 A.M. to 6 P.M. ET)
Fax: (609) 771-7088
Website: *www.collegeboard.com/clep*

CLEP Options for Military Personnel and Veterans

CLEP exams are available free of charge to eligible military personnel and eligible civilian employees. All the CLEP exams are available at test centers on college campuses and military bases. In addition, the College Board has developed a paper-based version of 14 high-volume/high-pass-rate CLEP tests for DANTES Test Centers. Contact the Educational Services Officer or Navy College Education Specialist for more information. Visit the College Board website for details about CLEP opportunities for military personnel.

Eligible U.S. veterans can claim reimbursement for CLEP exams and administration fees pursuant to provisions of the Veterans Benefits Improvement Act of 2004. For details on eligibility and submitting a claim for reimbursement, visit the U.S. Department of Veterans Affairs website at *www.gibill.va.gov/pamphlets/testing.htm*.

CLEP marks a special sweet spot with reference to the new Post-9/11 GI Bill, which applies to veterans returning from the Iraq and Afghanistan theaters of operation. Because the GI Bill provides tuition for up to 36 months, racking up college credits by testing out of general introductory courses with CLEP exams expedites academic progress and degree completion within the funded timeframe.

SSD Accommodations for Students with Disabilities

Many students qualify for extra time to take the CLEP Introduction to Educational Psychology exam, but you must make these arrangements in advance. For information, contact:

College Board Services for Students with Disabilities
P.O. Box 6226
Princeton, NJ 08541-6226
Phone: (609) 771-7137 (Monday through Friday, 8 A.M. to 6 P.M. ET)
TTY: (609) 882-4118
Fax: (609) 771-7944
E-mail: ssd@info.collegeboard.org

HOW TO USE THIS BOOK

What do I study first?

Read over the course review and the suggestions for test-taking, take the first practice test to determine your area(s) of weakness, and then go back and focus your study on those specific problems. Studying the reviews thoroughly will reinforce the basic skills you will need to do well on the exam. Make sure to take the practice tests to become familiar with the format and procedures involved with taking the actual exam.

To best utilize your study time, follow our Independent Study Schedule, which you'll find in the front of this book. The schedule is based on a four-week program, but can be condensed to two weeks if necessary by collapsing each two-week period into one.

When should I start studying?

It is never too early to start studying for the CLEP Introduction to Educational Psychology. The earlier you begin, the more time you will have to sharpen your skills. Do not procrastinate! Cramming is *not* an effective way to study, since it does not allow you the time needed to learn the test material. The sooner you learn the format of the exam, the more time you will have to familiarize yourself with it.

FORMAT AND CONTENT OF THE CLEP

The CLEP Introduction to Educational Psychology covers the material one would find in a college-level introductory educational psychology class. The exam emphasizes principles of learning and cognition, teaching methods and classroom management, child growth and development and evaluation and assessment of learning.

The exam consists of 100 multiple-choice questions, each with five possible answer choices, to be answered within 90 minutes.

The approximate breakdown of topics is as follows:

5%	Educational Aims or Philosophies
15%	Cognitive Perspective
11%	Behavioristic Perspective
15%	Development
10%	Motivation
17%	Individual Differences
12%	Testing
10%	Pedagogy
5%	Research Design and Analysis

PRACTICE-TEST RAW SCORE CONVERSION TABLE*

Raw Score	Scaled Score	Course Grade	Raw Score	Scaled Score	Course Grade
100	80	A	48	49	C
99	80	A	47	49	C
98	80	A	46	48	C
97	79	A	45	48	C
96	79	A	44	47	C
95	78	A	43	47	C
94	78	A	42	47	C
93	77	A	41	47	C
92	77	A	40	46	D
91	76	A	39	46	D
90	75	A	38	45	D
89	74	A	37	45	D
88	73	A	36	44	D
87	73	A	35	44	D
86	72	A	34	43	D
85	72	A	33	43	D
84	71	A	32	42	D
83	70	A	31	41	D
82	70	A	30	40	F
81	69	A	29	39	F
80	69	A	28	38	F
79	68	A	27	37	F
78	67	A	26	36	F
77	66	A	25	35	F
76	66	A	24	34	F
75	65	A	23	34	F
74	64	A	22	33	F
73	63	A	21	33	F
72	63	A	20	32	F
71	62	A	19	32	F
70	61	A	18	31	F
69	61	A	17	31	F
68	60	A	16	30	F
67	59	A	15	29	F
66	59	A	14	28	F
65	58	B	13	28	F
64	57	B	12	27	F
63	57	B	11	27	F
62	56	B	10	26	F
61	56	B	9	25	F
60	55	B	8	24	F
59	55	B	7	23	F
58	54	B	6	22	F
57	54	B	5	21	F
56	53	B	4	20	F
55	53	B	3	20	F
54	52	B	2	20	F
53	52	B	1	20	F
52	51	C	0	20	F
51	51	C	-1	20	F
50	50	C	-2	20	F
49	50	C	and below	20	F

*This table is provided for scoring REA practice tests only. The American Council on Education recommends that colleges use a single across-the-board credit-granting score of 50 for all 34 CLEP computer-based exams. Nonetheless, on account of the different skills being measured and the unique content requirements of each test, the actual number of correct answers needed to reach 50 will vary. A "50" is calibrated to equate with performance that would warrant the grade C in the corresponding introductory college course.

ABOUT OUR COURSE REVIEW

The review in this book provides you with a complete background of all the pertinent facts, principles, and concepts of educational psychology. It will help reinforce the facts you have already learned while better shaping your understanding of the discipline as a whole. By using the review in conjunction with the practice tests, you should be well prepared to take the CLEP Introduction to Educational Psychology.

SCORING YOUR PRACTICE TESTS

How do I score my practice tests?

The CLEP Introduction to Educational Psychology is scored on a scale of 20 to 80. To score your practice tests, count up the number of correct answers. This is your total raw score. Convert your raw score to a scaled score using the conversion table on the following page. (**Note: The conversion table provides only an *estimate* of your scaled score. Scaled scores can and do vary over time, and in no case should a sample test be taken as a precise predictor of test performance. Nonetheless, our scoring table allows you to judge your level of performance within a reasonable scoring range.**)

When will I receive my score report?

The test administrator will print out a full Candidate Score Report for you immediately upon your completion of the exam (except for the College Composition and College Composition Modular). Your scores are reported only to you, unless you ask to have them sent elsewhere. If you want your scores reported to a college or other institution, you must say so when you take the examination. Since your scores are kept on file for 20 years, you can also request transcripts from Educational Testing Service at a later date.

STUDYING FOR THE CLEP

It is very important for you to choose the time and place for studying that works best for you. Some students may set aside a certain number of hours every morning, while others may choose to study at night before going to sleep. Other students may study during the day, while waiting on a line, or even while eating lunch. Only you can determine when and where your study time will be most effective. But be consistent and use your time wisely. Work out a study routine and stick to it!

When you take the practice tests, try to make your testing conditions as much like the actual test as possible. Turn your television and radio off, and sit down at a quiet table free from distraction. Make sure to time yourself. Start off by setting a timer for the time that is allotted for each section, and be sure to reset the timer for the appropriate amount of time when you start a new section.

As you complete each practice test, score your test and thoroughly review the explanations to the questions you answered incorrectly; however, do not review too much at one time. Concentrate on one problem area at a time by reviewing the question and explanation, and by studying our review until you are confident that you completely understand the material.

Keep track of your scores and mark them on the Scoring Worksheet. By doing so, you will be able to gauge your progress and discover general weaknesses in particular sections. You should carefully study the reviews that cover your areas of difficulty, as this will build your skills in those areas.

TEST-TAKING TIPS

Although you may not be familiar with computer-based standardized tests such as the CLEP Introduction to Educational Psychology, there are many ways to acquaint yourself with this type of examination and to help alleviate your test-taking anxieties. Listed below are ways to help you become accustomed to the CLEP, some of which may be applied to other standardized tests as well.

Read all of the possible answers. Just because you think you have found the correct response, do not automatically assume that it is the best answer. Read through each choice to be sure that you are not making a mistake by jumping to conclusions.

Use the process of elimination. Go through each answer to a question and eliminate as many of the answer choices as possible. By eliminating just two answer choices, you give yourself a better chance of getting the item correct, since there will only be three choices left from which to make your guess. Remember, your score is based only on the number of questions you answer *correctly*.

Work quickly and steadily. You will have only 90 minutes to work on 100 questions, so work quickly and steadily to avoid focusing on any one question too long. Taking the practice tests in this book will help you learn to budget your time.

Acquaint yourself with the computer screen. Familiarize yourself with the CLEP computer screen beforehand by logging on to the College Board website. Waiting until test day to see what it looks like in the pretest tutorial risks experiencing needless anxiety into your testing experience. Also, familiarizing yourself with the directions and format of the exam will save you valuable time on the day of the actual test.

Be sure that your answer registers before you go to the next item. Look at the screen to see that your mouse-click causes the pointer to darken the proper oval. This takes less effort than darkening an oval on paper, but don't lull yourself into taking less care!

THE DAY OF THE EXAM

Preparing for the CLEP

On the day of the test, you should wake up early (hopefully after a decent night's rest) and have a good breakfast. Make sure to dress comfortably, so that you are not distracted by being too hot or too cold while taking the test. Also plan to arrive at the test center early. This will allow you to collect your thoughts and relax before the test, and will also spare you the anxiety that comes with being late. As an added incentive to make sure you arrive early, keep in mind that no one will be allowed into the test session after the test has begun.

Before you leave for the test center, make sure that you have your admission form and another form of identification, which must contain a recent photograph, your name, and signature (i.e., driver's license, student identification card, or current alien registration card). You will not be admitted to the test center if you do not have proper identification.

If you would like, you may wear a watch to the test center. However, you may not wear one that makes noise, because it may disturb the other test-takers. No dictionaries, textbooks, notebooks, briefcases, or packages will be permitted and drinking, smoking, and eating are prohibited.

Good luck on the CLEP Introduction to Educational Psychology exam!

CHAPTER 1
Educational Aims

CHAPTER 1

EDUCATIONAL AIMS

Teaching is one of the most noble professions. Teachers have the privilege and opportunity to work with and influence the lives of others in dramatic, significant, and long-lasting ways. When working with students today teachers must be aware of many social, political, psychological, and emotional variables, because society expects the schools to prepare each child to become a productive and contributing citizen.

SOCIALIZATION AND SOCIAL EFFECTS

During the past thirty-five years the effects of poverty on the educational progress and performance of children have become increasingly clear, especially for children living in urban areas (Massey & Denton, 1993). The neighborhoods in which children live profoundly influence their perception of their role in society and their belief in their ability to fit into the larger social order. Dropout rates in seriously distressed neighborhoods are more than three times higher than those in more economically advantaged neighborhoods. Additionally, the jobless rates for young high school dropouts exceed 80 percent in those neighborhoods (Kasarda, 1993).

The characteristics of specific neighborhoods have been shown to have a tremendous influence on the educational performance and achievement levels of children because these characteristics shape the role models children are exposed to outside the home. It is not unusual for the role models of children in distressed neighborhoods to provide negative, or at least antisocial, values that encourage children to engage in behaviors that are ultimately self-defeating and lead to failure. Further, these neighborhoods do not provide a sufficient number of stable adult role models who demonstrate the kinds of emotional, vocational, and interpersonal characteristics that are valued within American society and typically lead to success (Wilson, 1996). Negative models and social interactions can make life a confusing set of experiences for children. The reality presented to them in their immediate neighborhoods is in marked contrast with the larger social reality, where different kinds of skills and capabilities are required for success. Moreover, occupational, educational, and social opportunities for these children are often seriously limited. The kinds of behaviors esteemed within these impoverished communities are often counterculture in nature, with the values and influences of peers being stronger than those of parents. Many distressed neighborhoods have both formal (gangs) and less formal (generalized attitudes and values expressed among individuals) standards of social control that significantly govern the performance of youth. A lack of appropriate and responsible adult structure, complicated by the presence of adults who sometimes provide seriously negative structure and codes of conduct, further complicates children's lives.

Children in advantaged neighborhoods are more likely to be exposed to a positive social network of adults, some of whom can provide positive emotional and/or technical resources that encourage the children to pursue learning and develop skills. Advantaged neighborhoods also expose children to different kinds of information and opportunities that can be educationally beneficial, in both the short term and the long term. For example, more affluent communities may have elaborate and well-organized systems of athletics that enable children to nurture and develop skills in a systematic and focused manner beginning at very young ages. In addition, social or philanthropic groups, such as scouting programs for boys and girls, provide well-recognized and accepted opportunities for children to excel and become skilled. For example, attaining the rank of Eagle Scout with the Boy Scouts of America is an achievement that not only is well recognized by many very successful people throughout the United States, but also is valued because it is deemed to represent and reflect a set of personal, social, and emotional skills that the Eagle Scout developed in the process. It is not unusual, therefore, for many adult males to maintain their personal identification as an Eagle Scout throughout their lives. Some colleges strongly factor in this achievement when evaluating a student's acceptability for college.

The quality of the neighborhood in which a child lives usually has a profound influence on the quality of the schools and the educational process that occurs. Many inner-city, poor rural, and/or distressed areas have difficulty recruiting and retaining quality educators (Jencks & Mayer, 1990). As the teacher turnover rate increases, it becomes more difficult to maintain an appropriate school atmosphere in which student conduct is managed effectively so that learning and achievement can occur in a systematic and effective manner. It has also been argued that stressed and disadvantaged neighborhoods are more likely to have schools that provide an inferior educational experience and devote less time to tasks in which students are being taught and are actively learning.

MORAL AND CHARACTER DEVELOPMENT

Because of the diversity of children's socioeconomic backgrounds, many people have seen that one important role for the public schools is to provide a common ground for acquainting children with the appropriate rules and codes of conduct that govern American society. In essence, attending a public school becomes a social training experience. Research has shown that children's understanding of rules and behaviors reflect both environmental and intellectual characteristics. Children of different ages and intellectual abilities understand and implement rules in very different ways. Most children do not develop an appreciation and awareness of the need for rules until around the age of 12 years. It is also at this stage of development that some children begin shifting from obeying rules adults have told them to follow to developing their own rules to fit a particular situation.

Several studies have been done regarding the pattern of moral and character development in children. A classic series of studies conducted by Hartshorne and May (1929) consistently revealed that children who attended Sunday school or participated in civic organizations such as the Boy Scouts or Girl Scouts were just as likely to be dishonest as children who were not exposed to the kind of moral instructions provided by these and similar kinds of organizations. Even though a child might be able to state the right and wrong ways of behaving when presented with a hypothetical situation, research has found that many children do not actually use those standards when involved in real-life situations. In other words, there seem to be significant discrepancies between *knowing* what is appropriate to do and *doing* the appropriate thing.

Educators have made many attempts to develop character education programs to teach children correct moral reasoning and conduct. Leming (1993) conducted a review of the findings from research examining the effectiveness of these character education programs and reached the following three conclusions:

1. Telling students what they should or should not do is highly unlikely to have any long-lasting effects on character development or moral decision making.

2. Encouraging students to consider ways to resolve moral dilemmas and socially complex problems does not automatically increase the child's ability or willingness to engage in an accepted pattern of conduct.

3. The most important factor in determining the development of a child's character and moral structure appears to be the environ-

ment in which the child resides. When students live in a setting in which adults· model and consistently use virtuous behavior and morally appropriate decision making, students learn clear rules to guide their behavior and accept those rules as appropriate and important. Being rewarded for complying with these rules further increases the probability of children embracing and implementing the rules in their daily life decisions. This research also indicates the importance of using a long-term and well-conceived program of character development and moral education that is an integrated component of a child's entire life approach.

The best way for children to acquire moral values seems to be by participating in relationships with other people who support, guide, and encourage the development of natural moral tendencies (Damon, 1988). It is important for parents, teachers, and other adults to tell children the reasons why they must behave and interact with others in ways that reflect moral and character structures that are positive and healthy.

Further research has indicated that people determine what behavior is moral based on their beliefs about the validity of the information available to them at the time they made the moral decision (Wainryb & Turiel, 1993). In effect, if people believe that the consequences of their decisions and behaviors are effective, they will deem those decisions and behaviors moral and reflecting character.

Studies have shown that cheating within the public schools and universities is being viewed as an acceptable behavior by an increasing number of students (Schab, 1991). Many of the reasons given by students to justify cheating indicate that fear of failure is the primary motivator. The greatest frequencies of cheating seem to occur in mathematics and science classes.

Character is a pervasive and dominant set of underlying qualities of a person reflecting a general and consistent tendency to behave in ways that are courageous, honest, responsible, and respectful of the rights of others. A person's character is not the sum total of each of these individual traits; rather, the traits tend to be organized so that there is an overall positive outcome that represents the interaction of the traits in combination with each other. Character can be seen as the underlying foundation that orients a person's attitude and approach toward interactions with others.

Character education programs are designed to improve a child's character traits so that there is an increased likelihood the student will do what is proper and correct because it is the morally right course of action. Three basic types of character education models exist:

1. **Simple moral education programs** that usually occur within a classroom setting and discuss topics concerning abstinence-based sex education, abortion, extramarital affairs, cheating, and dishonesty. The impact of these kinds of programs is generally considered to be quite restricted and short lived. These programs have several disadvantages because they do not always achieve what they put forth (Davis, 2003). It is not unusual for conflicts to exist between what "good" character is and the way it is taught to children. Further, these programs sometimes emphasize doing the right thing (helping another person who is in need) but for the wrong reasons (avoiding being punished).

2. **Community-based education programs** that emphasize democratic decision-making processes in the real world of the community and the larger society, rather than merely in the classroom setting. This approach attempts to relate and apply knowledge and information learned within the classroom to real situations and encounters.

3. **Character education programs** that attempt to develop character and morals within the educational setting and to teach children how to apply this knowledge to real life by addressing specific character traits one at a time and identifying what makes up appropriate and unacceptable codes of conduct regarding these character traits.

CITIZENSHIP

Another very important goal for the educational system is the development of responsible, productive citizens within our society. The problems that confront people in their role as citizens often have strong underlying moral components. For example, consider a group of people who have ready access to resources such as housing and community protection. The necessity and obligation of these people to consider future generations when making laws and policies affecting the environment, and the conflicts that can occur when multiple stakeholders (e.g., developers, environmentalists, housing rights advocates) become involved in community decision making reflect the moral structure of this group of people as citizens in their community.

For students to be both civically engaged and morally responsible, they must have a deep understanding about how these two qualities affect each other. They must have values that reflect moral and social concerns, as well as a strong, clear sense of who they are as people.

Students must understand the mechanisms involved in dealing with different kinds of political issues to bring about successful and positive resolutions that benefit the larger society. Some of the core values involved in responsible citizenship are concern for truth and academic freedom, mutual respect for others, receptivity to and serious consideration of the ideas and views of others, and awareness that different viewpoints are healthy and important.

In the past, citizenship education programs in the schools largely embraced an **ideology of assimilation**, with conformity being the main goal (Banks, 1997). This approach has several implicit and significant negative consequences. Students often lose their identity with their first culture, language, and ethnic affiliation. Assimilation discourages students from developing strong emotional ties with their families of origin and ethnic communities. Consequently, students can become alienated from both their immediate families and their national origins, as well as from the new society into which they are supposedly being assimilated. It is not unusual for them to assume marginal roles in the new culture because they do not see themselves as fitting in with any particular strata or group.

Research conducted on citizenship education programs has shown that a positive relationship exists between students' knowledge of democratic processes and programs that stress

— voting as adults;

— obeying the law and being moderately trusting of government;

— being supportive of the economic and political rights of women, although females tend to be more supportive in this area than do males;

— being generally positive about immigrants and their rights;

— showing greater interest in working toward social goals and activities that are common to the society, such as the environment and basic human rights; and

— being more receptive to having open discussions about important issues that affect their communities and society.

Education about citizenship should specifically increase student knowledge about governmental processes, law, and politics. The core values that should be communicated include justice, authority, participation in the governing process, truth, equality, freedom, patriotism, diversity, privacy, due process, and property and human rights (Butts, 1988).

PREPARATION FOR CAREERS

The United States is quickly shifting from an industry-oriented economy to one that is highly information-based. In this new economic orientation many of the basic skills once needed for success in the workplace are no longer as important as they once were. For example, high school programs typically have emphasized and rewarded students for producing well in the areas of mathematics, science, English, and the language arts. These kinds of course subjects were considered essential for admission to college. Yet having a four-year college degree today is not necessarily a guarantee of success in the job market.

In a technologically oriented society the nature of literacy and the specific skills that make up literacy seem to be changing quickly (Berners-Lee & Fischetti, 2000). Critical communications skills such as reading, writing, speaking, and listening are now intimately merged with other skills, such as the ability to orally present new information to other people, computer mediation and use, and time and logistical management skills. People are increasingly being called upon to evaluate information, assess its validity and logic, and determine how to apply the information to reach insightful decisions and solutions.

The United States Department of Labor estimates that roughly 70 percent of the fastest-growing jobs in the country will require some form of postsecondary education (Employment Policies Institute, 2001). By 2010, 42 percent of all jobs are expected to require some form of postsecondary vocational certification and/or an academic degree (Hecker, 2001). Individuals with minimal academic skills will be eligible for only about 10 percent of all new job openings within the next four years in the United States (Employment Policies Institute, 2001).

These changes in the economy will have profound implications for schools, with significant changes in course work and emphasis required for students' success in the future. Schools will be challenged to try to identify the specific technological areas that are marketable and then develop educational curricula that enhance the essential technical and basic skills leading to success in those areas.

Surprisingly, little is known about what specific variables contribute to a person's success in a career (Sagen, Dallam, & Laverty, 2000). Some basic variables such as the specific degree an individual holds, the field of study, grade point average, and occasionally internship experiences seem to have some slight relationship to career success (Pascaralla & Terenzini, 1991), but these variables are not strong predictors of whether or not a student will be successful in procuring a job in the desired area.

The schools may have to consider assuming a multifaceted developmental approach to career education, which would include helping students learn to make satisfying career decisions. Career preparation programs may also need to attend to personal variables, such as students' feelings about themselves and what makes them feel fulfilled as human beings, as part of this retooling process. In Texas and a few other states, school districts must offer programming in broad areas of concentration such as arts and communications, business education, technology education, agricultural science and technology, family and consumer sciences, and health occupations technology (Christie, 2001).

LIFELONG LEARNING

Globalization and individualization—two by-products of technological advancement—have changed dramatically both the economic system of the entire world and the personal life of every individual (Glastra, Hake, & Schedler, 2004). People can no longer be confident about what skills they must acquire to gain and maintain employment, nor can they predict the consequences and outcomes of the educational and vocational choices they make as young adults.

People must continue to learn and acquire new skills through work and formal educational training programs if they are to keep pace with the technological changes that impact the kinds of jobs available to them and remain marketable as wage earners. If professionals fail to maintain their technical skills, they will lose their ability to provide effective answers to specific problems. Moreover, they could actually harm people by not keeping up-to-date with the most current advances in their fields.

This process of formalized training and educating, leading to further formalized training and reeducating, has become much more of a normal practice in our current technologically advanced society. There are a number of specific cognitive skills involved in lifelong learning that are very different from the basic academic skills and content taught in many public schools and even at the undergraduate university level. Lifelong learning skills include the ability to analyze and evaluate large amounts of data objectively to discern patterns, the ability to interpret these patterns in meaningful ways that are relevant and usable, and the ability to make complicated decisions that can have significant effects on large numbers of people. These changes present significant challenges to the schools and the specific kinds of skills, content, and teaching methods they use.

At one time in the United States the **standard biography** of a working person usually started with going to school during the childhood and adolescent years to learn and become educated. This was followed by completion of the educational program and entrance into the world of work, where the person would spend many years at the same or a similar position until reaching retirement. For women, this standard biography might deviate somewhat in that they might have periods of working interrupted because of childbearing and/or other caretaking duties that eventually became intermixed with returning to the workforce.

This standard biography has now become replaced by the **elective biography** (Castells, 1996). Now the lives of people, particularly in the United States, are characterized by periods of formalized learning during their childhood and adolescent years that culminate in their acquiring employment or additional education as adults. These periods of employment are sometimes interrupted by periods of unemployment because of economic downturns. People are forced to reenter the formalized educational system and acquire new skills and knowledge so they can reenter the workforce with a more marketable portfolio. This cycle may occur more than once during a person's working career and is not related to a specific gender. In addition, people now may leave the work world for periods of time to take care of other people in their family (maternity leaves, family illness leaves) or simply take personal leaves of absence or other periods of respite to rejuvenate themselves and/or acquire new technological skills.

REFERENCES

Banks, J. A. (1997). *Educating citizens in a multicultural society*. New York: Teachers College Press.

Berners-Lee, T., & Fischetti, M. (2000). *Weaving the Web: The original design and ultimate destiny of the World Wide Web*. New York: HarperCollins.

Butts, F. (1988). *The morality of democratic citizenship*. Calabasas, CA: Center for Civic Education.

Castells, M. (1996). *The rise of the network society*. Oxford, UK: Basil Blackwell.

Christie, K. (2001). Oh, no! Not Texas again. *Phi Delta Kappan, 83*(1), 5.

Damon, W. (1988). *The moral child*. New York: Free Press.

Davis, M. (2003). What's wrong with character education? *American Journal of Education, 110,* 32–58.

Employment Policies Institute. (2001). *State flexibility: The minimal wage and welfare reform*. Washington, DC: Employment Policies Institute.

Glastra, F. J., Hake, B. J., & Schedler, P. E. (2004). Lifelong learning has transitional learning. *Adult Education Quarterly, 54*(4), 91–307.

Hartshorne, H., and May, M. A. (1929). *Studies in service and self-control.* New York: Macmillan.

Hecker, D. E. (2001, November). Occupational employment projections to 2010. *Monthly Labor Review,* 57–84. Available at http://www.bls.gov/opub/mlr/2001/11/art4full.pdf.

Jencks, C., & Mayer, S. E. (1990). The social consequences of growing up in a poor neighborhood. In L. E. Lynn Jr. and M. G. H. McGeary (Eds.), *Inner-city poverty in the United States.* (pp. 111–186). Washington, DC: National Academy Press.

Kasarda, J. D. (1993). Inner-city concentrated poverty and neighborhood distress: 1970–1990. *Housing Policy Debate, 4,* 253-302.

Leming, J. S. (1993). In search of effective character education. *Educational Leadership, 51*(3), 63–71.

Massey, D. S., & Denton, N. A. (1993). *American apartheid: Segregation and the making of the underclass.* Cambridge, MA: Harvard University Press.

Pascarella, E. T., & Terenzini, P. T. (1991). *How college affects students.* San Francisco: Jossey-Bass.

Sagen, H. B., Dallam, J. W., & Laverty, J. R. (2000). The effects of career preparation experiences on the initial employment success of college graduates. *Research in Higher Education, 41*(6), 753–767.

Schab, F. (1991). Schooling without learning: Thirty years of cheating in high school. *Adolescence, 26*(104), 839–848.

Wainryb, C., & Turiel, E. (1993). Conceptual and informational features in moral decision-making. *Educational Psychologist, 28*(3), 205–218.

Wilson, W. J. (1996). *When work disappears: The world of the new urban poor.* New York: Knopf.

CHAPTER 2
Cognitive Perspective of Learning

CHAPTER 2

COGNITIVE PERSPECTIVE OF LEARNING

Cognitive psychology studies how people acquire, store, transform, use, and communicate information (Neisser, 1967). Thus the focus of the cognitive perspective of learning is on how people mentally assimilate and accommodate information from their world. A number of key processes are involved when a person interacts with and interprets the world: attention, perception, working memory, long-term memory, problem solving, and transfer of information. Decision making and reasoning are also typically part of the information-processing mechanisms.

Cognitive psychology views human beings as having an active and constructive role in the perception and interpretation of reality. External reality is represented by incoming information that enters the brain through the sensory organs (the eyes and ears are the primary organs used for most learning activities in school), is analyzed and stored in various areas of the brain, and then retrieved from those memory stores for use as needed. Information is processed in stages. Each stage affects the storage of new information entering the system and interacts with both past experiences that have been stored in the brain and the world that is currently being experienced. Learning is viewed as a change in a person's mental structures. This change provides the person with the capacity to behave differently based on past knowledge, beliefs, goals, and expectations about a specific situation.

The most widely accepted view of how people process information is the **two-store model** of memory developed by Atkinson and Shiffrin (1968). This model has three components that interact with each other during the processing of information from the external world. It is referred to as the two-store model because only two components of the model actually retain or store information for later use.

The model describes how information is held within the human memory, the various cognitive processes and actions involved in transforming information from the world into a meaningful language system, and how information is transferred from one component to the other. The model also addresses how human beings can take control over some of these cognitive processes to more effectively and efficiently retain and retrieve information that has been learned. These kinds of controlling mechanisms are referred to as metacognitive processes. A summary of the stages of the two-store model of memory and key components at each stage is presented in Table 2.1.

SENSORY REGISTER

All information from the outside world enters through the sensory register. The **sensory register** is a temporary, large-capacity storage mechanism that holds information as it is directly obtained through the various sensory modality organs. Two modality-specific stores have been identified within the sensory register. The first is the **iconic storage register**, which is involved with the processing of information taken in visually. It has a maximum storage capacity of 1 second. Following one second, the information in this store is lost through decay. The second component in the sensory register is called the **echoic storage register**. This storage mechanism has a maximum storage capacity of 4 seconds, after which the auditory-based information is lost permanently through decay.

The information that enters either the iconic or echoic stores is considered to be "raw" information directly received from the environment. No verbal labels are assigned to the information. People do not process every visual or auditory cue or stimulus going on around them. Rather, mechanisms such as attention and perception serve as regulators to detect pertinent and important information.

Attention is a cognitive process that has an extremely important role in the processing of information. Attention refers to consciously focusing on external stimuli. It is the beginning of the learning process, and it serves a very important purpose by helping a person sort out what is important from what is irrelevant. There is a long-standing body of research showing that individual differences exist in people's abilities to attend to their world (Neisser, 1967). The information that a person focuses on or attends to is highly influenced by the kind of information in that person's long-term memory. Attention operates in a selective manner so the person is not overloaded by the vast amount of stimuli that exists in the daily world.

Table 2.1
Characteristics of the Stages and Cognitive Processes Involved in the Two-Store Model of Memory

Stage 1				Stage 2
Sensory Register	Attention → Perception →	**Working Memory**	Encoding → Storage → Access → ← Retrieval	**Long-Term Memory**
Iconic storage register (1-second duration)		Span of 7 bits +/– 2 bits for adults		Semantic memory
Echoic storage register (4-second duration)		Conscious awareness of stimuli		Episodic memory
Sensory copy of stimuli from the world		Rehearsal to keep information active		Procedural memory
Information lost through decay		Can be a bottleneck to the long-term memory		Information stored as schemata Permanent record of information
No verbal labels for information		Chunking		Cueing for retrieval
		Automaticity		
		Information lost through interference		
		Transfers information to long-term memory		

WORKING MEMORY

The second stage in the two-store model of information processing is called the **working memory**, or the **short-term memory**. At this level in the processing chain, attention and a second cognitive process called perception become especially influential because they begin to focus the person on specific aspects of the outside world. Information in the working memory is maintained at a conscious level. The person must think about this information in a deliberate manner.

The working memory has been shown to have a limited capacity (Miller, 1956). The average adult can remember about 7 bits, or items, of information (plus or minus 2 bits) in the working memory, although there have been many studies showing that the working memory capacity varies among individuals. The working memory capacity has also been shown to vary with age, with the average adolescent having a short-term memory capacity of about 5 bits of information (Flavell, Friedrichs, & Hoyt, 1970; Webster, 1992). Information within the working memory must be rehearsed so that it is maintained at a conscious, deliberate level of awareness. Without active rehearsal or repetition of the information, the typical person will forget the material in about 20 seconds.

Research has shown that young children seldom rehearse spontaneously and need to be taught explicitly how to use **rehearsal** to retain information in short-term memory at a conscious level. The use of rehearsal varies even among people at older age levels. Two types of rehearsal exist. The first is **maintenance rehearsal** (sometimes called **rote rehearsal**), where the child simply repeats the information either out loud or mentally in the exact form in which it was processed. This type of rehearsal is most often used when the information that has been perceived has an immediate use. Some examples of situations where maintenance rehearsal is commonly used are musical numbers, dance routines, and the memorization of rote information (e.g., letters of the alphabet, numbers counted, and names of different parts of the body). This is the first type of rehearsal to develop in younger children (Berk, 1997), and it has been shown to be an inefficient method of transferring information to long-term memory.

The second type of rehearsal is elaborative, where the individual associates newly acquired information with information already learned and stored in long-term memory. Elaborative rehearsal, sometimes referred to as **elaborative encoding**, is a much more efficient and effective way to learn and retain information for long periods because it forms links to knowledge the person has already acquired. It is also a characteristic of mature learners.

Because of its limited capacity, the working memory can serve as a bottleneck that restricts the amount of information the person can deal with at any given time. People with small working memory capacities will be penalized during new learning experiences unless instruction is accommodated to the restrictions imposed by the limited capacity. In a very real way the working memory has a screening role for the person because information that is not actively processed and stored in the person's long-term memory is most commonly lost through interference and, to a lesser extent, decay.

Although the working memory capacity is limited by the number of bits of information that it can hold, there are no limits to the size of the individual bit of information. By combining information into larger and more meaningful units (Miller, 1956), one can increase the size of the bit. This process of combining elements into larger elements or units is referred to as **chunking**.

The working memory span is also significantly influenced and enhanced by the degree of automaticity involved in the tasks or operations that it must perform. **Automaticity** is the ability to perform an operation or a task with very little conscious effort (Schneider & Shiffrin, 1977). Some examples of activities that we do automatically on a daily basis include driving an automobile while talking or listening to the radio or typing on a computer while listening to music. Samuels (1988) has shown that children who can automatically identify and decode words are often better readers because they can devote more of their working memory capacity to understanding the message being communicated in the passage. They do not have to spend as much time trying to decode individual words before extracting the gist of the message being presented in print.

In the process of **encoding,** the individual forms a mental representation of stimuli that he or she has perceived through the sensory organs and processed in the working memory. It allows the person to develop a meaning for the new information by forming connections or associations between the new information and the ideas and information contained in the long-term memory (Siegler, 1991). During encoding the new information interacts with previously acquired and stored information. Rehearsal also allows newly acquired information to be organized logically so the person can use and apply the information in the future. It has been shown that various types of encoding mechanisms exist within the working memory system to include acoustic and visual codes.

Within the working memory newly received information is assigned meaning in a process referred to as **perception**. All information that has been attended to by the person and brought into the working memory is processed and analyzed through perception. At this level of processing, information about reality reflects the person's perceptions of reality and does not necessarily represent an absolute record of what actually occurred. People's perceptions are affected by their past knowledge and experiences. Knowledge and experiences serve to modify and sometimes elaborate on what has been processed so people can make sense of what they encounter within the parameters of how they have experienced the world and/or what they have learned about it.

LONG-TERM MEMORY

The second storage component in the two-store model of memory is the **long-term memory system**. This component has an unlimited storage capacity and is believed to provide a permanent record of information the individual processed and categorized as significant or important (Ashcraft, 1989). The key to accessing and retrieving this information resides in the person having enough cues available to trigger recall.

The long-term memory system comprises three separate but interrelated storage files. The first file is called **semantic memory** and involves retention of factual knowledge and information. This information is generic and has little relation to personal experiences. The kinds of knowledge contained in semantic memory include multiplication facts learned in school and, say, the dates of World War II. Usually, the person does not remember when this information was first learned or the circumstances under which it was learned, unless something personally significant occurred at around the same time as this knowledge was being taught.

The second file system in the long-term memory is the **episodic memory**, which contains memories of personal experiences and activities that the person has participated in or encountered. Many people recall both the facts they learned and the circumstances under which that learning first occurred if it was accompanied by a highly emotional experience, such as being in a motor vehicle accident or seeing television coverage of the attacks on the World Trade Center on Sept. 11, 2001.

Procedural memory is the final memory file in long-term memory. It retains knowledge about how to do things and defines the steps to take when specific conditions or circumstances exist. These rules and knowledge are referred to as **productions**. For example, although a person has not been on a bicycle for many years, after getting on the bicycle the necessary behaviors quickly return so the person can move forward without falling.

Within each of these files, information is organized into **schemata**, which are abstract stores of information that represent and contain knowledge describing what the world is like (Anderson, 1984). Schemata often contain both general knowledge about the world and information about specific events. By offering summaries of the information received and stored in the long-term memory system, schemata provide examples of past experiences and relate various concepts about information with each other. They allow people to generate expectations about the characteristics of objects and/or social events and transactions.

Two types of schemata exist. **Well-formed, specific schemata** provide the person with clear, useful expectations about situations and lead to comprehension and understanding of those situations. **Poorly formed, vague schemata** typically lead to unclear and uncertain learning because the person is unable to use or rely on previously learned and retained information to make judgments and predictions about what is happening at a specific point in time.

Schemata are formed to represent concepts, personal experiences, reasoning strategies and algorithms, and problem-solving approaches and techniques. A schema for "cat" could contain concepts, or **subschemata,** such as "fur, four legs, tail, and drinks milk." The "cat" schema could also include more personalized concepts such as "sits on my lap, called Maybelle, jumps on the couch, and scratches me." Collectively, these subschemata help the person predict and understand what stimuli in the world classify as a "cat."

All information contained within the long-term memory must come through the working memory first. Information within the working memory is encoded into a neurolinguistic or language-based code for storage. Once stored, this information must be accessed or located to be used; and once located, the information must be **retrieved**, or brought up from the long-term memory, and transferred to the working memory system.

TEACHING STRATEGIES TO ENHANCE LEARNING AT EACH STAGE OF INFORMATION PROCESSING

This section contains some teaching recommendations and strategies to use to enhance students' processing and retaining of information during each stage of learning. To help students remember information more effectively during the initial phases of learning, teachers should emphasize *drill, practice, and repetition* of new skills and concepts until students can use and apply this knowledge automatically. Visual, auditory, experiential, and other kinds of *multimodal learning experiences* using a variety of problem formats and situations can help students develop automaticity as well as provide interesting learning opportunities. During the course of these activities, teachers should *get feedback from the children* about what they are able to attend to and retain so that their working memory capacities are not overloaded.

Teachers may need to *organize newly presented information* in ways that maximize students' ability to derive and assign meaning to the information and connect it with information that they have already learned. Some ways to accomplish organizing information are by clustering knowledge into categories, patterns, or sequences that encourage the students to understand interrelationships among concepts while they are learning and memorizing (Mayer, 1987). Charts summarizing large quantities of information may help students form mental pictures or images that make their ideas and concepts more concrete and comprehensible. Imagery has been shown to be a very effective strategy to enhance learning, memory, and recall.

Visual models using color coding to emphasize various components can also be very effective to encourage imagery formation and development during learning (Webster, 1992). Using outlines with written narrative explanations or creating written hierarchies for students are two forms of elaborative encoding that may assist some students. Research by Clark and Paivio (1991) has shown that people can learn and recall concrete words better than abstract words and concepts, because concrete words and concepts are encoded as both visual images and verbal labels whereas abstract concepts are encoded only as verbal labels. This form of elaborative encoding is referred to as the **dual coding hypothesis**.

Other helpful teaching strategies include using **analogies**, which teach students to look for similarities between new concepts and previously learned concepts (Mayer & Wittrock, 1996), and using mnemonic devices. **Mnemonic devices** are memory and recall facilitators that enable students to form associations between knowledge and information that do not naturally exist. There are five kinds of mnemonic devices that can be used readily in school subjects. The first of these is **rhyming** mnemonics. One example of a rhyming mnemonic is the poem used to remember the number of days in the months: "30 days hath September, April, June, and November." Rhyming mnemonics are very useful to recall and remember factual information.

The second type of mnemonic device, the **acronym**, can be effective to learn and recall a short list of items. The first letter of each item in the list is used to create a shorthand and an easily remembered concept. For example, HOMES is an acronym to recall the names of the five Great Lakes (Huron, Ontario, Michigan, Erie, Superior). The SCUBA acronym refers to a self-contained underwater breathing apparatus. The acronym need not have a generally accepted format; it can be one that has unique cuing value only to the person using it. The primary goal of the acronym mnemonic device is to be an effective cue for retrieval.

Third, **acrostic mnemonic devices** involve creating a sentence based on the first letter of each word contained in a list of items to be remembered. A common acrostic used in graduate programs to help students learn the names of the 12 cranial nerves is, "On old Olympus's towering tops a Finn and German vend some hops." Although learned by this author more than 30 years ago, this acrostic still incites fresh recall of the names, in order, of the 12 cranial nerves. The first letter of each word is a cue for the name of the specific cranial nerve: olfactory, optic, oculomotor, trochlear, trigeminal, abducens, facial, ventriculo-cochlear, glossopharyngeal, vagus, accessory, and hypoglossal (some poetic license is taken with nerves 8 and 11).

Fourth, the **method of loci** is a mnemonic device that uses visual images with a set of well-known locations to recall large quantities of information. For example, a person might think about various locations in the kitchen as cues to remember what purchases to make during grocery shopping. The shopper might begin this mental tour with the refrigerator for meats and dairy, move to the oven for foods to be cooked during the week, go to a drawer where the storage bags and other paper products are stored, and conclude in the pantry to identify canned goods.

The fifth mnemonic device, the **keyword**, involves isolating part of a word, creating a visual image that represents the keyword, and using it to form a physical image. The keyword device is useful when trying to remember the meanings of words or in learning a foreign language. To remember the meaning of the Italian word *biblioteca*, for example, a person might focus on *biblio* and associate it with the Bible. This would then be associated with a place where books are kept, the library.

FORGETTING

Forgetting occurs when a person loses the ability to retrieve information from memory. Interference by new information (Postman & Underwood, 1973) and **decay**, the process of learned information simply fading away, are the two main reasons people forget. The role of each in forgetting remains a controversial issue (Altmann & Gray, 2002) that is beyond the scope of this discussion. In the working memory it is believed that interference causes much of the forgetting that occurs.

Forgetting information stored in long-term memory seems to represent an entirely different set of circumstances, though. Information stored in the long-term memory is "permanent." Therefore, it cannot easily be lost. Rather, it is believed that either previously learned information (**proactive interference**) or newly acquired information (**retroactive interference**) interferes with a person's ability to retrieve the target information on demand. The greater the number of retrieval cues present, the higher the probability that the information will be recalled from long-term memory. The more retrieval cues that exist during original learning, the more likely that the information will be recalled later when it is needed. As such, assuming normal neurological functioning, many instances of forgetting from the long-term memory are really failures by the person to have a sufficient number of retrieval cues available to access and regenerate the target knowledge.

PROBLEM SOLVING

The ability to solve problems is a very important skill for everyone, because people encounter problems every day in one or more areas of their lives. A problem exists when there is a discrepancy between a current situation and a desired outcome. A person solves a problem by closing the gap between desire and reality.

Although several different types of problems exist, all problems can be categorized as either well defined or poorly defined. A **well-defined problem** has a clear goal, and the possible strategies to reach that goal are either known or easily developed. A **poorly defined problem** has an unclear goal, and the strategies to reach the goal may be unclear or difficult to identify (Mayer & Wittrock, 1996).

A well-defined problem, also called a **routine problem**, has a ready-made solution. Basic arithmetic computations, such as addition and multiplication, are examples of routine problems. A poorly defined problem, also called a **nonroutine problem**, is more open ended and requires that the person develop a strategy to solve it. In general, most school-based problems are routine, whereas most problems faced in everyday life are nonroutine.

Regardless of the type of problem presented to the student, **problem solving** is the application of knowledge, skills, and information to achieve a desired goal or outcome. It is very important that teachers specifically address problem solving and teach students specific strategies and techniques to approach both routine and nonroutine problems.

Several different problem-solving strategies exist to help students focus on the sequence of steps necessary to achieve solutions. Bransford and Stein (1993) proposed the **IDEAL** strategy. This strategy involves a five-step sequence, with IDEAL being an acronym to cue students about each step in the process:

1. **Identify** problems and opportunities.

2. **Define** goals, and represent the problem by either breaking it into steps or using drawings, outlines, or charts to depict the information.

3. **Explore** possible strategies to approach solving the problem.

4. **Anticipate** outcomes and act.

5. **Look** back and learn.

Another problem-solving approach is **means-ends analysis**. The first step in this strategy is to identify the goal clearly and concretely. Next, the present situation is clarified, and then an analysis is done to determine the procedures required to reduce the gap between the goal and the situation. Finally, these procedures are implemented and evaluated.

A third strategy involves teaching the child to identify only the most important or relevant information in the problem. This requires the child to eliminate information that serves as a distraction. Once distracting information is eliminated, the child can use a means-ends analysis to solve the problem.

Finally, using **graphic representations** to illustrate a problem can often be a useful approach to clarifying a solution. A graphic representation can be a diagram, a flowchart, a brief outline, or a drawing of various parts of the problem using circles or other pictures (Katayama & Robinson, 1998).

A key element of effective problem solving is creativity, which enables a student to view a problem from many sides. Three variables that can seriously hamper a student's ability to engage in creative, and thus effective, problem solving include: the student's cognitive developmental status, response set, and functional fixedness.

Problem solving is an extremely complicated cognitive activity that involves fairly high levels of intellectual maturity and sophistication. It also requires that the child be able to view problems from different perspectives that reflect varying understanding about how the solution goal can be achieved. In general, young children will have a great deal of difficulty looking at problems in a creative, alternative manner because they simply have not attained the sophisticated level of cognitive development needed. Instruction in problem solving must be carefully adjusted to the cognitive developmental status of each child. Children functioning in the early concrete operational stage of development will have a great deal of difficulty reasoning abstractly and then applying these abstractions to situations that have little similarity to the situations in which they first learned the principle. This does not mean that children at this stage are not intelligent or are incapable of being taught problem-solving strategies. Rather, it means that these children have not reached the level of cognitive development required to begin making abstractions and generalizations.

The second variable affecting problem solving is the tendency of some people to respond to a problem in the way that they are most familiar. A student's **response set** may cause the child to respond in rigid and persistent patterns, even though these patterns fail to achieve a correct solution to the problem.

Finally, the third variable that can impede problem solving is functional fixedness. **Functional fixedness** is the inability of a person to use tools or objects creatively to solve problems (Duncker, 1945). Creative problem solving often requires the person to use tools or view the problem in unusual and/or different ways. An example of functional fixedness is when a person has a screwdriver available but spends 15 minutes looking for a specific paint-can-opening device to remove the lid from a can of paint. The screwdriver could serve the same purpose even though it has other uses in addition to prying off lids from paint cans.

A number of specific teaching strategies have been shown to be very useful in teaching problem solving. One effective technique is called **brainstorming** (Osborne, 1963). In this approach two or more students work together and suggest all the ways they can think of to solve a problem. None of the suggestions is evaluated as a possible solution until all suggestions have been made. This strategy encourages students to focus on more than one approach as a potential solution.

Setting a relaxed climate in the classroom can also encourage problem solving. In a relaxed climate students are more likely to open up and freely express their ideas and perspectives about solution options (Benjafield, 1992; Tishman, Perkins, & Jay, 1995).

Teaching students how to apply algorithms in problem solving can also be very effective. An **algorithm** is a step-by-step process to achieve a goal and is usually unique to a specific domain or subject area. Choosing the correct algorithm guarantees arriving at a correct answer. Mathematics and many of the sciences contain algorithmic procedures that result in the same outcome each time they are applied.

Heuristics are general strategies to use in problem solving that only sometimes lead to the correct answer. Heuristics are often applied to poorly defined problems for which no algorithms exist. Heuristic procedures are often very useful in subjects such as geometry or dealing with social and interpersonal relationships.

Sometimes it is appropriate to approach problem solving using a **working backward strategy**, in which a person begins with the goal and works backward to reach the unsolved initial question. This strategy is often useful in teaching subjects with poorly defined problems and no algorithms available to achieve solutions. It can also be a good way to set up intermediate time lines when working with a complicated or extended problem.

For example, an assignment in a world history class might be to discuss the significance of the building of the Berlin Wall following World War II. This is a complex topic because there are many reasons that led to this wall, some of which date back decades before it was constructed. Students will be easily overwhelmed by its complexity.

Using a working backward strategy, students would begin with the year the wall was built and the immediate circumstances associated with it. Instruction would then examine the political conditions existing during the war that preceded its construction. Next, pre-war political conditions might be addressed until each of the major factors leading to construction of the Berlin Wall are unraveled.

Finally, trying to verbalize the nature of the problem can sometimes give direction and focus and thereby lead to a successful solution. While talking about the problem, the student might engage in logical thinking, searching for solutions by examining other topics or situations that have something in common with the problem at hand.

TEACHING AND THE TRANSFER OF INFORMATION

In the final stage of information processing, students use the information they have learned and retained in memory. **Transfer of information** describes how skills, concepts, and facts that students have learned affect how they learn new skills, concepts, and facts in a different situation or in relation to a new problem.

Transfer depends on learning and memory. The child must learn a concept, skill, or fact well enough to be able to apply it accurately or perform it correctly. This information must then be retained in memory and available for use later. The child needs to know when a new problem can be solved using a certain piece of previously learned information. Because transfer requires understanding and insight, it is a high-level cognitive skill that reflects intellectual maturity and competence. Three types of transfer of information exist: positive, negative, and zero.

A transfer of information is **positive** when a student uses information in a constructive manner to solve new problems. It makes new learning easier. For example, learning Latin can often make learning Italian easier because of the large number of similarities between the two languages.

Transfer of information is **negative** when previously learned information interferes with new learning. Frequently a concept, skill, or fact that a student is learning is similar to one that the student has already learned. Because of this similarity, the student inappropriately uses what was first learned to try to solve the new task. For example, a racquetball player may try to use the same arm positions and stroke mechanics when playing tennis, even though these movements typically cause poor returns and many losses.

Zero transfer is when skills learned in one setting have no impact on the acquisition of new skills in a different setting. It is not likely that martial arts training will interfere with or enhance learning about the parts of a flower in botany class.

Transfer can be either specific or general. With **specific transfer** a skill or fact learned in one setting is used in almost the same way to solve a problem in a new but similar situation. Using multiplication facts learned in mathematics class to solve problems requiring multiplication in a chemistry class is an example of specific, positive transfer. With **general transfer** a concept, skill, or fact learned in one setting is applied to a new problem in a new setting that is not similar to the original. Usually, general transfer involves using cognitive strategies to solve problems rather than just specific skills. General transfer occurs, for example, when a student in a botany class learns about flowers and trees and then uses this knowledge in an art class to draw garden landscapes.

Salomon and Perkins (1989) have also proposed the concepts of low-road transfer (specific skill development focused) and high-road transfer (rule and strategy focused). In **low-road transfer** of knowledge the student automatically uses a previously learned concrete skill or behavior in a new setting that is very similar to the one in which the student learned the skill. This kind of transfer requires high levels of practice in a number of situations so the student masters the skill to the point of it being automatic. Learning to change the spark plugs in an automobile transfers directly to changing the spark plug in a lawn mower. A student who has learned to use a word-processing program usually has little trouble learning to use the newest version of this same word-processing program on a faster, more powerful computer. Other examples of low-road transfer are riding a bicycle or driving a car. However, the skill of driving a car may not necessarily directly apply to driving a piece of construction equipment or a tractor-trailer.

The processes involved in **high-road transfer** are more abstract and refer to applying learned rules, strategies, or algorithms to new tasks and problems. The student intentionally and consciously identifies the rule or strategy and then relates it to solving a problem that may only vaguely resemble the original problem or situation. High-road transfer requires the student to know how the principles operate across different contexts and situations. The student also must be able to determine when the rule is relevant to the new task and how to adapt it, if necessary. Students taking a course in study skills should learn ways to take notes, read chapters in textbooks, organize and prepare for tests, and adopt metacognitive learning strategies that they can use in all their courses, regardless of the content.

Teachers must explicitly teach students both of these transfer strategies. If a student simply learns a concept, skill, or fact in isolation, it will likely be very difficult for the student to transfer the information independently. The essential components of transfer are the student knowing the necessary concept, skill, or fact very well, recalling this information correctly, and applying the information flexibly. Specific teaching approaches that encourage the transfer of information include

— offering students many opportunities to practice the information so it becomes automatic;

— helping students understand the general procedures and applications of the information;

— providing students with a wide variety of learning experiences in which they can use the information and the rules defining the information;

— using many different cues during teaching (verbal, visual, auditory, experiential) that help students learn, store, retain, and retrieve the information so it can be accessed and used in the future;

— providing students with clearly expressed objectives and advance lesson organizers to enhance initial learning of the information, which leads to better performance on the transfer task and may reduce the effects of negative transfer; and

— encouraging students to apply the newly learned information to both well-defined and poorly defined problems.

This kind of teaching approach enables most students to appreciate much of the information they are given in school. Because transfer strategies can make education a more relevant and practical experience, many students are motivated to invest the effort in learning them.

METACOGNITION

Knowing ways to learn and remember efficiently and effectively and then consciously and deliberately using those strategies is known as **metacognition** (Flavell, 1985). This kind of knowledge can produce significant positive advantages for students. First, it helps students perceive knowledge more accurately because they will defer making judgments until they acquire all the data available. Second, it enhances attention because students will choose carefully where to sit to gain the best and most advantageous viewpoint in a learning experience. Third, metacognition encourages students to organize new information in meaningful ways that capitalize on personal learning strengths and preferences while minimizing weaknesses or less preferred modalities. Finally, it increases students' awareness of what they need to learn and remember to be successful in school.

Semb and Ellis (1994) note that most forgetting in school occurs within four weeks after initial learning has taken place. However, in classes where students are actively involved in learning by participating in field trips, making observations and drawings about what they are learning, and answering questions, the amount of information lost can be greatly reduced. A **mastery learning** approach—having students study the material until they have developed automaticity with it—produces higher levels of recall for longer periods after the material is no longer being taught. Strategies such as frequent testing with corrective feedback given close to the time the testing occurs, peer tutoring, and experiential learning activities are all very effective strategies to facilitate initial learning acquisition and enhance long-term memory and recall.

These general instructional strategies also have been shown to enhance learning and retention:

— Using rote rehearsal for short-term memory tasks (although this approach does not lead to elaborative encoding and long-term retention).

— Using self-guiding questions that emphasize the who, what, where, when, why, and how of material.

— Providing students with clear objectives about where to focus their attention and effort.

— Encouraging students to link new information to knowledge they have already learned.

— Having students engage in distributed practice sessions to increase their exposure to the material using drill and repetition. In contrast, massed practice sessions are not effective in producing learning and retention.

— Presenting important information early in the lesson and then reviewing it at the conclusion of the lesson, thus lessening the effects of proactive and retroactive interference on retention and recall.

REFERENCES

Altmann, E. M., & Gray, W. D. (2002). Forgetting to remember: The functional relationship of decay and interference. *Psychological Science, 13*(1), 27–33.

Anderson, R. C. (1984). Some reflections on the acquisition of knowledge. *Educational Researcher, 13*(9), 5–10.

Ashcraft, M. (1989). *Human memory and cognition.* Glenview, IL: Scott, Foresman.

Atkinson, R. C., & Shiffrin, R. M. (1968). Human memory: A proposed system and its control processes. In K. Spence & J. Spence (Eds.), *The psychology of learning and motivation,* (Vol. 2, pp. 742–775). New York: Academic Press.

Berk, L. (1997). *Child development* (4th ed.). Boston: Allyn & Bacon.

Bransford, J. D., & Stein, B. S. (1993). *The ideal problem solver* (2nd ed.). New York: W. H. Freeman.

Benjafield, J. G. (1992). *Cognition.* Englewood Cliffs, NJ: Prentice-Hall.

Duncker, K. (1945). On solving problems. *Psychological Monographs, 58* (5, Whole No. 270).

Clark, J., & Paivio, A. (1991). Dual coding theory and education. *Educational Psychology Review, 3,* 149–210.

Flavell, J. (1985). *Cognitive development* (2nd ed.). Upper Saddle River, NJ: Prentice-Hall.

Flavell, J., Friedrichs, A., & Hoyt, J. (1970). Developmental changes in memorization processes. *Cognitive Psychology, 1,* 324–340.

Katayama, A. D., & Robinson, D. H. (1998, April). *Study effectiveness of outlines and graphic organizers: How much information should be provided for students to be successful on transfer tasks?* Paper presented at the annual meeting of the American Educational Research Association, San Diego.

Mayer, R. E. (1987). Learnable aspects of problem solving: Some examples. In D. E. Berger, K. Pezdek, & W. P. Banks (Eds.), *Applications of cognitive psychology: Problem solving, education, and computing* (pp. 109–122). Hillsdale, NJ: Erlbaum.

Mayer, R. E., & Wittrock, M. C. (1996). Problem-solving transfer. In D. C. Berliner & R. C. Calfee (Eds.), *Handbook of educational psychology* (pp. 47–62). New York: Macmillan.

Miller, G. A. (1956). The magical number seven, plus or minus two: Some limits on our capacity for processing information. *Psychological Review, 63,* 81–97.

Neisser, U. (1967). *Cognitive psychology.* New York: Appleton-Century-Crofts.

Osborne, A. F. (1963). *Applied imagination.* New York: Scribner's.

Postman, L., & Underwood, B. (1973). Critical issues in interference theory. *Memory and Cognition, 1,* 19–40.

Salomon, G., & Perkins, D. N. (1989). Rocky roads to transfer: Rethinking mechanisms of a neglected phenomenon. *Educational psychologist, 24,* 113–142.

Samuels, S. (1988). Decoding and automaticity: Helping poor readers become automatic at word decoding. *Reading Teacher, 41*(8), 756–760.

Schneider, W., & Shiffrin, R. (1977). Controlled and automatic human information processing: Detection, search, and attention. *Psychological Review, 84,* 1–66.

Semb, G. B., & Ellis, J. A. (1994). Knowledge taught in school: What is remembered? *Review of Educational Research, 64*(2), 253–286.

Siegler, R. S. (1991). *Children's thinking* (2nd ed.). Englewood Cliffs, NJ: Prentice-Hall.

Tishman, S., Perkins, D. N., & Jay, E. (1995). *The shrinking classroom.* Boston: Allyn & Bacon.

Webster, R. E. (1992). *The Learning Efficiency Test and Manual.* (2nd ed.). Novato, CA: Academy Therapy Publications.

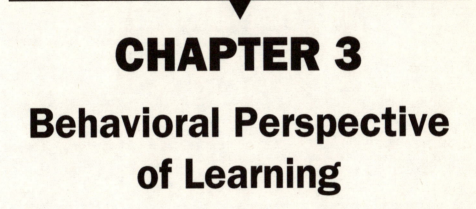

CHAPTER 3
Behavioral Perspective of Learning

CHAPTER 3

BEHAVIORAL PERSPECTIVE OF LEARNING

The behavioral perspective of learning is one of the most widely accepted and utilized approaches within American public schools. Among the reasons for the approach's appeal are that it has a strong research base to support the effectiveness of its interventions, it is practical, its impact is often quickly apparent, and it is relatively easy to implement its strategies for one student or an entire class. Human behavior is seen as the result of **conditioning**, where two events or stimuli are consistently paired so that the presence of one evokes the occurrence of the second. This contiguity among stimuli leads to learning.

Two types of conditioning exist: **classical conditioning** and **operant conditioning.** Four people have made especially distinguished contributions to the study of conditioning: **Ivan Pavlov** (1849–1936) developed the procedures described as classical conditioning, while **Edward Lee Thorndike** (1874–1949), **John Broadus Watson** (1878–1958), and **Burrhus Frederic Skinner** (1904–1990) are responsible for the operant conditioning perspective, which emphasized the role of reinforcement in learning.

CLASSICAL CONDITIONING

Pavlov, a physiologist and 1904 Nobel Prize recipient (for his work on the physiology of digestion), began his research on conditioning while trying to locate the causes of emotional disorders in humans. He believed that these disorders were caused by a disturbed nervous system. While researching this problem he observed that the dogs used in his experiments would react in predictable ways when it was their feeding time. It soon became evident that the laboratory assistants carrying food buckets, their footsteps, and the sight of meat powder were strong auditory and visual cues that caused the dogs to stop what they were doing, go to the closest part of the cage, and begin salivating.

From these observations he devised an experiment in which he paired a sound with meat powder. He then measured how much the dogs salivated in response to the meat powder paired with the sound and then the sound alone. When he presented just the sound (**neutral stimulus**, or **NS**) the dogs did not salivate. When he presented only the meat powder (**unconditioned stimulus**, or **UCS** or **US**) the dogs salivated (**unconditioned response**, or **UCR** or **UR**). The dogs had not learned to salivate to the meat powder—it was a natural and uncontrollable response.

Pavlov then presented the sound (NS) followed closely by meat powder (UCS) and found that the dogs would salivate (UCR). He repeated this process several times and then presented only the sound without the meat powder. He found that the sound alone caused the dogs to salivate. The previously neutral sound had become a **conditioned stimulus** (**CS**) that evoked salivation. At this point in the process the salivation by the dogs was referred to as a **conditioned response** (**CR**) because the dogs had learned to associate the sound with the presence of the meat powder. It was later found that the optimum time between presenting the NS and the UCS was between *0.5 and 1.0 second*. This interval produced the quickest and strongest association in the animals. Pavlov's classical conditioning is sometimes called **type S conditioning** because of the importance of the stimulus in evoking the desired response.

In summary, the steps involved in classical conditioning are:

1. Present sound (**NS**) → No response from dog

2. Present meat powder only (**UCS**) → Dog salivates (**UCR**)

3. Present sound only, wait a second, and then present meat powder → Dog salivates

4. Present sound (**CS**) → Dog salivates (**CR**)

Later research showed that conditioned responses could also be prompted from humans. Some examples are taking your foot off the accelerator when you see blue flashing lights in front of you on the highway, even if you are doing the speed limit; sneezing when you are exposed to bright sunlight after being in a dark theater; and not talking when you are in a classroom and someone turns the lights off. These principles have also been successfully used to develop treatment programs for autistic and seriously emotionally disturbed children and substance abusers.

OPERANT CONDITIONING

Thorndike was the first American researcher to develop a theory of human learning based on experimentation. He studied the time it took cats to escape from a box in which they had to pull a chain or push against a pole to open a door, escape, and get food. He found that the cats got progressively quicker in escaping as they became more familiar with the box and how to pull the chain or push against the pole. Thorndike also used chickens in a maze-running task and found that they could not perform as well as cats.

He hypothesized that all learning initially involves trial and error. Once a person solves a problem, he or she can then solve that problem again, as well as solve similar types of problems, quickly and accurately. Thorndike proposed several laws about learning, the most important of which was the law of effect. The **law of effect** states that if a behavior is followed by a satisfying change in the environment, the probability of that behavior being repeated in similar situations in the future is very high. On the other hand, if the behavior results in an unsatisfying outcome, then the probability of it occurring again is very low. This law is the basis of operant conditioning.

Watson, often considered the founder of behaviorism, devised an experiment in which he used an 11-month-old infant named Albert (Watson & Rayner, 1920). First, Albert was allowed to see a white rat. Initially, the infant showed no fear of the rat and actually tried to touch it. Subsequently, an experimenter standing behind Albert would strike a steel bar loudly with a hammer each time Albert reached for the rat. The child first would jump, then whimper, and eventually cry whenever the rat was present. It was later found that Albert's fear of white and furry objects *generalized* to a rabbit, dog, fur coat, cotton, and Santa Claus mask. The significance of the results is that Watson was the first to show that human emotions could be classically conditioned.

Skinner, ranked in 1991 as the eighth most influential American psychologist (Korn, Davis, & Davis, 1991), greatly expanded on Watson's research and its relevance to human learning. His approach is referred to as **type R** or **operant conditioning** because the strength of the conditioning is shown by the frequency of responding. He proposed that **respondent behavior** (elicited by a known stimulus) and **operant behavior** (not clearly related to a stimulus) are governed by two general principles:

1. A response followed by a reinforcer tends to be repeated.

2. A **reinforcer** is anything that increases the likelihood of the behavior occurring again.

Five kinds of reinforcers exist:

1. **Positive:** something that the person desires and is given or added for an acceptable behavior; for example, a child receives a token or money for completing an in-class assignment.

2. **Negative:** something that the person does not desire and is taken away when the person shows a target behavior; for example, a teacher stops blowing a whistle when students sit in their seats, or the buzzer stops when a driver fastens the seat belt. Stopping the whistle blowing or the buzzing increases the likelihood of students being in their seats or the driver using the seat belt.

3. **Primary:** something that is naturally occurring and related to survival, such as food, water, or heat.

4. **Secondary:** a neutral stimulus that is paired with a primary reinforcer, such as money, a token to exchange for candy, or good grades in school.

5. **Generalized:** a secondary reinforcer that is paired with more than one primary reinforcer and does not depend on the condition of deprivation to be effective; for example, athletic achievements or social status.

Two variables determine how reinforcement will be given:

1. **Schedules of reinforcement** refer to *how* the reinforcement will be given. There are two types of scheduling:

   a. **Continuous scheduling** involves the reinforcement being given every time a student shows the desired target behavior. For example, a student would receive a piece of candy for every in-class assignment completed with 80 percent or higher accuracy. Continuous scheduling is best used to strengthen a new behavior so it occurs more often, and it is the fastest way to get a student to behave in a desired manner. It is often used in the preliminary stages of shaping. The liability of continuous scheduling is that it can become very expensive for the teacher to use because it requires giving the student many primary or secondary reinforcers. It also has the high potential to lose its effectiveness rather quickly because the student can become satiated and stop working for the reinforcer. Further, once the desired behavior is not reinforced, it disappears very quickly. This disappearance of the target behavior is called **extinction**.

b. **Intermittent scheduling** involves giving the reinforcement based on a predetermined number of responses displayed by the child or the passage of time. This is the most cost-efficient and effective way to maintain a behavior once it has become established as a regular part of a student's behaviors. Because the student does not receive the reinforcer every time he or she shows the target behavior, there is a lower probability of the student becoming satiated and not responding to the reinforcer. This approach shows much greater resistance to extinction.

2. **Categories of reinforcement** refer to *when* the reinforcement is given (based on the number of behaviors shown or the passage of time). There are two types of categories:

   a. A **ratio category** makes reinforcement depend on the number of target behaviors shown by the student.

   — A **fixed ratio** (**FR**) category provides reinforcement after the student shows a specified number of the target behavior. For example, an **FR3** means that the student will be reinforced every third time he or she shows the target behavior. Fixed categories tend to have little persistence and extinguish quickly when the reinforcement ceases.

   — A **variable ratio** (**VR**) category provides reinforcement for target behaviors based on the *average number* rather than a predictable number of responses. A **VR4** means that the student is reinforced on the average for every fourth target behavior shown. This means that the student could show three target behaviors and get reinforced on the first and third behavior but not receive any reinforcement for the next five target behaviors shown. There are a variety of ways in which the reinforcement pattern can be organized using the VR category. VR shows the greatest durability and resistance to extinction.

   b. An **interval category** depends on the passage of time to determine when the student receives reinforcement. The student gets reinforced for the first target behavior shown after the specified period has expired. During the beginning portions of the period the student may not respond at high rates with the target behavior. But as the end of the time interval approaches, there is generally an increase in the target behavior as the likelihood of receiving the reinforcer approaches.

Students often show a pattern of studying that reflects the interval category when they postpone studying until the night or two before an examination. Then they show increased rates of studying when the examination is looming the next day. Interval category strategies encourage the student to show the desired behavior at higher levels than do the ratio categories once the behavior has become established. There are two types of interval categories:

— A **fixed-interval category (FI)** reinforces the student for the target behavior when a predetermined period of time has passed. An **FI5** category means that the reinforcement is given for the first target behavior shown after five minutes have elapsed.

— A **variable-interval (VI)** category provides reinforcement for target behavior based on the average time period that has elapsed. A **VI5** category offers reinforcement on the average following the passage of five minutes and when the target behavior is shown.

Punishment reduces the likelihood of an unwanted behavior occurring again in the future. The use of punishment techniques *suppresses* unwanted behaviors but does not teach the child new behaviors that are more adaptive. Skinner argued that punishment is generally temporary and ineffective in the long term because it often creates many negative emotional side effects. When the threat of punishment does not exist, however, the unwanted behavior often recurs. Two types of punishment exist:

1. **Positive punishment** involves *adding something negative* for the child based on an inappropriate behavior. One example of positive punishment would be scolding. Such techniques involve presenting something highly negative for the child to reduce the probability of misbehavior.

2. **Negative punishment** involves removing *something desirable* when the child displays an undesirable behavior. An example of this is restricting the child's time with peers for not behaving acceptably.

It is important to remember that punishment involves either applying something that is undesirable or denying something that is desirable. The ultimate goal of punishment is reducing the target behavior, which can

Table 3.1 Reinforcement and Punishment

Action	Effect on Child Displaying Target Behavior	Effect on Frequency of Target Behavior
Reinforcement		
Positive	Receives something desired	Increased
Negative	Has something undesired taken away	Increased
Punishment		
Positive	Receives something undesired	Decreased
Negative	Has something desired taken away	Decreased

only be determined by either taking away a privilege or evaluating the effect of the punishment on the child. For some children a time-out can actually be a reinforcer, depending on how they view it.

Using punishment with anyone raises many problems. It has been argued that punishment tends to weaken a negative behavior. In fact, it simply suppresses the behavior based on the situation and people involved. Some of the *uncontrollable, negative side effects* of using punishment include:

1. The child is not given corrective feedback about how to behave.

2. The child is shown that "might makes right" or that the more powerful you are the more you can dominate another person.

3. It often makes the child angry and can generate various kinds of aggression of a subtle or covert nature from the child.

4. Punishment often generates undesirable side effects in the person giving the punishment.

5. The punished child often develops fear and avoidance for the person giving out the punishment and/or the setting associated with the punishment.

A summary of the various approaches to both reinforcement and punishment is shown in Table 3.1.

PRACTICAL APPLICATIONS OF BEHAVIORAL PSYCHOLOGY

When a child does not show a desired behavior at a sufficiently high level of frequency, or at all, the teacher cannot immediately implement a reinforcement program. It is also difficult to predetermine what can be an effective and motivating reinforcement for a particular child. Two strategies can help raise the child's behavior to the desired level of occurrence. The first is the **Premack principle**, which states that a preferred activity should be used to strengthen a less preferred behavior (Premack, 1959). For example, to get a desired dessert, a child must eat all the collards on the dinner plate. Eating the collards leads to the desired dessert. No collards, no dessert! There are many ways in which this principle can be applied effectively, without conflict or argument.

The second strategy is **shaping**, in which the child who shows the desired behavior infrequently or not at all is taught how to behave in the desired way. Shaping consists of eight steps:

1. Select the target behavior.
2. Break down the target behavior into a sequence of sub-behaviors.
3. Evaluate the child to determine which of these sub-behaviors are shown and at what level of occurrence.
4. Select an appropriate reinforcer.
5. Determine the sub-behavior in the sequence that the child displays most frequently and reinforce it; gradually reinforce more complex sub-behaviors that are closer to the target behavior.
6. Use a continuous schedule of reinforcement initially to stabilize the sub-behavior.
7. Shift to a fixed interval or fixed ratio category of reinforcement.
8. Transition to a variable interval or ratio category of reinforcement.

Behavior modification is a very popular set of management techniques to help children perform better behaviorally and academically. The principles of behavior modification can be used in a classroom setting in at least six different ways: time-out, token economies, contingency contracting, response cost system, planned ignoring, and corporal punishment.

Time-out is a generally effective type of negative punishment that requires removing the student from the classroom because the teacher believes that attention from other students is reinforcing the undesirable behavior. One implementation of time-out is to remove the student from the larger class setting but keep the student in the room, able to see what is happening from the time-out area. Alternatively, the student can be moved to an area of the classroom where they cannot see what is happening, but remains in the general class setting. A third way to implement time-out is by secluding and isolating the student from the class, putting the student in a low-stimulus, safely monitored setting for a given period with no contact with anyone. Time-out works best when it is paired with a positive reinforcement program and is especially useful with aggressive children. Yet it can be reinforcing to some children who find being alone preferable.

A **token economy** uses a positive reinforcement strategy in which the teacher identifies a set of desired behaviors for a student and awards a token—for example, a poker chip, colored paper clip, or hash mark on an index card—each time the child shows a target behavior. The student accumulates these tokens and can trade them in for reinforcers such as candy, free time on the computer, or some other valued activity. A token economy can be very effective to enhance positive behaviors and increase the student's productivity in completing both in-class and homework assignments, especially when there is a home-based component to support the program used at school. To be most effective, a token economy must be used consistently. The point values for desired behaviors must be carefully set and the student required to put forth a good deal of consistent effort so satiation effects are minimized.

Contingency contracting involves the teacher and student jointly developing a written contract specifying a set of mutually agreed-on academic and/or social behavioral goals. The teacher agrees to grant the student certain desired privileges or rewards when the goals are achieved. Goals can be both short term and long term and can be used for one student or an entire class. Using a home-based reinforcement system will intensify the effectiveness of this positive approach to student behavior.

With a **response cost system** the student has something desirable taken away when an undesirable behavior is shown. This approach is typically used as part of a token economy system. The tokens or points the student earns for appropriate performance, encourage positive conduct and performance, while the response cost system serves to suppress unwanted behaviors.

Planned ignoring simply involves a teacher ignoring inappropriate behavior by not reacting verbally or nonverbally to the student. This strategy can be useful with students who behave inappropriately to get the teacher's attention. The primary limitation of this technique is that some students will interpret being ignored as tacit approval and reinforcement of the behavior by the teacher, with peers sometimes serving as additional sources of attention. This is not an effective technique to use with children who are seriously troubled, highly disruptive, or aggressive.

Corporal punishment is the use of physical punishment, such as spanking by using a hand or an object. It is a practice that is currently banned in 27 states in this country (National Coalition to Abolish Corporal Punishment in Schools, 2001). This approach has questionable effectiveness and should be used with a great deal of caution and discretion. Corporal punishment is not acceptable to most learning theorists and mental health professionals. Skinner was consistent in asserting that physical punishment merely serves to suppress behavior in specific situations and has limited educational value.

Behavior modification programs in schools and mental health settings are highly appealing for many reasons. These programs emphasize that learning occurs in small steps or intervals, that immediate feedback is best to facilitate learning, and that each child learns at a unique pace and rate. These approaches focus professionals' attention on how a child behaves, and the setting reinforces the behavior. It also clarifies the impact of consequences on behavior and enhances the teacher's level of management influence in the classroom. Finally, all behavior is viewed as the result of logical laws of learning that have been reinforced and rewarded by the child's environment.

COGNITIVE LEARNING THEORY

Cognitive learning theory is similar to behavioral learning in that both approaches see learning as dependent on experience and feedback that reinforce behavior. Whereas behavioral approaches view children as passive learners who are shaped by reinforcement, cognitive learning views children as having an active role throughout the entire learning process. Children form ideas, make inferences, arrive at conclusions, and try to understand their world. They learn by observing other people's behavior. They then determine if those behaviors are appropriate for them to use to reach their own goals.

Reciprocal determinism (Bandura, 1986) describes the relationships among how children behave, the environments they live in, and how they see and think about their behaviors and their environments. None of these three variables can be viewed in isolation or as separate from each other. Each variable interacts with the others in an active, continuous, and influential manner.

People learn to expect certain outcomes to occur when they behave in specific ways by seeing how these behaviors work for others. These **ex-**

pected outcomes become reinforcers or punishers. When an expected positive outcome does not occur, the child experiences this as punishment. If the expected outcome from a behavior is negative and it does not occur, the outcome becomes a reinforcer. If an expected outcome is positive and a positive outcome occurs, the behavior is also reinforced. In brief, reinforcement occurs when the outcome from a behavior is consistent with the child's expectations.

Bandura (1965) proposed that all human behaviors occur from **observational learning** and that the child does not necessarily use this information immediately. People observe how others behave and the specific results those behaviors produce. The people being observed are **models** who influence children's decisions about their own behaviors. Three types of models exist: direct models, symbolic models, and synthesized models.

In **direct modeling** the child simply imitates the model's behavior without any real understanding of the purpose of the behavior. For example, children who are hesitant to pet a dog may do so when they see their father pet the dog. **Symbolic modeling** occurs when the child views models in movies or reads about them in books and then decides to behave like them. A very common form of symbolic modeling occurs in television commercials that show famous athletes doing phenomenal athletic performances while wearing a certain brand of shoes. The implication is that anyone wearing the same brand of shoes will be able to perform similar amazing feats of athleticism. People buy the shoes with the implicit expectation that they will then possess some of the characteristics of the model who wears the same shoes.

Synthesized modeling occurs when the child takes parts of behaviors seen used by several different models and integrates those behaviors into a new set of behaviors to reach a goal. An example of this kind of modeling is when a young male college student begins to emulate two professors whom he views as scholarly examples by dressing in a style similar to each one. The student may grow a beard, wear a bow tie, and smoke a pipe because one of the professors has a beard and wears a bow tie to class each day, while the other smokes a pipe.

The impact of watching a model is magnified when children directly witness the results of behaviors for the model. This process, called **vicarious learning**, will usually motivate children to modify their own behaviors. Vicarious learning can either be reinforcing (vicarious reinforcement) or punishing (vicarious punishment). **Vicarious reinforcement** increases the probability of a behavior occurring, while **vicarious punishment** decreases or suppresses the frequency of the behavior. A reduction in the frequency of behaviors is called **inhibition**, because the children voluntarily choose to stop or inhibit these behaviors based on seeing the consequences for the person who shows them. Vicarious punishment would occur when students stop talking in the classroom unless they have permission because they see one of their peers punished for talking without the teacher's permission. Vicarious reinforcement exists when these same students see a peer rewarded for speaking only when given permission by the teacher. The other students in class begin raising their hands to get the teacher's permission to speak so they can also be rewarded.

The ability to control and change behaviors based on either direct experiences with reinforcement or by vicariously observing the behaviors of other people being reinforced indicates that human behaviors are generally self-regulated. **Self-regulation** means that children learn to set standards about their behavior based on their experiences. Once developed, **performance standards** become the way children evaluate their own levels of performance. If a child's performance standards are too high, the child typically becomes emotionally distressed and frustrated. People generally do not perform well or feel satisfied emotionally when personal performance standards consist of goals that are too difficult to attain or lie too far in the future. Performance goals should be **moderately difficult** so that the child is motivated to achieve them while receiving an ongoing sense of personal gratification when doing so.

Critical to performance standards is **perceived self-efficacy**, which is the belief a child holds about what he or she is capable (and incapable) of doing. Perceived self-efficacy evolves from the child's direct or vicarious experiences with success and failure. Verbal persuasion and encouragement may temporarily motivate a child, but it is perceived self-efficacy that will determine how successful the child is over the long term.

Children with high perceived self-efficacy try more activities with a greater sense of focus and determination, accomplish more, and are more persistent with the task than are children with low levels of perceived self-efficacy. A child's perceived self-efficacy does not necessarily have to be consistent with his or her **real self-efficacy**, or how the child truly performs in life activities. It is possible for a child to have high perceived self-efficacy and low real self-efficacy, and the discrepancy between these two views will create a great deal of frustration and disappointment because of continued failure in many activities the child attempts. Yet, if the child has high real self-efficacy and low perceived self-efficacy, there will also be feelings of frustration and disappointment because the child will not fully grow and develop.

Several variables affect observational learning. If a child is to learn by observing a model, the child must first be *attentive* to the characteristics and specific behaviors of the model. Once the child has paid attention to the characteristics of the model, the child must *retain* this information using visual images and verbal information. The verbal information also stimulates recall of the visual imagery, just as the visual imagery evokes recall of the verbal information.

After the child has paid attention to the model and retained the information mentally, the child must have the *necessary physical and behavioral characteristics* to perform the behaviors in their world. If the child does not have the physical characteristics to perform the behaviors or does not remember the information accurately, there will be a discrepancy between the child's actual behaviors and those of the model. This discrepancy can encourage the child to develop a **feedback loop** that redirects the child's behaviors so they gradually begin to match those of the model. The child changes the behaviors using *self-correction* and *self-observation* procedures.

Finally, the child must be *motivated* to use the behaviors seen in the model. As the child makes progress toward imitating a model's behavior, there is often a strong **self-reinforcement** experience. This feeling of self-reinforcement usually creates a deep sense of personal accomplishment that is highly motivating. It also encourages continued development and refinement of the behaviors.

Cognitive learning theory presumes that emotional and behavioral problems result from bad learning that leads to *faulty cognitive processes*. These processes come about in one of three ways. Children can develop a false belief because they *misperceive a situation*, such as seeing a teacher's constructive verbal feedback as being critical and antagonistic. Children can also develop a faulty cognitive process when a decision or judgment is made on the basis of *incomplete information*. Some teenagers create an unrealistic and inappropriate sense of entitlement and expectation about what their parents should purchase for them or allow them to do by watching certain kinds of television shows depicting teenagers driving expensive cars, wearing designer clothes, and skipping school to go to Acapulco for stress management. These teenagers erroneously believe that television is portraying the way life really is for most teenagers and, therefore, should be for them. These kinds of false beliefs often become self-perpetuating and lead to additional faulty beliefs that create bizarre social and personal behaviors. Finally, children can have *information-processing problems* that interfere with their ability to comprehend and understand language or social feedback.

Faulty cognitive processes cause children to develop inaccurate expectations and anticipations about the world that generate inappropriate behaviors. The goal of counseling is to help the child reduce the gap between their expectations about what the world has to offer them and the realities of their world.

REFERENCES

Bandura, A. (1965). Influence of a model's reinforcement contingencies on the acquisition of imitative responses. *Journal of Personality and Social Psychology, 11,* 589–595.

Bandura, A. (1986). *Social foundations of thought and action: A social-cognitive theory.* Englewood Cliffs, NJ: Prentice-Hall.

Korn, J. H., Davis, R., & Davis, S. F. (1991). Historians' and chairpersons' judgments of eminence among psychologists. *American Psychologist, 46,* 789–792.

National Coalition to Abolish Corporal Punishment in Schools. (2001). *Facts about corporal punishment.* Available at http://www.stophitting.com/NCAPS/index.html.

Premack, D. (1959). Toward emirical behavior laws: 1. Positive reinforcement. *Psychological Review, 66*(4), 219–233.

Watson, J. B., & Rayner, R. (1920). Conditioned emotional reactions. *Journal of Experimental Psychology, 3,* 1–14.

CHAPTER 4
Cognitive Development

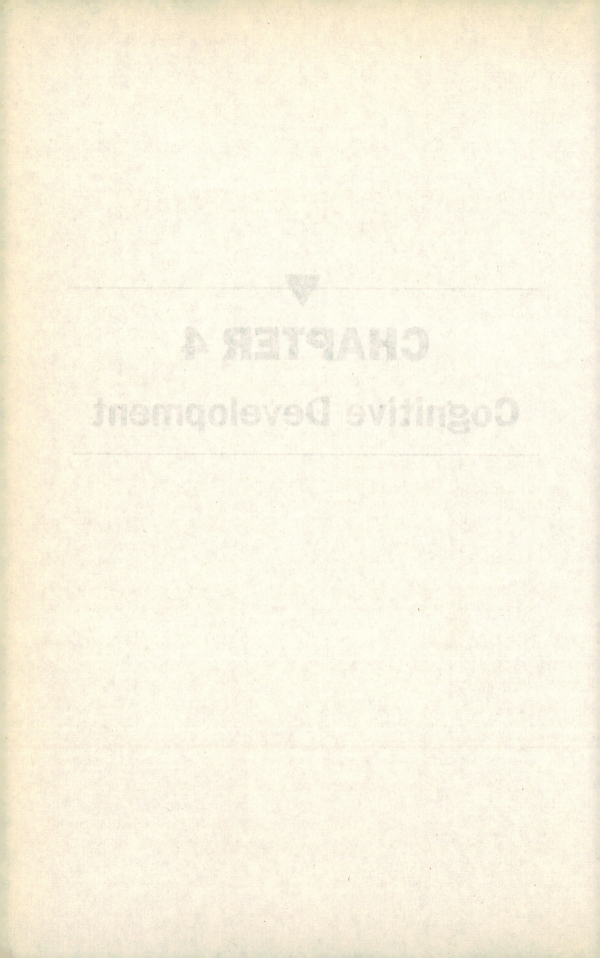

CHAPTER 4

COGNITIVE DEVELOPMENT

A person's **development** involves orderly changes that occur over time and improve the person's overall adaptation to the world. This adaptation also reflects complex patterns of behaviors and interpretations of the world. Coexisting with development is maturation. **Maturation** involves the natural and spontaneous changes that occur within a person because of genetically programmed codes. Maturation processes are typically of a physical nature and involve body structures and functions.

There are three important premises that underlie all types of development: (1) Individual differences exist in the *rates* at which people develop; (2) all development generally proceeds in an *orderly* fashion and is essentially the same for each individual; and (3) development occurs gradually, and its effects are long-standing improvements to adaptation.

This chapter examines two very prominent theories of cognitive development (Piaget and Vygotsky); a widely accepted theory of emotional and social development (Erikson); and two theories of moral development and values (Kohlberg and Gilligan). Adolescence, gender identity, mental health, and school readiness are then discussed. The chapter concludes with an examination of how children acquire language.

PIAGET'S GENETIC-EPISTEMOLOGICAL THEORY OF COGNITIVE DEVELOPMENT

Jean Piaget (1896–1990) is considered one of the most influential contributors to understanding children's intellectual development. His initial area of study was biology, but his research interests gradually focused on how knowledge emerges and evolves in people. Sometimes referred to as a *genetic epistemology,* Piaget's theory emphasizes the strong interdependency between genetics and the environment. He viewed **intelligence** as a set of behaviors that allows individuals to deal effectively and optimally with their world.

Key Terms

An in-depth study of Piaget's theory of intellectual development requires an understanding of several important terms. Piaget used the term *development* to describe how systematic changes occur within a person as a result of the effects from learning, personal experiences, and physical maturation of the central nervous system. Development begins in utero and continues until death. As people develop, their perceptions and interpretations of the world around them change, as does their understanding of the world. These concepts underlie much of Piaget's approach to cognitive development.

He viewed development as an active, *continuous process* that progresses through a set of *clearly identifiable stages* that apply to all people. He proposed that all children are born with an innate tendency to interact with the world and attempt to make sense of it. People organize and process information differently based on age and the kinds of experiences they have had.

The process of attempting to understand and make sense of the world is called **organization**. Organization requires that the child form **schemes**, or **schemata**, which are mental patterns within the mind that describe how the child thinks about and interprets the world. Schemes vary according to the child's age. Some examples of schemes are the understanding of quantity as applied to mathematics learned in the classroom and the application of that classroom knowledge in practical experiences outside the classroom, such as using money or counting objects.

As the child develops and matures, existing schemes typically become inappropriate or ineffective to explain events and experiences in the world. When this occurs the child is forced to reexamine these schemes and make adjustments to them—a process called **adaptation**. The goal of adaptation is to help the child achieve a state of **equilibrium**, which leads to a new understanding of how the world operates. Equilibrium occurs when the child is able to comprehend how the world operates so there is order, structure, and predictability that make it sensible. Piaget believed that seeking equilibrium is an innate tendency that maximizes adaptation to the world.

Adaptation also requires the child to undergo alternating processes, which Piaget termed accommodation and assimilation. **Accommodation** is the basic mechanism for human growth and it occurs when the child must modify an existing scheme so that it can be applied to new situations in a more accurate way that allows for adaptation, structure, understanding, and predictability. **Assimilation** occurs when the child takes new information from the world and incorporates it into an existing scheme. Children will assimilate only that information from the world that they are able to process cognitively. For example, a young child may first learn the concept *kitty* and use the word to refer to the family's cat, which is orange and white with a very short tail. As the child gets older, he or she begins to associate a number of other physical characteristics with this concept so that more than just one cat with only those physical attributes is described when the child uses the word *kitty*.

Cognitive development in children occurs through the interaction of assimilation and accommodation. This interaction forces children to achieve new levels of equilibrium in their understanding of the world. Each of these processes is necessary to maintain equilibrium. Without this active and ongoing interaction between these two processes, children would have a great deal of difficulty adjusting to the world and the change that is an inevitable part of life.

How a child thinks is also influenced by maturation, social experiences, and personal experiences in the physical world. Within the context of existing schemes the child processes information from each of these three sources. No new information is ever processed or understood without being related to preexisting schemes that the child has already developed.

Maturation is the process of physical and biological change that occurs within a child as a result of the interaction between the child's genetic characteristics and the environment in which he or she lives. Genetics provides the plan for development, while the environment interacts with genetics to influence how genetic characteristics will become visible, or manifested. It is possible that extreme environmental conditions, such as a head injury during infancy or an infant-onset disease, can impede or stop the emergence of genetically determined characteristics. In general, though, Piaget believed that a child's genetic characteristics and the environment interact with each other to lead to normal growth and development.

The second characteristic affecting development is the child's social experiences and interactions. As the child develops new schemes, experiences with other people allow the child to determine the veracity or accuracy of these schemes. If the child's schemes are generally consistent with those of others, the child achieves a state of equilibrium. On the other hand, if the child's schemes are not consistent with those of others, the child enters into a period of **disequilibrium**, and new information must be assimilated and accommodated. Disequilibrium encourages the development of new schemes to more appropriate and effective conceptualizations about the world. Children's ability to develop new schemes depends on the kinds of experiences they have within their families, the opportunities

Table 4.1
Summary of Piaget's Stages and Important Developmental Concepts

Stage	Key Concepts
Sensorimotor	Goal-oriented behaviors
	Object permanence
	Imitation of behaviors of others
Preoperational	Language development rapidly increases
	Centration
	Conservation
	Egocentricity
	Reversibility
	Transformation
Concrete Operational	Logical reasoning
	Engages in alternative perspectives, reversibility, and conservation
	Class inclusion
	Seriation
	Transitivity
	Classification
Formal Operational	Symbolic, systematic, and abstract reasoning
	Understanding of quantitative concepts
	Capacity to deal with hypothetical situations logically

they have to experience enriched cultural and educational activities, the kinds of peer experiences they encounter, and their parents' child-rearing practices.

The third variable affecting development is the child's experiences within the physical world. Children form schemes based on their transactions with their environment. Specific information that they are taught, the opportunity to use this information across a variety of different settings and problems, and the kinds of instruction and guidance they receive from adults and teachers are very significant variables that influence development as well as the emergence of new, appropriate schemes to understand reality.

With the key terms defined in this section serving as a foundation, it is now possible to examine Piaget's four stages of cognitive development:

the **sensorimotor stage** (0 to 2 years), the **preoperational stage** (2 to 7 years), the **concrete operational stage** (7 to 11 years), and the **formal operational stage** (11 years through adult). These stages are described in the following sections and summarized in Table 4.1.

Sensorimotor Stage

At this stage of development a child interacts with the world primarily through sensory and motor functions. Crying, sucking, breathing, and reflexes emerge first. Some of these reflexes are replaced slowly by voluntary behaviors, such as pushing or reaching for objects, and in the later phases of this stage the child develops increased mobility that allows experimentation with the world.

Many of the child's behaviors at this stage can be described as **goal oriented** because the behaviors are performed to achieve a certain outcome, such as being fed or changed. The major milestone attained toward the end of this stage is **object permanence**, which is the capacity to hold objects in memory. A simple example of object permanence is when a child plays with a jack-in-the-box toy: the child understands that when the jack is pushed down under the lid, it is hidden but still exists.

Of secondary importance is the child's imitation of behaviors, which begins to emerge during the later part of the sensorimotor stage. The child smiles as a response to an adult smile, and some children at this stage make cooing noises in reply to adult language. As the child grows older the ability to imitate behaviors will have increasing importance.

Preoperational Stage

At this stage of cognitive development children undergo many important changes in how they view their world. Language development grows rapidly, as does the ability to think using symbols and concepts. Children at this stage start to use the language of adults, but words and expressions do not have the same meanings as they do for adults. Children equate obedience with pleasing the parent. Most play is self-focused. Children presume that everyone thinks and sees the world exactly as they view it. Piaget defined five important cognitive characteristics that influence the processing of information from the world during the preoperational stage of development, although many children at this stage do not acquire all five characteristics.

The first characteristic is **centration**, or the ability to focus on one object or event while excluding other objects or events. Second is **conservation**, which is the notion that the quantity or amount of a substance remains the same regardless of its shape or the number of pieces into which it is divided. The classic illustration of conservation involves using two glasses with different shapes: Water is first poured into a glass that is short and wide. Then the water is poured from that glass into a glass that is tall and thin. During the initial phases of the preoperational stage many children will say that there is more water in the second glass than in the first.

The third characteristic of children at this stage of development is **egocentricity**, which reflects an inability to interpret events or situations from another person's point of view. Being egocentric can lead to some significant difficulties in peer relationships.

The fourth characteristic of the preoperational stage is **reversibility**— the ability to reason from a conclusion to its starting point. Children at this stage of development have tremendous difficulty performing this kind of mental operation. For example, a child may be presented with two lines of tokens, with five tokens in each line. When the tokens in each line are aligned most children, when asked if the two rows have the same number of tokens, will respond yes. However, when the distance between the tokens is expanded in the top row (but the number of tokens in the two rows remains the same), most children will say that the row with the widely spaced tokens has more tokens.

Finally, **transformation** is the ability to mentally retain an object when it is changed from one physical state to another. Because children at the preoperational stage tend to be highly focused in the immediate reality of their world, they have difficulty comprehending the concept of object change. When shown a ball of clay and then shown the same ball of clay formed into a cylinder, most children at the preoperational stage will be unable to say or understand that the clay in the cylinder is the same clay appearing first as a ball.

Concrete Operational Stage

At this stage children's cognitive development achieves a new level of sophistication. The ability to order and organize thoughts emerges as well as the mental capacity to relate these thoughts to life experiences. Children begin to be able to solve problems and understand relationships that are primarily concrete. The capacity for logical reasoning and understanding emerges, but children at this stage are restricted in their ability to use these skills across a wide variety of situations; they mainly use them in dealing with familiar situations. Concrete operational children acquire the ability to process information from a reversible perspective and begin to be able to take an alternative perspective or view about situations. Further, children at this stage begin to understand and use conservation in reasoning.

Four important cognitive characteristics emerge during this stage of development that allow children to interpret the world in unique and more mature ways. The first ability is **class inclusion**. This skill enables children to think and process a number of objects simultaneously and to begin to discern the relationships among objects that are related to each other. For example, concrete operational children are able to see that a banana, a watermelon, and an apple are all fruit. Prior to this stage of development children might see each of these fruits as different because they are focusing on the color or size of the fruit.

Seriation describes the ability to organize objects in a sequential order based on some overriding and organizing concept such as volume, weight, ranking, or size. In other words, children now begin to organize and classify the world according to some dimension or criterion. As children become more proficient with seriation, a second skill emerges that Piaget called transitivity. **Transitivity** is the ability to infer relationships between two objects or to compare and arrange two objects. An example that illustrates the use of transitive reasoning skills involves telling a child that John is shorter than Linda and Frank is taller than Linda. Younger children at the concrete operational stage cannot identify correctly whether John is shorter or taller than Frank. The older child at this stage, however, can make this distinction on the basis of height as the classifying dimension.

Classification reflects the child's ability to organize and group objects or concepts on the basis of common characteristics. Classification forms the foundation for the development of higher-level abstract reasoning skills.

Formal Operational Stage

The final stage of cognitive development is that of formal operational thought. Reasoning now goes beyond immediate sensory experiences and becomes transformed into symbols and symbolic thinking. An understanding of quantitative concepts develops in the order of objects and events, length and distance, volume, and object and ordering activities. Children at this stage develop the capacity to comprehend multidimensional measurements, such as area and volume. Full cognitive maturity is expected by the age of 15.

At this stage adolescents begin to examine the world in a more abstract and conceptual manner, analyzing problems systematically and deriving conclusions and generalizations from analysis. Adolescents begin to think and reason abstractly and systematically. They develop the capacity to generate hypotheses as well as the ability to deal with hypothetical situations rather than requiring the presence of concrete models. Logical reasoning skills evolve, and the ability to solve problems becomes more effective.

VYGOTSKY'S SOCIOCULTURAL THEORY OF COGNITIVE DEVELOPMENT

In recent years the contributions of the Russian-born developmental psychologist Lev Vygotsky have become increasingly appreciated and applied to educational settings. Although he died at the age of 37 (in 1934) from tuberculosis, he made two very important contributions to the study of cognitive development: the concepts of internalization and the zone of proximal development (ZPD).

Internalization is the process by which people mentally store and integrate information they see and experience in the environment. The primary source of information is social interaction. Children watch what other people do and say, as well as how people interact with and treat each other. On the basis of these observations of others' behaviors, they recreate within themselves how interactions in their world should proceed. Vygotsky places a strong emphasis on the impact of social feedback and interactions within the child's environment on the development of cognitive and mental structures.

The **zone of proximal development**, sometimes called the **zone of potential development**, represents the difference between the abilities a child actually develops and those the child might acquire if living in the most appropriate setting. In other words, the "zone" is the gap between a child's potential and his or her real-life behaviors, which are the product of the child's environment.

The notions of internalization and the ZPD offer some exciting and profound implications regarding the education of children. Presently, most educational systems use a **static assessment approach**, in which the child must give closed-ended responses to specific questions. The examiner does not help the child arrive at an answer, nor does the examiner give the child feedback about the correctness or incorrectnessness of any response. By constrast Vygotsky suggested that testing should proceed from a **dynamic assessment perspective**, in which the examiner provides the child with guided hints during problem-solving activities. The examiner focuses on the child's ability to use this feedback and make changes in problem-solving behaviors to reach a correct solution. The **Learning Potential Assessment Device** is the best-known instrument that uses this approach to evaluate children's cognitive characteristics (Feuerstein, 1979).

Feuerstein extended Vygotsky's work by emphasizing the role of parents in enhancing their children's learning through **mediated learning experiences** (**MLE**). The role of the adult is to introduce the child to an interesting environment or task and then help the child to learn by interpreting experiences, relying on language the child understands. The adults can also give direct instruction to the child about specific information as part of this educational developmental process.

This type of assisted instruction from adults teaches children strategies to use when they are faced with challenging tasks or problems. An MLE can also occur when a child **imitates** what an adult does or through **collaborative learning**, with peers working together to solve problems.

A critical component in Vygotsky's process of mediated learning is **language**, which may be the most important system of symbols that characterizes cognitive development in children. Vygotsky posited that children engage in **self-talk**, or **private speech**, which guides their thinking patterns and behaviors. As children mature their self-talk becomes internalized into an inner speech system that focuses their attention, assists with planning and concept formation, and helps children develop self-control.

Children's social and emotional development has a very significant influence on how they approach learning and school. Much of this influence occurs outside the school setting and is the result of children's interactions with important adult caretakers in their world.

ERIKSON'S THEORY OF PSYCHOSOCIAL DEVELOPMENT

Erik Erikson (1968) theorized that psychosocial development comprises eight stages. A person must advance through every stage to become a psychologically and mentally healthy individual. Each stage presents key social-emotional issues the person must resolve. The less able the person is to resolve the issues at any stage, the greater the probability that he or she will be emotionally troubled and have difficulty adjusting to life's demands.

There are two novel aspects of Erikson's theory of development. He believed that human development is based on the emergence of *predictable developmental crises* at different points in life. These crises emerge as a function of life experiences and are not necessarily related to chronological age. Moreover, he proposed that *development is a lifelong process*. Most theories of social and emotional development prior to Erikson's concluded at the adolescent stage. It was presumed that no further development of a significant nature occurred after the adolescent years.

Erikson's theory is based on several important presumptions: (1) All people have the **same basic needs**, and a person's **sense of self** develops in response to these needs; (2) development proceeds in **stages**, and each stage is characterized by a specific and unique psychosocial challenge or crisis; (3) **resolution of this challenge** or crisis provides opportunities for the person to develop into a more fulfilled individual; and (4) different stages represent different types of motivation that influence **how the individual focuses his or her energies** at that time.

The **eight stages of development** that Erikson devised, the approximate age levels at which each stage occurs, and the key challenge or crisis experienced at each psychosocial developmental stage are described in the following paragraphs.

Stage I, birth to 1 year old: trust versus mistrust. On the basis of life experiences with their caregivers infants learn either that they can trust the world and other people to meet their needs or that the world is a hostile, unforgiving place that is cold and without support. Infants who pass through this stage successfully can be expected to develop a positive and optimistic outlook toward life.

Stage II, 1 to 3 years old: autonomy versus shame. During this period children become increasingly independent and learn to master a substantial number of challenges, such as walking, talking, bowel control, and language. They also begin to increase their level of mobility within the world. The amount of support that children receive from significant adult caretakers, linked with the degree of success they have in mastering each of these challenges, serves to create a sense of competence and personal mastery. On the other hand, negative feedback from significant adults and/or difficulty in mastering these essential life skills can cause children to doubt their competency and feel ashamed of themselves for their failures.

Stage III, 3 to 6 years old: initiative versus guilt. As children gain independence from their parents, they are often led into direct conflict with parental authority. If conflicts are dealt with in healthy and encouraging ways, children develop a sense of confidence and eventually realize how to channel their energy into positive and constructive activities. If feedback from parents is negative because children are assertive, they may then begin to feel guilty whenever they try to take the initiative. An underlying sense of guilt can have significant influences on children as they continue to mature and affect the quality of their lives as well as create difficulties for them in developing a sense of purpose and meaning.

Stage IV, 6 to 12 years old: industry versus inferiority. Children at this stage develop a much wider range of experiences in their world and begin to develop a sense of **competence** about their ability to be successful in a variety of tasks and activities. Once again, support and encouragement within an affirming and structured setting serve to enhance children's feelings of competency and generate positive feelings of self-worth and self-regard. Failure and negative adult feedback undermine children's sense of self-worth and generate feelings of frustration and futility that interfere with their ability and willingness to take on challenges in life.

Stage V, adolescence: identity versus role confusion. The primary challenge during the adolescent period is clarifying personal **identity** (a person's sense of who he or she is and what values, priorities, and views of the world the person holds) based on the individual's gender and social status. During this stage adolescents begin to integrate information on social, cultural, intellectual, and sexual role identity into a unified sense of who and what they are as unique individuals. Difficulty in meeting this challenge can lead to an unclear sense of personal identity that has significant and lifelong repercussions.

Stage VI, early adulthood: intimacy versus isolation. The formation of emotionally meaningful and intimate relationships with other people becomes extremely important at this time. Young adults begin to learn how to offer love and commitment to other people in an altruistic manner. An inability to form emotionally intimate relationships with others can create a sense of loneliness and isolation as well as result in significant difficulties in social and interpersonal relationships.

Stage VII, middle adulthood: generativity versus stagnation. At this stage of life many adults take on careers or pursuits that allow them to make a contribution to the larger community, society, and even future generations. Many adults become highly productive and creative, which enhances their sense of purpose and meaning in life. Adults who do not complete this stage tend to be selfish and self-centered, leading lives that are often described as boring and lacking in a sense of purpose or fulfillment.

Stage VIII, old age: integrity versus despair. During the latter part of adulthood many people begin to address whether or not they have lived a life of meaning, purpose, and authenticity. It is not unusual for older adults to review their lives and past choices to determine if their decisions were successful or ineffective. Adults who are able to meet this challenge often gain wisdom and insight from the years of life that they have experienced. Adults who are unable to meet this challenge can become full of despair and have a sense of meaninglessness in their lives.

Although Erikson's psychosocial theory has been widely accepted in educational circles, it does not address the issue of **cultural relativity** in any of its stages. For example, do all societies value identity as a unique individual, which is an important element of Stage V? If a person has difficulty reconciling his or her past life, does it necessarily mean that all people will fall into despair in later adulthood, regardless of the culture in which they live? It has been very difficult to conduct research studies to support the validity of Erikson's assertions.

Perhaps the most important and educationally relevant aspect of Erikson's psychosocial theory is that it focuses educators on the significance of verbal and nonverbal feedback in the instructional process. It also highlights the need for educators to be sensitive to, and aware of, the environments that students come from and how these environments have served to shape students' attitudes and values about the educational process.

MORAL DEVELOPMENT

As children get older they gradually develop a better understanding of how other people may see things. This increased capacity to take another person's viewpoint is a very important component of socialization and healthy mental functioning. As part of this development children also continually develop moral standards. Social conventions may vary, but morality is universal because it defines standards for conduct that nearly all societies view as appropriate and inviolable. For example, in most societies murder and theft are viewed as inappropriate and unacceptable behaviors that are generally not tolerated. In most societies parents are viewed as authority figures.

There are two major viewpoints about how moral development proceeds. The first is that proposed by Lawrence Kohlberg (1984), which emphasizes an increasing understanding of justice. An alternative perspective, advanced by Carol Gilligan (1982), proposes that women are more concerned about caring than are men and that women's notions of justice have a far greater influence on the decisions women make every day regarding other individuals. The following sections discuss the salient points of each of these two perspectives on moral development.

Kohlberg's Stages of Moral Reasoning

Kohlberg (1984) proposed that moral reasoning evolves in levels and stages. He identified six stages and organized the six stages into three levels. The three levels are preconventional, conventional, and postconventional, and each level contains two stages of moral reasoning and development.

Level 1, preconventional moral reasoning tends to be guided mainly by a system of reward and punishment. Children think that they should not break rules because they will get punished. They also believe that they should follow rules to get rewarded. These two premises guide obedience to authority. Children presume that the authority figure's position is correct and will comply without questioning or challenging. The interests of other people are not important.

Stage 1 morality begins at around age 7 and concludes at about 10 years of age. At this point children are rigidly locked into compliance with authority to gain rewards and avoid punishment. Their behavior and moral decision making are highly self-focused. It is important to obey authority figures because they are more powerful than the child.

During **stage 2** children's moral reasoning slowly begins to shift toward more of an individualistic and social transaction perspective. At this point children follows rules that appear to serve their own best interests. Children make decisions without regard for how their behaviors will affect other people. They continue to make moral decisions according to the rewards gained for themselves.

Level 2, conventional moral reasoning, begins at **stage 3**. At this stage moral reasoning is largely guided by mutual expectations and group conformity. Externally given rules are becoming increasingly internalized. Children begin perceiving themselves as behaving appropriately to please other people. There may even be times when children's moral reasoning places their own personal interests secondary to those of family or peer groups. An almost rigid adherence to maintaining rules and systems of authority reinforces socially expected behaviors.

As young teenagers begin to mature and enter **stage 4**, they begin to recognize the importance of having a socially organized set of rules to govern people's conduct. The typical child complies with and shows respect for authority so that a particular social order and hierarchy can be maintained. Sometimes teenagers at this stage begin to realize the difference between a social point of view and an individual's point of view. As a result, they may be able to see that even though they view a particular situation in a certain way, their view might not be consistent with the expectations of the larger social group.

Level 3, postconventional moral reasoning, is characterized by the individual's increasing recognition of the importance of individual rights and socially approved standards of conduct. People at this stage may recognize that laws sometimes need to be changed for the betterment of individuals and the larger society.

At **stage 5** people may embrace a wide variety of opinions, perspectives, and values and may recognize that standards are relative rather than absolute; prior to this stage people have largely viewed standards as absolute codes of moral reasoning. People begin to see themselves as part of a larger society and understand that members of the society have an implicit contract with the larger group. Although the group's moral standards must be maintained, stage 5 individuals also recognize that individuals have implicit rights and values, such as liberty, appropriate education, justice, fairness, equal opportunity, and perhaps even medical care. These rights and values should be safeguarded, regardless of what the majority of people in the society believe. Kohlberg believed that only about 20 percent of adolescents ever reach the fifth stage of moral reasoning.

The highest level of moral reasoning and development exists at **stage 6**. Kohlberg believed that few people ever attain this level of moral development. It is characterized by having universal principles of justice and general codes of ethical principles that apply cross-culturally. People become committed to these general principles. If laws violate the general principles, then people must take action to uphold personal values and universal belief systems.

Both stages 5 and 6 are closely interrelated and represent essentially the same perspective regarding abstract principles of a universal code of ethics that should govern moral judgment and reasoning. Developmental changes in moral development are usually essentially fixed by early adulthood, although additional educational experiences may encourage people to reexamine their values from different perspectives.

Kohlberg's position has been highly controversial for numerous reasons. The primary criticisms focus on the stage perspective, arguing that some people may be able to skip early stages altogether while others may advance into a higher stage and then regress to an early stage because of personal experiences in their lives. Questions have also been raised challenging whether there is a relationship between how people think morally and the actions they will show in real-life situations. People may embrace one set of beliefs but lack the willingness to implement those beliefs in their daily decision making. Finally, much of the data for his theoretical viewpoint was based on research using a small sample of middle-class white American males who were less than 17 years old. This limited sample calls into question the cultural relativity and generalizability of Kohlberg's findings to persons from other backgrounds, educational experiences, and socioeconomic positions.

Gilligan's Model of Moral Development

Gilligan (1982) hypothesized that men and women differ substantially in how they view and interpret moral decision making and standards. She proposed that men focus more on general principles (e.g., fairness, justice), while women view morality more from an interpersonal perspective that embraces or emphasizes caring and compassion. She argued that women are more concerned about relationships, are not competitive when dealing with other people, and try to resolve moral issues within a socially sensitive and respectful manner. Men show more competitiveness when making moral judgments.

Gilligan claimed that women pass through three levels of moral development. Not all women reach the third level of moral development, though. At the first level women are concerned primarily for their own welfare and advancement. As women progress into the second level they become more involved with self-sacrifice and concern for other people when making moral decisions. The third level involves balancing responsibilities and liabilities between a commitment to other people and good self-caretaking. As with so many areas in psychology, research findings for Gilligan's model have been mixed. Some research has failed to show that men and women perform at different levels or in different ways when faced with moral dilemmas (Rest, 1986).

ADOLESCENCE

A child becomes an adolescent beginning with the onset of puberty. During adolescence the child undergoes rapid physical, social, and intellectual changes. In American society it is also one of the most difficult and challenging times of a person's life. Although most adolescents are too old to be managed and controlled like children, they are also too young to have complete independence and relative financial autonomy. Moreover, adolescence is a period of tremendous emotional confusion, uncertainty, and insecurity.

Among the physical changes that occur during adolescence is the ability to reproduce. Other physical changes affect nearly every organ in the body. The child begins to develop secondary sexual characteristics such as the appearance of pubic hair, girls develop breasts and begin menses, facial hair appears and the voice deepens in boys, and both sexes experience increases in height and weight. These physical changes occur within the context of cognitive and social-emotional issues that serve to create a good deal of confusion for the adolescent.

According to Piaget's theory of cognitive development, this time of life is viewed as a transitional stage from concrete operational to formal operational thinking. Adolescents begin to engage in more abstract thinking that goes beyond their immediate reality or concrete situations. They develop the capacity to view situations from a more complicated perspective and may engage in a good deal of analytical reasoning. Sometimes, though, their analytical reasoning perspective is flawed, while at other times it reflects efforts on their part to comprehend their world in a more logical and integrated manner. It is important to remember that not all adolescents achieve Piaget's level of formal operational thought.

The central issue for most adolescents is the search for their individual identity and clarifying who they are as unique human beings. **Identity** reflects a person's perceptions and beliefs about his or her unique abilities (intellectual, social, academic, athletic), values, and priorities that motivate and focus that person's efforts and self-perception as a social being. In short, a person's identity reflects his or her internal views about what it means to be a human being. These views become translated into real-life behaviors and patterns of social interactions.

Marcia (1991), using Erikson's theoretical perspective on social development, identified four levels of identity status for adolescents. Each level reflects the degree to which adolescents have developed a clear sense of thinking about themselves as individuals.

The first status level is **foreclosure**. Adolescents at this level have developed their identity as a person based on the input they have received from their parents. They have not made their own choices freely and after careful consideration about who they want to be or where they want to focus their life energies. Rather, their occupational, religious, and social belief systems are largely reflections of those that their parents have imposed on them, either overtly or covertly. Adolescents with this type of identity typically have difficulty meeting the crises of life because their views about themselves and the world are fixed and rigid. Often they have not explored for themselves the various complexities that characterize nearly all aspects of life, nor have they achieved some resolution and closure based on their unique perceptions and interpretations of these situations.

At the second level of identity status for adolescents, **identity diffusion**, adolescents have no basic idea about their belief system, occupational focus, or the kind of people they would like to be socially. These adolescents have typically made little progress in each of these areas to achieve closure and may simply drift along without any clear focus or goal.

Adolescents at the third level of identity status, **moratorium**, have begun to experiment with a variety of belief systems and choices. They typically have not made any definite commitments to a particular course of action or belief system in their life. They may experience various identity crises throughout this stage of life as they examine alternative perspectives about how to create their individual lifestyles.

The final level of identity status is **identity achievement**. Adolescents at this level have developed a rather clear and consolidated perspective about who and what they are as human beings. They have reached these decisions independently and consciously. They also believe that the decisions they reached were the result of their own free choices rather than the input or influence of their parents. They typically will see these decisions as reflecting their true inner natures and priorities.

Many adolescents achieve the identity achievement status by roughly 22 years of age. Research has indicated that levels of anxiety are greatest for adolescents who are in the moratorium stage and lowest for those in foreclosure. Self-esteem is greatest for those at the identity achievement and moratorium status levels and lowest at the foreclosure and identity diffusion levels. Identity achievement and moratorium are considered to be healthy approaches toward life at this stage of development.

Adolescence is an opportunity for teenagers to experiment with different perspectives and outlooks about life. Adolescents must remain flexible to arrive successfully at a clear understanding about their identity and uniqueness. Trying out new ways of presenting themselves socially, testing and examining these new ways, and modifying their approaches based on the feedback they receive can be helpful mechanisms that allow the adolescent to become more clear and constant in reaching conclusions about who and what they are. This process requires a high degree of self-confidence to experiment and vary their behaviors, especially when these experimental behaviors are not those that are supported or approved of by parents. This process is made easier and can be much more successful and meaningful for adolescents when their parents are stable and accepting of these life experiments.

Adolescents also begin to develop specific concepts about themselves in five areas of life (Marsh, 1993): academic and verbal, academic mathematics, parent relations, same-sex relationships, and opposite-sex relationships. Adolescents begin to formulate clear and concrete notions about their degree of success and competence in each of these areas.

Many adolescents also experience a **personal fable**—the sincere belief that they are uniquely destined for fortune and fame. Some also demonstrate an **invincibility fallacy**—the belief that they are not vulnerable to the bad things that happen to other people. This fallacy can create some very difficult situations for some adolescents because of the risk-taking behaviors that typically accompany it. Further, it is not uncommon for adolescents to experience an **imaginary audience fallacy**—the unrealistic belief that other people are constantly watching them, paying attention to them, and evaluating what they do.

The final area of significance during adolescence relates to social and interpersonal relationships. It has been found that adolescents often can be categorized into one of four distinct social groups (Newcomb, Bukowski, & Pattee, 1993). **Popular adolescents** are socially skilled and well liked by most of their peers. **Rejected adolescents** typically do not fit in with their peer group either because they show high levels of verbal or physical aggression or are highly withdrawn socially. **Controversial adolescents** are often socially engaged but also show aggressive behaviors at times; peer reactions to them are mixed, and they may be disliked by some peers. Finally, **neglected adolescents** are less social and less aggressive than their peers and are simply overlooked or ignored by other adolescents in the group.

During adolescence the friendships of boys and girls go through several stages (Douvan & Adelson, 1966). Eleven- to thirteen-year-old girls tend to participate in joint activities with other girls and boys and enjoy sharing fun activities together. As girls mature they become more focused on developing emotional intimacy with other female friends. This usually begins and continues from ages 14 to 16 years. Trust is a critical component at this time as the girls develop increased emotional intimacy through their friendships. At around 17 years of age and older the emphasis for females shifts to compatibility with shared personalities. Male relationships during adolescence are oriented toward participation in joint activities with others. Individual achievement and personal independence are very important for boys throughout this period in relation to their friendships with others.

Although adolescents of both genders are capable of showing consideration for other people socially, they tend to show very high levels of egocentricity, as is often seen in children who are much younger (Elkind, 1985). This characteristic can make it very difficult to deal with some adolescents both at home and in the school setting. One of the best predictors of school failure and dropping out from school is the degree of social rejection that an adolescent experiences from their peers (Rubin, Coplan, Nelson, Cheah, & Lagace-Seguin, 1999). Greater peer rejection encourages leaving school before graduation. The major problems experienced during adolescence are emotional disorders, such as depression and anxiety; eating disorders; bullying and verbal taunting from peers; drug and alcohol abuse; pregnancy; and sexually transmitted infections.

GENDER ROLE IDENTITY AND SEX ROLES

People are not born with attitudes about how girls and boys or men and women should behave in society. These beliefs evolve from the various kinds of learning experiences that people have within their cultures and can be shaped through classical conditioning, operant conditioning, observational learning, or some combination of these three basic learning models.

Gender role identity refers to the set of beliefs a person holds about the specific characteristics associated with either feminine or masculine traits. It is part of a person's self-concept, and most people tend to view themselves as ranking high or low in either trait. Although it is difficult to specify precisely how a person's gender role identity develops, the identity present during early childhood is probably affected by physiological and hormonal activities that influence how aggressive or passive the child is as well as how physically active or restrained he or she may be. Clearly, though, it is very early in a child's life that they begin to learn what it means to be a boy or girl, male or female. These experiences are strongly influenced by parental attitudes and the quality of parents' interactions with the child during the first years of life. Research indicates that parents generally interact more vigorously and physically with sons than with daughters. This kind of parental interaction begins to create a mental set within the child about how to respond socially to others. Parents are also more likely to react favorably to sons who show assertive or aggressive behavior than to daughters. Parents are more likely to reinforce emotional sensitivity and compliance in their daughters (Fagot & Hagan, 1991). These differences become magnified as the child grows older because parents tend to touch male toddlers less and keep them at a greater physical and emotional distance than they do female toddlers.

Research has consistently demonstrated that differences do exist in the rates of development for boys and girls. Girls generally develop faster and show greater development in verbal and motor skills earlier on than do boys. During the early grades in school girls perform as well as or better than boys on most standardized measures of achievement and psychological well-being. By the time they complete high school or college, however, these differences reverse.

Gender bias is an individual's belief that because males and females behave differently and have different strengths and weaknesses, one gender is better than the other. Gender bias is pervasive within society and has typically been represented throughout the educational curriculum, which often portrays girls and boys in very traditional, conventional, and stereotypical social roles.

Observational learning experiences, especially those presented by the media and television, have been shown to exercise serious and extensive influences on gender bias and gender stereotypes. In general, children's television programs show males performing in important roles more often than females. Males are more likely to be portrayed in proactive roles, are rewarded for their actions, and make things happen. Women who take on action roles in television programs are more often punished for their activities than are males in the same roles (Basow, 1992). Women are typically depicted on television as being concerned about their physical appearance, engaging in household chores and duties to take care of the family, or serving in supporting roles to males (Gan, Zillmann, & Mitrook, 1997). Further, around 70 percent of the main characters performing on prime-time television programs are white males.

A number of social, educational, and family practices significantly influence sex role definitions and gender identity. Parents have different expectations for sons and daughters. These different expectations can influence how girls and boys approach learning in school. For example, girls are discouraged from participating in science and mathematics classes while boys are discouraged from participating in home economics and dance.

Within the school setting research has indicated that boys and girls are indeed treated differently by their teachers. Teachers typically view boys as being independent thinkers who are more likely to do better in mathematics and science. Girls tend to be viewed by teachers as more conforming, compliant, and not analytical in how they approach problems (Grant, 1984). Teachers generally interact more often with boys and will ask them more conceptual and abstract-oriented questions. Boys often receive more direct and explicit approval, are listened to more, and are taught using more direct instruction methods than are girls. Males are also more frequently rewarded by teachers for their creativity (Torrance, 1983).

Boys have been found to ask more questions during class and offer more comments and observations during class discussions than girls. As they continue to progress to the upper grade levels these kinds of gender-related differences become even more obvious.

It has been found that gender stereotyping has a strong impact on the decisions that students make about their careers. These kinds of career choices often become apparent as early as kindergarten. According to the U.S. Bureau of the Census (1996), only 20 percent of physicians, 21 percent of lawyers, and 8 percent of engineers are female. Girls are less than half as likely to become involved in careers that emphasize engineering, computer science, or the physical sciences (American Association of University Women, 1992).

MENTAL HEALTH

Children's feelings and emotions can have a very significant effect on their achievement levels and social adjustment in school. There are a number of disorders that can present substantial obstacles for children and disrupt their ability to learn at levels that are consistent with their intellectual ability.

Six types of disorders are especially prominent: attention-deficit/hyperactivity disorder (ADHD), physical and sexual abuse, exposure to domestic violence, depression, anxiety, and suicidal ideation. In addition, bullying and being the victim of a violent crime are also substantial life experiences that have seriously negative effects on a child's ability to adjust socially at school and learn successfully.

ADHD has reached epidemic proportions in this country, with as many as 12 percent of young boys receiving this diagnosis and subsequent psychotropic medical interventions. Although this type is discussed more fully in Chapter 6, a brief introduction of this disorder is appropriate. There are three types of ADHD. The first type is ADHD. These children are very physically active, impulsive, have poor self-control, and difficulty paying attention to what is happening in the classroom. The second type of ADHD is the predominately inattentive type. Children with this disorder have difficulty paying attention but show no obvious physical, behavioral, or motor restlessness and increased activity. The third type of ADHD is the combined type, which is characterized by hyperactivity, impulsivity, and difficulty paying attention. Common medications prescribed for children diagnosed with ADHD to control their behaviors and reportedly increase attention levels include Ritalin, Adderall, and Strattera.

Another common experience for children is either physical and/or sexual abuse. The impact of these traumas varies dramatically among children (Webster, 2001). The most common reactions include dissociating and externalizing problems, aggression and oppositional defiant disorder, delinquency, ADHD, poor school achievement and adjustment, depression, and anxiety (Webster & Hall, 2004). A strong and consistent body of empirical research shows that children who have been sexually abused typically reside in families with significant problems in child-rearing and child management.

Research has shown that children exposed to domestic violence in their own families can experience significant emotional problems with a wide range of negative effects. Many children have emotional and/or learning problems several years after the violence has ended. Witnessing abusive interactions between caretaking adults generates intense levels of emotional stress, lowered self-esteem, increased anxiety, and somatic complaints.

Depression, sometimes called dysthymia or dysthymic disorder, is another very common emotional problem for both children and adolescents. In general, girls and boys show different symptoms of depression. It is not uncommon for girls to withdraw emotionally and remain distant from people in general. On the other hand, boys often become aggressive verbally or behaviorally.

Anxiety disorders, discussed more completely in Chapter 5, are conditions in which children or adolescents have a constant and chronic underlying sense of apprehension and uneasiness about the circumstances of their lives. They often have difficulty concentrating and paying attention, may be fearful in both new and familiar situations, and sometimes show unusual behaviors or gestures in an effort to try to keep these very uncomfortable feelings under control.

Finally, suicide has increased substantially over the past 20 years, particularly among adolescents. This increase reflects the negative effects of social and educational pressures, the decline of emotional support provided by the family, and improved record keeping. Many adolescents experience difficult and uncomfortable feelings, such as loneliness, a sense of social isolation, feeling like they do not fit in, and resentment at being treated like children but not being sufficiently independent to function on their own. Suicidal gestures or comments from a child or adolescent should never be interpreted as simply attention-seeking in nature. These threats or gestures are clear pleas for help from the child or adolescent and should be interpreted and responded to accordingly.

SCHOOL READINESS

Most states require that schools have some kind of prekindergarten readiness testing (Kirst, 1991). Many of the tests used to evaluate a child's readiness for kindergarten have been criticized for being inappropriate to the developmental age of the child and not measuring the important skills necessary for success in the early grades. Many people have recommended that assessment at this age involve an ongoing process that examines the cognitive, social-emotional, physical, and language characteristics of children as they mature (Engel, 1991).

Early school failure can affect a child in many significant and long-lasting ways. Early failure can lead to a decreased sense of self-competence and self-esteem that discourages the child from trying at school. This poor self-image can lead to poor achievement and behavior problems, as the child continues in school.

During the early school years, gross motor and fine motor development have been found to be very important skills that form a foundation for later academic success. Visual motor coordination and control, visual motor integration, and gross motor skills have been identified as being especially important. The ability to recognize the alphabet and name letters has been shown to be a strong and consistent predictor of later reading achievement (Badian, 1982). The degree of self-control that the child displays during kindergarten has been shown to be highly predictive of both social competence and social success later in life (Mischel & Peake, 1990). An unusual pencil grip is sometimes associated with fine motor deficits that can lead to difficulties in handwriting (Thompson, 1996). A child's development in gross motor and fine motor skills during the kindergarten year has also been shown to be a factor in determining whether or not the child is at risk of failing in school (Huttenlocher, Levine, Huttenlocher, & Gates, 1990).

DEVELOPMENT AND ACQUISITION OF LANGUAGE

The ability of human beings to communicate using spoken and written language is a unique and highly complicated process that involves thinking, reasoning, attention, memory, and perception of symbols either visually or orally. Communication is different from language in that a **language system** must contain a **grammar,** or a system of rules that govern how the language is expressed. A language system must also be **productive** in that these grammatical rules allow for an infinite number of combinations of the symbols to be expressed to represent the world. **Communication** on the other hand involves the exchange of feelings and thoughts through verbal and nonverbal expressions such as gestures or glances. The range of communicative verbalizations or vocalizations is limited in structure, lacks complexity, and is not spontaneously acquired. Studies with chimpanzees have highlighted the differences between language as used by human beings and communication as used by nonhuman species.

Human language also has several other characteristics in addition to being productive and containing a grammatical structure. Human language is **arbitrary** in that there is not necessarily a similarity between a word or sentence and what it refers to specifically. For example, the word *hot* can refer to the temperature outdoors, the flavor of a food, an object such as an automobile being desirable, or a member of the opposite sex being highly appealing. Interpretation of the word's exact meaning must occur within the context in which it is uttered.

Human language is also **discrete** in that the overall language system can be subdivided into identifiable and recognizable parts such as **sentences**, **phrases**, and **word**s. Words make up phrases and sentences. Phrases can make up sentences.

Human languages contain sounds called phonemes. A **phoneme** is the smallest unit of sound that affects the meaning of spoken words. The English language is made up of 53 phonemes. Changing one phoneme can change the entire meaning of a word. The word *house* is made up of three phonemes that blend with each other. If the first phoneme /h/ is changed to to /m/, then the meaning of the word is changed radically. Similarly, changing the phonemes within words can produce the same result, as with the words *battle* and *babble*, in which changing the third phonemes affects the word meaning.

Phonology is the process of putting different sounds or phonemes together in some systematic and meaningful way so that the sound units express meanings in the form of language. Phonemes can refer to the letter sound for an individual letter or for a letter cluster, such as /th/ or /ph/.

Spoken language has several other characteristics. **Morphemes** are the smallest meaningful units of language. Many morphemes are often words, but morphemes can also be prefixes, suffixes, root words, and endings for words. **Syntax** is the grammatical structure within each sentence and usually describes the set of rules that determine how words are organized to create phrases and sentences. **Semantics** is the study of the meaning of words used in the language. Finally, **pragmatics** is the study of the social aspects of spoken language and includes the qualities related to a person's tone when speaking (such as polite or rude) or quality of conversational interactions (such as not interrupting others). Young children tend to speak without relating to what others are saying. Although this behavior might seem to reflect a lack of attention, it simply shows that the child is more focused on personal thoughts than on what others are expressing.

The perception of speech is a highly complicated and intricate process. Speech is **continuous**, which means that there are rarely pauses surrounding each sound in a word. Further, different sounds from the same word may sometimes blend into each other and create a new sound. For example, decoding the word *butterfly* cannot be done by sounding out each individual letter in the word and then saying each individual sound or phoneme rapidly. Rather, the word must be broken into its components— its syllables. Then the beginning and ending consonant phonemes can be integrated with the medial vowel sounds. Finally, the individual syllable phonemes can be synthesized to create the word *butterfly*.

Another difficulty in the perception of speech is that sometimes a single phoneme or sound is different depending on the context in which it is used or the letters surrounding the particular phoneme. For example, examine the phoneme /ch/. The specific sound of the phoneme changes depending on its location in the word, as with chart, schedule, and tachometer. The actual sound of these two letters differs greatly based on the letters that surround it in the word. The social context may also influence the sound of a word, as is the case for words such as *potato, tomato, vase,* and *Caribbean*.

Stages in the Acquisition of Language

The development of language begins with listening and responding to language from other people. As children grow older, making a variety of different sounds and noises becomes a way for them to initiate interactions with others. Children then progress to using the sounds they hear to communicate with others using language.

In summary, the acquisition of language in human beings proceeds as follows:

1. Prenatal influences

2. Cooing

3. Babbling

4. Holophrastic speech (one-word utterances)

5. Telegraphic speech (two-word utterances)

6. Development and refinement of basic adult language communication that is typically present in most children by age 4

Several stages emerge in sequence as the child acquires language competency. The first stage reflects prenatal influences on the child. Some research has shown that a baby in utero can recognize its mother's voice, and within a few days after birth the typical newborn clearly prefers its mother's voice over the voices of other women (DeCasper & Spence, 1986). Shortly after being born infants will try to imitate sounds they hear (Kuhl & Meltzoff, 1997). Further, studies have found that infants' emotional expressions often match those shown by their caregivers (Fogel, 1994).

The maturing infant gradually begins to produce sounds spontaneously. These sounds typically are signals to the caretaker that the infant wants attention, is experiencing discomfort, or is hungry. These spontaneously produced sounds usually begin as cooing. **Cooing** allows the infant to explore all the sounds that human beings are capable of making. Research has shown that infant cooing around the world is highly similar in terms of the sounds produced. Infants will produce many of the sounds that make up their own unique language as well as the sounds found in other languages.

With increasing age the child begins to babble, usually starting around 1 year old. At this point the young child is beginning to lose the ability to make the full range of sounds capable of being made by human beings and begins to vocalize the sounds unique to his or her native language. **Babbling** specifically involves the infant producing only those distinct phonemes that are characteristic of their language.

Eventually, the child utters a first word, which is usually used to express a demand or indicate a desired object. This type of one-word speech is called **holophrastic speech** and typically reflects the use of nouns to describe objects familiar to the child. For example, the child uses familiar words such as *Mommy, Daddy, ball,* or *go* to indicate specific concrete objects and actions. By around 18 months of age most children have a vocabulary of between 30 and 100 words (Siegler, 1986). Because the child lacks enough words to describe all the important things in their world, the child may over extend the meaning of words. **Overextension** occurs when the child uses one word to cover many different concepts and meanings. For example, a child might call all animals "cat" because he or she has a pet cat at home.

Sometime between 15 and 30 months of age (and sometimes earlier) children begin to combine single words into two-word expressions. This is the stage of **telegraphic speech**. The speech is not fully grammatical because many of the key elements required in spoken language are omitted. Words such as conjunctions, prepositions, and articles are typically absent. The child uses phrases like "go bye-bye" or "eat milk" to communicate with others.

A child's vocabulary expands rapidly and may include up to 1,000 words by the time the child is 3 years old (Bloom, 2000). It is not unusual in the United States for a 3-year-old child to have a speaking vocabulary of 1,000 to 10,000 words. By fifth grade many children have speaking vocabularies of roughly 40,000 words, or half the normal adult speaking vocabulary (Anglin, 1993). Most children have learned the basics of adult spoken language, syntax and grammar, by around 5 years old. By 10 years of age many children have oral language competency that is essentially the same as that of adults. These children may have difficulty dealing with certain aspects of language, such as comprehending abstractions or colloquial phrases, but these kinds of concepts are also difficult for many adults.

During the language acquisition process children may make errors in the grammatical structure of their spoken language. For example, they may **overregularize** by applying grammatical rules to much of their spoken communication even if those rules are not appropriate. For a brief time some children may use phrases such as "my leg hurted" as they try to rigidly apply grammatical rules. Most children eventually mature and stop this behavior.

Theories of Language Acquisition

There are three different explanations about how human beings acquire language: conditioning, imitation, and the existence of critical periods. The **conditioning or behavioral perspective** argues that children hear vocalizations and are rewarded by their parents and other people when they use these same vocalizations to express themselves. The second perspective, **imitation**, indicates that children imitate the speech patterns and language used with them in their home settings. Mother is the main person providing these rewards, and it is believed that children typically model her language patterns most clearly. These kinds of language patterns, called **motherese**, consist of short sentences with simple constructions. Parents model the ways in which the child uses language as well as how loudly they should speak, their vocal inflexions (volume and pitch), and the social and emotional characteristics that accompany spoken language.

The third perspective, proposed by Chomsky (1959, 1975), argues that people possess a **language acquisition device** (**LAD**). This device is innate and predisposes an individual to learn language. In other words, people are genetically wired to learn language. Certain periods of a child's life are critical to acquiring language. If language development is interfered with during these critical periods it will be difficult for the child to compensate and acquire the relevant skills later. There also appear to be critical periods for human beings to acquire an understanding of syntax. Support for this position comes from studies examining the development of language in "wild children." These children have consistently shown significant deficits in their ability to develop spoken language despite substantial professional intervention.

REFERENCES

American Association of University Women. (1992). *How schools shortchange girls.* Annapolis Junction, MD: Author.

Anglin, J. M. (1993). Vocabulary development: A morphological analysis. *Monographs of the Society for Research in Child Development,* Serial No. 238, Vol. 58, No. 10.

Badian, N. (1982). The prediction of good and poor reading before kindergarten entry: A four-year follow-up. *Journal of Special Education, 16,* 309–318.

Basow, S. A. (1992). *Gender: Stereotypes and roles* (3rd ed.). Belmont, CA: Wadsworth.

Bloom, P. (2000). *How children learn the meanings of words.* Cambridge, MA: MIT Press.

Chomsky, N. (1959). A review of Skinner's verbal behavior. *Language, 35,* 26–58.

Chomsky, N. (1972). *Language and mind* (2nd ed.). New York: Harcourt Brace Jovanovich.

DeCasper, A. J., & Spence, M. J. (1986). Prenatal maternal speech influences newborns' perceptions of speech sounds. *Infant Behavior and Development, 9,* 133–150.

Douvan E., & Adelson, J. (1966). *The adolescent experience.* New York: Wiley.

Elkind, D. (1985). Egocentrism redux. *Developmental Review, 5,* 218–226.

Engel, P. (1991). Tracking progress toward the school readiness goal. *Educational Leadership, 48*(5), 39–42.

Erikson, E. H. (1968). *Identity, youth, and crisis.* New York: Norton.

Fagot, B. L., & Hagan, R. (1991). Observations of parent reactions to sex-stereotyped behaviors: Age and sex effects. *Child Development, 56,* 1499–1505.

Feuerstein, R. (1979). *The dynamic assessment of retarded performers: The Learning Potential Assessment Device, theory, instruments, and techniques.* Baltimore: University Park Press.

Fogel, A. (1992). Movement and communication in human infancy: The social dynamics of development. *Human Movement Science, 11*(4), 387–423.

Gan, S., Zillmann, D., & Mitrook, M. (1997). Stereotyping effect of black women's sexual rap on white audiences. *Basic and Applied Social Psychology, 19,* 381–399.

Gilligan, C. (1982). *In a different voice: Psychological theory and women's development.* Cambridge, MA: Harvard University Press.

Grant, L. (1984). Black females "place" in desegregated classrooms. *Sociology of Education, 57,* 98–111.

Huttenlocher, P., Levine, S., Huttenlocher, J., & Gates, J. (1990). Discrimination of normal and at-risk preschool children on the basis of neurological tests. *Developmental Medicine and Child Neurology, 32,* 394–402.

Kirst, M. (1991). Interview on assessment issues with Lorrie Shephard. *Educational Researcher, 20*(2), 21–23.

Kohlberg, L. (1984). *Essays on moral development: The psychology of moral development.* New York: Harper & Row.

Kuhl, P. K., & Meltzoff, A. N. (1997). Evolution, nativism, and learning in the development of language and speech. In M. Gopnik (Ed.), *The inheritance and innateness of grammars* (pp. 7–44). New York: Oxford University Press.

Marcia, J. M. (1991). Identity and self-development. In R. M. Lerner, A. C. Peterson, & E. J. Brooks-Gunn (Eds.), *Encyclopedia of adolescence* (vol. 1, pp. 527–531). New York: Garland.

Marsh, H. W. (1993). The multidimensional structure of academic self-concept: Invariance over gender and age. *American Educational Research Journal, 30,* 841–860.

Mischel, W., & Peake, P. (1990). Predicting adolescent cognitive and self-regulatory competencies from preschool delay of gratification. *Developmental Psychology, 26*(6), 978–986.

Newcomb, A. F., Bukowski, W. M., & Pattee, L. (1993). Children's peer relations: A meta-analytic review of popular, rejected, neglected, controversial, and average sociometric status. *Psychological Bulletin, 113,* 99–128.

Rest, J. R. (1986). *Moral development: Advances in research and theory.* New York: Praeger.

Rubin, K. H., Coplan, R. J., Nelson, L. J., Cheah, C. S. L., & Lagace-Seguin, D. G. (1999). Peer relationships in childhood. In M. H. Bornstein & M. E. Lamb (Eds.), *Developmental psychology: An advanced textbook* (4th ed., pp. 451–501). Mahwah, NJ: Erlbaum.

Siegler, R. S. (1986). *Children's thinking.* Englewood Cliffs, NJ: Prentice-Hall.

Thompson, S. (1996). *I shouldn't have to tell you! A guide to understanding non-verbal learning disabilities.* San Ramon, CA: S. Thompson.

Torrance, E. (1983). Status of creative women past, present, future. *Creative Child and Adult Quarterly, 8,* 135–144.

United States Bureau of the Census. (1996). *Statistics.* Washington, DC: Author.

Webster, R. (2001). Symptoms and long-term outcomes for children who have been sexually assaulted. *Psychology in the Schools, 38*(6), 533–547.

Webster, R., & Hall, C. (2004). School-based responses to children who have been sexually assaulted. *Education and Treatment of Children, 27*(1), 64–81.

CHAPTER 5
Motivation

CHAPTER 5

MOTIVATION

Motivation describes a set of desires, impulses, or needs that can give a person impetus and direction to engage in behavior over a given time (Baron, 1998). Motivation varies both in its intensity and focus because it reflects the needs or desires of one individual at a particular time. Motivation can be the result of certain personality characteristics of an individual, a person's implicit interest in a particular task or subject area, or the expectation of the extrinsic rewards to be gained by doing well in the task or subject area.

A number of important issues are involved with motivation. For example, how does motivation energize a person to take action? What feelings motivate a person to begin taking action? Why do some people persist in performing a task longer than do other people? What is it that causes a person to become highly intense or passionate about a particular activity to the exclusion of other activities? Why do some students make good choices about where to put their energy, while others do not?

On early theory of motivation argued that people were motivated by inherited instincts that caused them to behave in predictable ways (Darwin, 1859). This theory was replaced by the drive theory, which posited that the basic physiological need for food, warmth, sleep, and sex was the driving force underlying all behaviors. Neither of these theories was validated by research.

Modern theories of motivation include physiological theories, which discuss motivation as arising from the operation of the central nervous system or from people behaving in ways that bring them to a state of inner equilibrium. Four contemporary theories are most appropriate to discussing motivation within the educational system: behavioral theory, human needs theory, attribution theory, and social learning and expectancy theory. The chapter concludes with an examination of the personal attributes and situational characteristics that affect motivation in positive or negative ways.

BEHAVIORAL THEORY

Behavioral theory views reinforcement as the primary source of motivation for all individuals. If a person is consistently reinforced for certain behaviors, then those behaviors become routine patterns that influence the person's daily life choices. **Extrinsic**, or **external**, **reward** is the key to motivation.

The major difficulty with the behavioral approach is that rewards and punishments can vary significantly from one person to the next. It is difficult to determine precisely what is serving as a reward, or reinforcer, for an individual. Is it the actual physical reward or is it the social status that the reward represents? Does the person giving the reward increase or decrease the value of the reinforcer? People cannot presume that what is reinforcing for them will also be reinforcing for others. The use of external reinforcers emphasizes that people should work to receive material objects, and it is these objects that generate motivation. Another risk with using external reinforcers is that the person can eventually become saturated and no longer find a reward to be reinforcing.

For an external reward to be effective, four factors must be present: (1) The person must *expect* to receive a reward for performing the desired behavior; (2) the reward must have *value* and importance to the person, because if the reward is irrelevant, its extrinsic motivating force diminishes; (3) the reinforcer must be *tangible* and concrete so it is clear that the person has achieved the reward after completing the desired behavior; and (4) the reward must be *contingent* on performance, so each performance of the behavior consistently and regularly leads to the reinforcer.

HUMAN NEEDS THEORY

Human needs theory emphasizes the role of intrinsic sources of motivation, especially the need for self-actualization and self-determination (Deci, Vallerand, Pelletier, & Ryan, 1991). The ultimate motivational goal is the satisfaction of basic human emotional or physical needs. These needs become strong motivating forces that influence how a person behaves and views life. Maslow (1954) proposed that human beings have a hierarchy of needs that begin with basic physiological needs and extend to needs for love and esteem from others and oneself. This hierarchy comprises four *deficiency needs* and three *growth needs*. The deficiency needs are **survival** (food, water, air, warmth); **safety** (freedom from emotional or physical threats); **belonging** (acceptance and love from family and others); and **self-esteem** (recognition and approval from other people). The growth needs are **intellectual achievement**; **aesthetic appreciation** (understanding of the world and appreciation of truth and beauty); and **self-actualization**, which Maslow (1954) defined as "the desire to become everything that one is capable of becoming."

He believed that very few people ever reach the highest level of self-actualization but that most people strive to be self-actualized. Self-actualized people are able to view reality objectively, are independent and creative, have meaningful relationships with a few people rather than superficial relationships with many, and are accepting of other people, themselves, and the world in which they live.

ATTRIBUTION THEORY

According to **attribution theory**, a person's behavior and motivation is determined by how the person thinks about and views the world (Rotter, 1966). Extrinsic rewards and punishment for behavior have only a minor role in motivation. Rather, people develop their own plans that regulate or control their behaviors. The critical factor in determining whether or not a person is motivated to behave a certain way is the significance the person gives to the behavior. This approach emphasizes *intrinsic motivation* as the primary source of reinforcement for all people. A more detailed description about intrinsic motivation is presented later in this chapter.

Attribution theory tries to explain motivation by examining the reasons people give for their successes and failures (Weiner, 2000). The theory's underlying premise is that all people attempt to maintain a sense of positive self-image. When people do well in an activity, they attribute it to their own individual efforts and abilities, but they may attribute failure to factors or variables over which they had no control.

Four factors are seen as being especially important when people formulate the reasons why they succeeded or failed: ability, effort, difficulty of the task, and luck. Ability and effort are personal characteristics. Ability is a relatively stable characteristic that does not change regardless of what the person does. On the other hand, the amount of effort that a person gives to a task can be changed. The amount of time spent performing a task, practicing, and studying are all under the person's control.

The difficulty of the task is also essentially stable and unchanging. It is external to the individual, and the individual has little control over how difficult or easy a task is to learn and master. The subject matter in chemistry or the specific items on a test are not under the direct control of a student. Similarly, luck is outside the control of the individual and is viewed as unstable and unpredictable.

Weiner (2000) believed that three dimensions affect a person's motivation in any given situation. The first dimension, which is called **locus**, refers to whether or not the person sees the situation as beng under his or her direct control. With an **internal locus of control,** a person believes that success or failure is the direct result of his or her own efforts and capabilities. For example, students have direct control over the amount of time they spend studying and preparing, the amount of practice they engage in, and whether they have read the textbook carefully and taken notes. Students who pay attention to these attributions often succeed because they make changes in their studying approach if they have earned an unacceptable grade. These students believe that they can make a difference in how a situation will conclude.

With an **external locus of control**, a person believes that regardless of what he or she does, the person has no control over his or her success or failure. Success and failure are largely the result of the actions of other people or situational variables over which the person has no control or influence. Variables associated with an external locus of control include students believing that they lack the necessary intelligence to learn, feeling that the teacher dislikes them regardless of how they perform on a test or in class, or insisting that they cannot do well in school because no other family members have done well in school. These kinds of attributions often lead students to have poor study habits and a high probability of failure.

The second dimension affecting motivation is stability. **Stability** means that the cause of success or failure either remains the same over time and across different situations or it changes. If students see that practicing skills leads to success, they are likely to engage in large amounts of practice regardless of the content or skill they are learning. On the other hand, if students believe that practice is important in athletic activities but not academic activities, the probability is much lower that the students will practice academic-related skills.

The third dimension is **responsibility**—that is, whether the student can control the causes leading to success or failure. A student who attributes success or failure to a stable factor, such as ability or preparation, is likely to be successful. In contrast, a student who attributes success or failure to an unstable factor, such as being in a good mood, may have some hope in the future that things will be different if he or she has failed in the past, but the probability is lower than if the student had viewed the situation as being more under his or her control.

These dimensions are often affected by the feelings students have in response to success and failure. Sometimes students become angry, ashamed, or guilty when they fail. These feelings will interfere with their expectations for success or failure by either motivating them further or demoralizing them.

Attribution theory can help teachers be more sensitive to how students might interpret feedback and use that feedback to increase their academic performance and learning achievement levels. Comments that are clear, concrete, solution-focused, and constructive are generally more effective in motivating students than is vague, critical, or negative feedback.

SOCIAL LEARNING AND EXPECTANCY THEORY

The **social learning and expectancy** theory of motivation suggests that people develop expectations about their ability to reach a goal and whether that goal has value to them. In short, a person may view behavior by asking, "If I work hard, can I achieve this goal?" If the person responds "no" to either part of this question ("I do not want to work hard" or "I cannot reach this goal"), then the probability is low that the person will be motivated to succeed. This approach emphasizes both intrinsic and extrinsic motivation within the context of setting goals based on a person's perceived probability of being able to reach those goals. **Self-efficacy** refers to a person's beliefs about personal competence and skill in a particular situation or subject area.

Bandura (1995) identified a sense of self-efficacy as stemming from four kinds of social experiences. First are experiences the child has had either succeeding or failing in a particular area. The greater the degree of success the child has had in past experiences, the more likely the child will feel a sense of mastery and able to be successful in new experiences of a similar nature.

Second, a child's sense of self-efficacy is influenced by **vicarious experiences**. Children watch other children engaged in tasks. Many children closely observe others who have characteristics similar to those they see in themselves. When children see other children like themselves having success, they are likely to believe they also can be successful in that same activity. Children base their own beliefs about their ability to succeed on their vicarious observations of others who are like them.

Third, the amount of support and encouragement a child receives, described as **social persuasion**, also has a significant influence on perceived self-efficacy. The greater the social support and persuasion, the higher the probability that children will believe they can be successful.

Finally, the kind of **emotional feedback** children receive from significant adults serves either to encourage or discourage. Many children interpret feedback as an indication that either they have the ability to succeed or they lack that ability. In fact, many children rely on adult opinions about them as standards to set their goals.

Self-efficacy can have a strong impact on children's levels of motivation and their expectations of being successful or failing. Children who have a high sense of self-efficacy in a particular area set higher goals for themselves. They are less afraid to fail. In fact, they do not expect to fail, and this frees them to set up challenges that they strive to overcome. These students also persist longer, even when they encounter substantial difficulties or failures when trying to meet challenges and goals. Research suggests that children with high levels of self-efficacy achieve more than do children of equal intellectual ability who have low levels of self-efficacy.

Children with a strong sense of self-efficacy typically see failure as the result of a lack of sufficient effort on their part. In this respect, they believe they have a high degree of control over the behaviors and strategies necessary to be successful. This allows them to make the necessary changes in a problem-solving approach, which in turn increases the likelihood of their being successful.

Children with a sense of self-efficacy also tend to be optimistic about their future because they have high expectations for themselves, are often less depressed than other children because of the positive feedback they get both intrinsically and extrinsically, and are likely to believe they can and will be successful in meeting their goals (Flammer, 1995).

Self-efficacy has also been found to be related to how teachers view themselves as professional educators. Teachers who have a high sense of self-efficacy have been found to work harder and persist longer even when their students are difficult. High-self-efficacy teachers believe they are capable of getting students to learn and are willing to modify their teaching approaches and management styles to help students meet high standards of achievement. This is often referred to as **teaching efficacy**, or the belief that a teacher can be successful, even when teaching very difficult students.

There are a number of things that teachers can do to increase students' feelings of self-efficacy. Helping students learn to set up short-term goals that are concrete and easily identifiable helps students develop a clear sense of making progress toward achieving a larger and more difficult goal. It is important for students to learn to use specific kinds of **learning strategies** (outlining, summarizing, note taking, color coding) that focus their attention on important information. These learning strategies can also provide students with a good deal of extrinsic reinforcement when their performance levels are increased as a result of using them. Increased performance on tests means that students are improving in their skill and competency levels (Graham, 1996).

In many ways the behavioral attitudes and characteristics of students with high levels of self-efficacy are very similar to those who are described as having an internal locus of control according to attribution theory. The primary difference is in the assumptions about what influences students to develop and maintain positive views of learning and achievement.

ACHIEVEMENT MOTIVATION

McClelland, Atkinson, Clark, and Lowell (1953) proposed the concept of **achievement motivation** to describe the degree to which a person desires, pursues, and actively strives to excel. There are two basic views about achievement motivation. The first view conceives it as a *stable and unconscious trait* that has a strong *generalized influence* on how a person approaches life. The person develops this trait early in life by the way in which his or her parents emphasized and reinforced achieving, taking the initiative, and competing with others. Parents also communicate that the child has a strong individual responsibility and the child's behaviors will determine the outcomes of his or her efforts (Schunk, 1996).

The second view of achievement motivation is as *a set of conscious values and beliefs* shaped by a person's experiences with success and failure. This viewpoint recognizes that the likelihood of success or failure varies from one task to the next. It is affected by the incentives available to the child for excelling. As such, achievement motivation is viewed as an *unstable personality characteristic* that varies from one task to the other and from one situation to another.

In school a student's level of achievement motivation can be seen in the degree of desire and personal effort he or she devotes to being successful and participating in the activities that are essential for success. Students who have high levels of achievement motivation are generally very successful with school activities. Research has indicated that achievement motivation in many students declines as they continue in school (Hidi & Harackiewicz, 2000), although the reasons for this trend are not clear.

Achievement need theory predicts that students with a high achievement need will seek out tasks and activities that are moderately challenging and that encourage them to grow and improve in their knowledge and skills. These students will persist at these tasks longer and are very likely to be highly successful. This theory also predicts that these students will be more successful in their occupations because of these characteristics. It is commonly believed that children develop a high achievement need because of pressure from their parents. However, the key element is how children perceive what their parents are communicating, not necessarily what the parents actually do to the child.

In general, girls have been found to see themselves as being less competent than boys (Juvonen & Weiner, 1993). Consequently, girls often expect less of themselves. **Cultural differences** have also been found regarding achievement need. Cultures that emphasize individual achievement over the needs of the larger group tend to have higher crime rates, greater incidence of alcoholism, and higher suicide rates (Triandis, 1994).

INTRINSIC AND EXTRINSIC MOTIVATION

Intrinsic motivation is a natural tendency to seek out challenges as part of pursuing personal interests. **Intrinsic motivators** are rewards that the student generates internally for successful performance. Research has suggested that intrinsically motivated people often do very creative work (Amabile, 2001) and are often high achievers who will work hard to master new skills and achieve goals because they value those skills and goals. Intrinsically motivated people have greater success meeting their goals and persist at working toward these goals for a longer period compared with people who are not intrinsically motivated.

Persons with a strong orientation toward their future tend to have high levels of intrinsic motivation. They are able to *postpone gratification* in the short term with an outlook toward achieving more important and personally relevant goals later. Intrinsically motivated people enjoy the activities in which they participate and it is this inner sense of pleasure that serves as their immediate reward. Intrinsically motivated learners often study hard because they see the act of studying and the knowledge acquired as important for them.

Extrinsic motivators are rewards given by someone else. Extrinsically motivated learners often study hard simply to get a high test score. The person giving the reward usually defines the standards for performance and the conditions under which the reward is given. This person also determines whether the standard has been attained. Extrinsically motivated people are oriented by this system of rewards and punishments. When the system of rewards and punishments is taken away, extrinsically motivated people typically will not continue in the activity. Extrinsic motivators can serve to undermine intrinsic motivators because they diminish the sense of personal inner satisfaction one often derives from performing some activity.

In real life it is often difficult to determine the cause of a student's behavior because an intrinsically motivated person often receives an extrinsic reward for success. Although the extrinsic reward was not the primary reason the instrinsically motivated student engaged in the behavior, it did serve as an additional source of reinforcement that may have encouraged the student in the behavior. Further, motivation for an individual can vary from one situation to the next and can also change over time. In the ideal educational setting teachers would have only intrinsically motivated students. In reality this is not usually the case.

Regardless of the source of the motivation, helping students establish clearly *identifiable and concrete goals* has been shown to be a significant and important way to improve their performance in school (Locke & Latham, 1990). Setting goals help the students *focus attention* in a clear and distinct way to the tasks they need to achieve. They also help students *mobilize* their cognitive and emotional energies and efforts in behavioral ways to achieve these goals. Goals can also *increase persistence* and encourage students to develop new problem-solving strategies or approaches when the old ones do not work.

REINFORCEMENT CONTINGENCIES

The public schools place a great deal of emphasis on the use of extrinsic motivators in an effort to encourage students to perform well. There are many reasons why schools use extrinsic rewards. Much of the information taught in schools has little apparent and direct relevance or practical use for most students. Many students do not see the value to learning unless they are shown how it is relevant and useful. Few teachers take the time to explain to students how the information they are learning in class will apply to their lives outside the school setting.

Also, much school learning is not implicitly interesting to students. It may be presented in ways that are abstract and not consistent with students' cognitive developmental status or in ways that make the information appear trivial and of no consequence. Many educators believe that using extrinsic incentives or rewards compensates for these deficiencies and encourages students to perform well.

Using extrinsic rewards to motivate children is a complicated and delicate process because it can interfere with students' ability to develop a perspective of motivation that is intrinsically focused (Kohn, 1993). Initially, extrinsic rewards may be necessary to get students interested in a particular subject. However, these extrinsic rewards need to be phased out slowly and consistently and replaced with activities that encourage students to enjoy learning and acquiring the information being presented. Providing students with experiences of success with the knowledge and skills they are taught is essential. There are a number of ways that teachers can orient instruction to enhance the development of intrinsic motivation.

First, it is very important to show students that the information they are being taught is *relevant* and will be of use to them at some point later in their lives. Teachers need to explicitly tell students how the information being taught in their classes can be used in the real world.

Using *various approaches* to present information can generate students' curiosity and stimulate their interests. The use of films, guest speakers, experiments, demonstrations, and multimodal learning experiences can increase students' motivation to be successful as well as enhance learning, memory, and recall of the information.

Teachers should consider assisting students to set their own *learning goals* for classes. Once these goals are defined, teachers can help students develop the individual steps and procedures needed that logically will conclude with meeting established goals.

Teachers who choose to use extrinsic rewards should have *clear expectations* for students about what the standards of performance are for receiving the rewards. Students should have a clear idea about how they will be evaluated and what the specific criteria are that go into the evaluation. Students should also be aware of the outcomes associated with success and failure in each task.

Teachers also need to provide students with clear, concrete, and immediate *verbal corrective feedback* about the quality of their performance on an assignment or test. The feedback must be specific and given close in time to the activity so the information is fresh in the students' minds. Frequent feedback during the initial learning of new information is also very important so students do not learn things incorrectly. A student who learns something incorrectly must unlearn that information and replace it with the correct information. This teaching-unteaching process makes the learning experience difficult and frustrating for many students.

When using extrinsic rewards to motivate students, teachers must pay attention to the *power or value of the rewards* being given. Many students do not see grades or teacher praise as a valuable or rewarding outcome. Some students actually perceive teacher praise as a punishment. It is important for teachers to know the kinds of extrinsic rewards that will be of value to students and that students will be willing to work toward. Some children may value having special class privileges, receiving homework passes, or getting extra time in physical education class rather than being praised or getting high grades.

In general, extrinsic reinforcers tend to lose their power for many students beginning in the middle school years. They also may not be very reinforcing for students who come from high socioeconomic backgrounds that provide them with access to a great number of material rewards and objects. Underachievers typically do not respond well to external reinforcers. For many middle school students adult approval becomes a much weaker reinforcer while peers become a much more significant source of feedback.

Rewarding all students when they complete a task detracts from motivation because it communicates to the students that any level of performance is acceptable regardless of how much effort or quality they put into the assignment. Therefore, the use of extrinsic rewards requires some type of concrete, measurable criteria to evaluate work products.

LEARNED HELPLESSNESS

Everyone needs to have a sense of control over the ability to be successful. Seligman (1975) proposed that people develop a sense of **learned helplessness** when they believe that the events and outcomes in their lives are not within their control and occur as the result of chance or other factors over which they have no influence. Learned helplessness is an extremely powerful mechanism. It can undermine motivation in all areas of life, whether the motivation is intrinsic or extrinsic, and cause people simply to give up and see their goals as beyond their reach.

Learned helplessness interferes with children's ability to become motivated intrinsically and learn for the sake of learning and personal growth. It is very important for teachers to be aware of the effects of their verbal and nonverbal feedback on children's self-perceptions about learning. Some students learn or believe that they are destined to fail or be unsuccessful in school regardless of how much effort they put into studying. This belief is often the result of experiencing a great deal of failure in a particular area, such as school achievement, and receiving large amounts of negative verbal and nonverbal feedback, indicating they are incompetent.

Learned helplessness has significant *negative emotional side effects*. Some students actually become *hopeless* because they expect to fail. They become *demoralized* and give up. Sometimes the students will *miss opportunities* to improve skills and abilities because they refuse to practice. They are unable to see that practice, drill, and repetition often lead to success. They sometimes develop emotional disorders such as *anxiety* and *depression* because of the negative feedback accompanying frequent failure.

There are a number of things that teachers can do to help students increase their chances of success in school. Although the following techniques will not necessarily change students' self-perceptions, they can lead students to develop increased self-confidence and a desire to at least try to succeed. Presenting information in small sequenced steps can often lead to success, especially when teachers provide immediate corrective feedback so students do not practice the skill incorrectly.

It is important for teachers to emphasize the positive characteristics of students rather than focusing on their weaknesses and deficits. Teachers need to remind students frequently that it is a lack of effort, rather than a lack of ability, that causes people to be unsuccessful in school. Teaching should begin with information the student already knows and gradually integrate new information within these preexisting knowledge stores. Experience-based learning, advance organizers, and guided discovery teaching can be useful to encourage students to persist and succeed. These strategies are discussed more fully in Chapter 8.

Teachers will also need to help students confront their learning deficits and weaknesses in realistic ways to minimize their effects on achievement. It is important for teachers to remind students that many people have learning weaknesses and that there are ways to work around any weaknesses students may have, rather than allow them to dominate and contaminate success.

Teachers should use praise and criticism judiciously and concretely. Verbal feedback should be specific and constructive. Teachers should not become emotional when giving feedback. They should clearly communicate to students that they are accessible and available to help students learn and be successful. Clear and visible emotional support can be highly motivating for students who have given up on school.

Most children try to arrive at some explanation for their failures in school. Many successful students who fail make internal but controllable attributions about the cause of their failure: I didn't understand the directions, I didn't study enough, or I didn't do the assigned readings. These internal, controllable attributions help focus students to develop remedial strategies that they can control and change, and the changes they typically make lead to success and an enhanced internal locus of control.

On the other hand, students who believe that success is outside their control often attribute it to their own lack of intelligence, lack of motivation and interest in school, or to the teacher not liking them. These kinds of attributions are themselves largely uncontrollable and lead to the students concluding that no matter what they do they cannot be successful. This attitude leads to further failure in a repeating cycle.

THE EFFECTS OF ANXIETY ON SCHOOL PERFORMANCE

Anxiety describes a generalized and underlying sense of tension and uneasiness. It is not uncommon for students to experience varying degrees of anxiety during their school experience. These kinds of experiences are generally normal and do not have significant negative effects on achievement. However, some students experience very high levels of anxiety much of the time about their school performance because they are afraid of failing. These students equate failure with lowered self-esteem, peer rejection, and parent disapproval. High-level anxiety is clinically significant and can interfere with students' ability to learn information and perform well on tests. Although a relatively high level of anxiety can improve a student's performance on simple, well-learned tasks, when the student must learn a new or challenging task, that relatively high level of anxiety decreases the student's performance (Covington & Omelich, 1987). Most learning in the typical school setting involves new and difficult tasks.

There is a great deal of research showing that anxiety has profound negative effects on children in most aspects of their school performance and achievement. Many anxious children fail to learn appropriate information, which eventually affects their personality characteristics and the quality of their social interactions. High anxiety appears to consist of both intellectual and emotional variables. It is not unusual for anxious children to have a variety of negative and intrusive thoughts about the dire consequences of failing. These thoughts lead children to worry and ruminate, interfere with attention, and decrease their ability to develop effective and efficient problem-solving skills.

Some children have such high anxiety levels that they begin to show physical symptoms. Some of the more common physical symptoms include having an upset stomach, an increase in heart rate, feeling afraid and apprehensive, having sweaty palms, or being openly depressed and verbally or physically negative.

The following characteristics are often seen in highly anxious students:

— Poor reaction to time limits, especially when being tested

— Increased anxiety in competitive situations

— Poor study habits and ineffective test-taking skills, leading to forgetting during test-taking

— Tendency to be easily distracted by irrelevant aspects of a task

— High levels of self-consciousness and concern with how other people see them

— Difficulty identifying important or significant details

— Difficulty taking information learned in one situation and transferring it to a new learning situation, especially when the new learning situation is a test

— Difficulty learning because they are disorganized and rely on rote memory rather than more effective ways of integrating new information

— Attention divided between learning the material and focusing on how frightened or fearful they are when learning (Tobias, 1985)

Students with high levels of anxiety can represent challenges in the classroom. Teachers should strive to create a classroom setting that is consistent and predictable, free from criticism and degradation, and relatively accepting of others. A success-oriented learning approach, with appropriately given positive reinforcement, is important. Allowing students enough time to complete assignments and tests can help some students control their anxiety more successfully. A good approach to use in testing is to begin the test with easy items and then gradually increase the difficulty. Experiencing success at the beginning of the test can serve to boost students' self-confidence and lower self-generated anxiety.

Some other strategies that teachers can use to support anxious students are:

— provide students with a quiet study area;

— help students set realistic studying goals according to their ability levels and the difficulty of the task on which they are working;

— allow students to slow down during test taking so they do not make careless errors; and

— encourage the students to do some relaxation exercises before and during testing.

REFERENCES

Amabile, T. M. (2001). Beyond talent: John Irving and the passionate craft of creativity. *American Psychologist, 56,* 333–336.

Bandura, A. (1995). Exercise of personal and collective efficacy in changing societies. In A. Bandura (Ed.), *Self-efficacy in changing societies* (pp. 1–45). New York: Cambridge university Press.

Baron, R. A. (1998). *Psychology* (4th ed.). Boston: Allyn & Bacon.

Covington, M., & Omelich, C. (1987). "I knew it cold before the exam": A test of the anxiety blockage hypothesis. *Journal of Educational Psychology, 79,* 393–400.

Darwin, C. (1859). *On the origin of species by means of natural selection.* London: John Murray.

Deci, E., Vallerand, R. J., Pelletier, L. G., & Ryan, R. M. (1991). Motivation and education: The self-determination perspective. *Educational Psychologist, 26,* 325–346.

Flammer, A. (1995). Developmental analysis of control beliefs. In A. Bandura (Ed.), *Self-efficacy in changing societies* (pp. 69–113). New York: Cambridge University Press.

Graham, S. (1996). How causal beliefs influence the academic and social motivation of African-American children. In G. G. Brannigan (Ed.), *The enlightened educator: Research adventures in the schools* (pp. 111–126). New York: McGraw-Hill.

Hidi, S., & Harackiewicz, J. M. (2000). Motivating the academically unmotivated: A critical issue for the 21st century. *Review of Educational Research, 70*(2), 151–179.

Juvonen, J., & Weiner, B. (1993). An attributional analysis of students' interactions: The social consequences of perceived responsibility. *Educational Psychology Review, 5,* 325–345.

Kohn, A. (1993). Why incentive plans cannot work. *Harvard Business Review, 71,* 54–63.

Locke, E. A., & Latham, G. P. (1990). *A theory of goal setting and task performance.* Englewood Cliffs, NJ: Prentice-Hall.

Maslow, A. H. (1954). *Motivation and personality.* New York: Harper & Row.

McClelland, D., Atkinson, J. W., Clark, R. W., & Lowell, E. L. (1953). *The achievement motive.* New York: Appleton-Century-Crofts.

Rotter, J. B. (1966). Generalized expectancies for internal versus external control of reinforcement. *Psychological Monographs, 80* (1), Whole No. 609).

Schunk, D. H. (1996). Goal and self-evaluative influences during children's' cognitive skill learning. *American Educational Research Journal, 33,* 359–382.

Seligman, M. E. P. (1975). *Helplessness: On depression, development, and death.* San Francisco: W. H. Freeman.

Tobias, S. (1985). Test anxiety: Interference, defective skills, and cognitive capacity. *Educational Psychologist, 20,* 135–142.

Triandis, H. C. (1994). *Culture and social behavior.* New York: McGraw-Hill.

Weiner, B. (2000). Intrapersonal and interpersonal theories of motivation from an attributional perspective. *Educational Psychology Review, 12*(1), 1–14.

REFERENCES

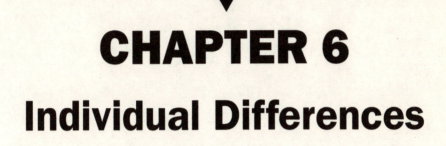

CHAPTER 6
Individual Differences

CHAPTER 6

INDIVIDUAL DIFFERENCES

During a lifetime an individual goes through a set of physical, cognitive, social, and moral developmental patterns that are similar for all people. However, each person perceives, interprets, integrates, and reacts to these common developmental experiences in unique ways that reflect the significance of these events for that person. It is the interpretation of these developmental experiences within specific cultural, social, and environmental settings that creates an individual.

Children bring into the school setting rather well-defined views, beliefs, social behaviors, and expectations about how other people will react to them based on their ability to interpret and integrate the world mentally, the cultural and familial influences they have been exposed to during their early childhood years, and whether they have any cognitive or emotional impairments that interfere with their ability to adapt socially to their world. The study of individual differences addresses the unique influences of intellectual functioning, cultural background, and atypical patterns of cognitive functioning on a child's success in the school setting.

This chapter begins with a discussion of the roles of genetics and the environment in a child's educational success. The concept of intelligence is examined, along with a discussion of how to interpret an intelligence test score, the uses and limitations of the scores in the schools, and some commonly used intelligence tests. It then examines the distinctions between aptitudes and abilities as they relate to testing approaches and their relevance in the educational system. This section concludes with a discussion of creativity as it relates to intelligence.

The second section of the chapter examines environmental influences on individual development and identifies at-risk children.

Finally, this chapter addresses exceptional learners. Some of the major kinds of learning difficulties that can impede educational performance are examined, and specific teaching recommendations and strategies are provided. A brief discussion of reading approaches and the cognitive skills needed for success and reading follows. The chapter concludes with an extensive discussion of the factors that influence a child's ability to be successful in school.

THE NATURE-NURTURE CONTROVERSY

There has been a long-standing debate regarding whether individual differences are the result of genetically based characteristics that predetermine and fix how a person will function and succeed in society, or whether environmental and living conditions are the primary influence on the degree of success that a person encounters in a lifetime. This topic becomes even more controversial when genetic characteristics are examined according to racial or ethnic variables.

This is not a trivial or academic argument. It is an important issue that has a significant impact on how a person perceives the role and effect of education on children. If a person believes that genetics are the primary determinants of an individual's intellectual and social emotional characteristics, then there is little that the environment can do to modify or influence genetic influences and alter the fate of the individual. On the other hand, if a person believes that the environment has a very significant impact on an individual's success and adjustment in life, then providing the appropriate social, educational, and cultural experiences becomes critical in facilitating the growth and development of the individual into a productive adult.

The two basic positions of the nature-nurture controversy are that **genetics** (nature) dominates and determines the course of a person's life or that the **environment** (nurture) does. In the first position researchers argue strongly that genetics is the primary variable that provides clear and concrete limits to how much a person can achieve or succeed in life (Herrnstein & Murray, 1994). This position argues that any positive effects contributed by the environment are trivial in altering "genetically determined fate." To support this position, Herrnstein and Murray examined the results of national studies in which group-administered intelligence tests were given. They compared the results of these studies and found that, on average, African Americans scored about 15 points lower on group-administered intelligence tests than did Caucasian Americans. The authors use these data to justify the position that there are genetically and racially based differences in intellectual ability and potential between the two ethnic groups.

Many studies have compiled data that strongly contradict the position that intelligence is strictly an inherited and permanent trait. Intelligence has been found to change over time. It is not unusual for a person's scores on intelligence tests to change up to 28 points between early childhood and adolescence (McCall, Appelbaum, & Hogarty, 1973). Other studies have shown that teaching methods devoted to showing children how to take intelligence tests can improve test performance significantly and consistently over long periods. For example, teaching a child the specific cognitive skills necessary to solve abstract nonverbal problems using blocks to make various designs can significantly enhance the child's ability to perform in similar tasks typically included in individually administered intelligence tests. These results have been found for children at the preschool and elementary levels, as well as for children with learning disabilities and adults.

Countering the argument that intelligence is genetically determined is a large body of research showing that intelligence is a reflection of the kind of social environment to which the child is exposed (Rifkin, 1998).

The most reasonable perspective regarding whether nature or nurture is more important is one that views a person's intellectual and emotional abilities as affected by nature and nurture interacting with each other. It is highly likely that genetics do place limits on a person's intellectual ability and potential. But what are the exact boundaries of those limits? It is very important to involve children in stimulating and intellectually challenging environments that encourage the development of cognitive skills that may have genetically determined limits. Stimulating activities and experiences will increase the chances that children reach genetically imposed caps, whatever they are. It is clear that genetic factors play a strong role in areas such as physical development, but the environment appears to have a much stronger role in the development of social behaviors and moral development (Berk, 2001).

Socioeconomic status (SES) has been found to be one of the most important variables affecting a child's performance in school. SES represents a combination of how much money the child's parents earn annually, their level of education, and jobs in which they are employed. This variable has been shown to consistently predict a child's scores on intelligence and achievement tests, the grades the child will receive in school, and the probability that the child will drop out of school, be truant, or be suspended (Macionis, 1994). In fact, high school dropout rates for children from low-SES families are nearly twice as high as those for the general population. The dropout rates for students who live in the poorest families typically exceed 50 percent (Catterall & Cota-Robles, 1988).

It seems clear that children's SES reflects the opportunities and experiences they have outside school that serve to enhance their learning activities in school. High-SES children tend to engage in more cultural and athletic activities outside school; are more frequently involved in getting tutoring for activities such as tennis, art, or dance; and have greater and freer access to important learning devices within their homes, such as calculators, newspapers, personal computers, and encyclopedias.

High-SES parents have been found to spend more time talking with their children, discussing the causes and possible outcomes of events and situations, engaging in conversations involving a great deal of interactive discussion and explanation, and encouraging independent thinking. High-SES parents are likely to ask questions that focus on who, what, when, where, and why. These kinds of questions encourage the development of language skills, both expressively as well as internally.

Low-SES parents tend to tell their children what to do using direct statements and commands, use verbal communications that lack appropriate grammatical structure, and provide vague directions and instructions that can be confusing to their children. Low-SES parents often do not encourage their children to engage in independent problem-solving activities and thinking.

In general, research has shown that children who have high-achieving parents are also likely to be high achievers. Some studies have also examined the effects on children's intelligence when children born to low-SES parents are adopted into high-SES families. These studies have shown strong and positive effects on the children's intelligence test scores, in that their test scores actually increase the longer they reside with the adoptive families (Capron & Duyme, 1991).

Ceci (1991) found that the longer a child remains in school, the higher the child's intelligence becomes as measured on intelligence tests. These increases are probably the result of the child receiving a great deal of ongoing mental stimulation, enrichment, active teaching that fosters the development of intellectual abilities and potential, and increased opportunities to practice test taking.

INTELLIGENCE

The nature-nurture controversy is probably most important and relevant when concerns arise about the nature of intelligence, how to measure a person's intellectual ability and potential, and whether predictions about a person's future behavior and performance can be made on the basis of intelligence test scores. The concept of intelligence means different things to different people. It can represent the person's *potential ability to learn* new information. It has also been seen to reflect the *total amount of knowledge* and information a person has acquired during a lifetime. Others believe that intelligence reflects a person's *ability to adapt* successfully to new situations and circumstances.

A great deal of disagreement surrounds the structure of intelligence. Some researchers believe that intelligence represents a single entity that is used in all different kinds of situations, while others believe that intelligence comprises separate abilities and that there are specific intelligences for specific tasks. There seems to be more consensus that intelligence represents high-level thinking processes, such as abstract verbal and non-verbal reasoning, problem-solving skills, and the ability to make effective and logical decisions.

Views of Intelligence

Early views of intelligence held that it was a single entity, sometimes referred to as *g*. Later research identified the various components of intelligence, and it soon became clear that intelligence consisted of a variety of characteristics and applications. According to various contemporary views, there are anywhere from 2 to 120 kinds of intelligence.

Cattell (1971) proposes that two types of intelligences exist. The first type he describes as **fluid intelligence**, which represents a general ability to solve new problems and tasks. An example of tasks requiring fluid intelligence would be the ability to solve block design puzzles or assemble a new bookcase using a diagram. **Crystallized intelligence** reflects the amount of education a person has had and accumulated over the course of a lifetime. Vocabulary knowledge, the ability to solve math problems, and reading comprehension skills are some examples of crystallized intelligence.

Guilford (1967) sees intelligence as consisting of 120 areas: four content areas, five areas involving cognitive operations, and six areas involving products. Guilford's model, referred to as the **structure of intelligence** (SOI), emphasizes memory for factual information and definitions while minimizing processes such as the ability to make evaluations or to identify relationships underlying concepts. The significance of this model is that it encouraged research to broaden the definition of intelligence. In reality, though, this model is far too complex to have any substantial or practical educational implications. Its significance lies primarily in the theoretical area.

A much more practical approach is offered by Gardner (1983) and his concept of **multiple intelligences**. He posits that there are eight dimensions of intelligence and that a person may be strong in one or two dimensions but cannot be competent in all eight dimensions. The following eight dimensions comprise Gardner's model of intelligence (Gardner & Hatch, 1989):

1. **Linguistic intelligence:** ability to understand the meaning and uses of words and language.

2. **Logical mathematical intelligence:** ability to understand, identify, and recognize order and patterns in information.

3. **Musical intelligence:** sensitivity to perceive and comprehend harmony, melody, pitch, and tone.

4. **Spatial intelligence:** ability to perceive the world accurately on the basis of visual and visual- spatial perceptions.

5. **Bodily kinesthetic intelligence:** ability to handle objects or use the body in highly coordinated and creative ways.

6. **Interpersonal intelligence:** ability to understand and be aware of other human beings.

7. **Intrapersonal intelligence:** deep understanding of how feelings and thoughts affect personal behaviors and social decisions.

8. **Naturalist intelligence:** ability to understand similarities and differences that exist within the physical world.

Gardner does not imply that his approach to intelligence should encourage teachers to try to teach all students to become excellent or highly competent in every area. The model simply alerts people to the fact that there is more than one kind of intelligence and that intelligence can mean more than simply performing well in an academic setting. Intelligence applies to life in general and it consists of many different facets, some of which are not easily seen or displayed in an educational setting.

Sternberg (1990) views intelligence as consisting of three components, each comprising multiple abilities. He describes his theory of intelligence as the **triarchic theory**. The three components of intelligence according to Sternberg are as follows:

1. **Processing components** are used to solve problems. These components are the rules and strategies necessary to arrive at a correct solution, whether the problem is one of adding two numbers together or solving an equation in chemistry.

2. **Contextual components** reflect the application of intelligence skills to daily life situations. In essence, contextual components describe the kind of situation or setting where a person is func-

tioning and how this setting either increases or interferes with the person's ability to be successful.

3. **Experiential components** describe how a person's intelligence becomes modified through social, educational, and emotional experiences as the person matures.

Triarchic theory places a high level of importance on a person's ability to deal with new challenges and experiences successfully, efficiently, and automatically. The major underlying premise is that an intelligent person will learn from experience and relate new experiences to old ones that are similar in important ways. Intelligence can be modified through experiences the individual has and continues to change over time as the person gains more experiences in the world. The more experience that a person has, the better and more efficiently they can adapt to new situations.

Although there may appear to be wide differences among the various definitions of intelligence, it is generally agreed that intelligence represents the ability to understand abstract verbal or nonverbal information, the ability to develop logical and effective solutions to problems, and the ability to acquire or learn new information relatively quickly and effectively.

Whether there is a general characteristic of intelligence or several kinds of intelligence is an interesting theoretical question. Yet its relevance to school learning is quite trivial. It is clear that the amount of knowledge a child has about a specific content area, the child's level of motivation to be successful, and the quality and type of teaching the child receives are much more important variables related to learning and achievement than definitions of intelligence or intelligence test performance levels.

Interpreting Intelligence Quotient Test Scores

Intelligence quotient (IQ) test scores are interpreted using the normal curve, with a mean of 100 points and a standard deviation of 15 points as the standard by which to compare how an individual's score ranks or compares with others of the same age. This curve defines the numbers of people expected to achieve each IQ score.

The *average range of intelligence* falls between a score of 90 and 109, with a score of 100 viewed as being exactly average. The following shows the expected numbers of people who fall between a given IQ score range:

IQ score of 101 to 115: 34.13 percent of people are expected to fall in this range and are considered **above average** in intelligence;

IQ score of 116 to 129: 13.59 percent of people are expected to fall in this range, which is called the **superior** range;

IQ score of 130 and higher: 2.1 percent of people are expected to fall in this range, called the **very superior** range.

Because the normal curve is symmetrical, these same percentage expectations apply to persons whose IQ scores fall between 85 and 99 (below average range); 70 to 84 (borderline range); and below 70 (mentally defective range).

Most IQ tests have a standard deviation of 15 points. The **standard deviation** indicates the way in which scores are spread around the mean of the test. If the standard deviation for a test is small, it means that nearly everyone had the same score on that test. If the standard deviation is large, it means that the scores vary widely across individuals on that test. The selection of 15 points as the standard deviation for most intelligence tests seems to represent the most suitable solution to representing scores without exaggeration.

Intelligence tests are examples of **norm-referenced tests** because an individual score is interpreted by comparing it to the performances of others in a specific group. The person's raw score is converted into some relative measure and, in this case, can be used to rank the person in terms of relative intelligence. This relative measure allows us to determine whether the person is either more capable or less able than others in that same age group. Another way of viewing the meaning of an IQ score is that the IQ score reflects a person's *mental age* divided by his or her *chronological age* and then *multiplied by 100*.

Numerous studies using large groups of people at different age levels have shown that scores obtained on IQ tests are generally **stable over time**, meaning that a person's score and relative ranking to other people in the same age range does not change significantly as they grow older. Yet it is important to remember that there are also a number of studies showing *much less stability* of IQ test scores for individuals, and especially those who are exceptional learners or who come from impoverished backgrounds. IQ test scores can vary dramatically, even over a three-year span. Intelligence test scores have been used in the past to assign students inappropriately to special education programs or ability groups (Hilliard, 1994). Several significant federal court cases have determined that a great deal of additional objective testing and real-life behavioral data are needed to justify placing a child into a special education program.

How children actually perform in school should be seen as being more important than their scores on either group or individual intelligence tests. It is clear that educational and cultural enrichment activities can have significant positive effects on children's performance on IQ tests. Therefore, even though research shows that IQ test scores are stable for large groups of people, their stability is much less clear when dealing with individuals.

Other problems can occur when using IQ test scores in the public schools:

— Misinterpretation of the meaning of the scores by professionals using them

— Inaccuracy of the score because of either racial, ethnic, or situational variables that occurred during the testing

— Test scores influencing teacher expectations about student levels of potential and therefore affecting the quality of teaching in a negative way

Test-taking experiences as well as general cultural and educational experiences can also have an important influence on children's performance on IQ tests. Children who possess a good vocabulary, have a wide range of understanding about different verbal and language concepts because they come from verbal families, and have had specific experience with the tasks or similar tests used on intelligence tests (e.g., manipulating puzzles, working with a pencil, copying and drawing designs) are probably at an advantage relative to children who have not had similar kinds of experiences.

Aptitude and Achievement Testing

Aptitude tests are designed to evaluate how a student is functioning in the present. This assessment is then used to make predictions about how the student will perform in the future.

Intelligence tests are examples of aptitude tests because the scores are often used to predict how well a student will perform in school. Aptitude tests are believed to measure abilities that have developed over many years. These abilities are believed to be predictive of success in future learning with new material.

The main goal of many aptitude tests is to predict how well a person will do in a particular program, such as college or professional school (Anastasi, 1988). Two widely used aptitude tests usually given in high school are the PSAT and the SAT Reasoning Test. The SAT is designed to indicate how well a student will perform in college and determine the level and quality of college the student should attend.

Achievement tests are designed to measure a student's final performance level in a course or subject area. These tests are generally standardized and norm-referenced tests that reflect the amount of learning that has taken place. They can be either group or individually administered. Sometimes achievement tests are given to children to determine if additional and more in-depth evaluation is needed. Some commonly used achievement tests are the California Achievement Tests, the Iowa Tests of Basic Skills, and the Metropolitan Achievement Tests.

Aptitude testing has sometimes been used to make teaching more appropriate for students by grouping them on the basis of a common set of characteristics in a particular aptitude area. Typically, students are homogeneously grouped into one class on the basis of the performance in an aptitude test. In some high schools there are distinct courses of study (college preparatory, general, or vocational), and students are placed into these courses of study on the basis of aptitude test results. As a student continues in one particular course of study, it may become difficult to shift to another, especially if the course of study the student has been enrolled in has not provided the same kind of content or intensity of instruction as has occurred in the course of study toward which the student aspires.

This practice, sometimes referred to as **tracking**, has been criticized for a number of reasons. In general, students placed in lower-aptitude classes tend to receive lower-quality instruction. Their teachers often have lower-level objectives for them to achieve, less of an academic focus during instruction, and an emphasis on learning routine procedures rather than encouraging creative and intellectual development (Garmon, Nystrand, Berends, & LePore 1995; Slavin, 1990). Lower-track classes often include a high number of minority group and economically disadvantaged students. Assignments given to the students are often made more on the basis of intelligence test scores rather than the subject area that they are studying. Possibilities for friendships become limited for the students because they are placed in classes where they have limited access to students from other backgrounds or aptitude levels.

Many elementary schools use aptitude test results to group students in the same class into smaller groups (e.g., bluebirds, vultures, aardvarks). This is a common practice to teach reading and mathematics. It is simply another manifestation of tracking, but it occurs within the same classroom rather than in a separate classroom. There has been no consistent research indicating that this type of class grouping is beneficial to students in terms of increasing learning and academic performance levels. Teachers choosing to use this approach should consider the following recommendations (Good & Brophy, 1994):

— Student groupings should be formed on the basis of the students' current performance in the subject being taught and not on the basis of their scores on an aptitude test.

— Students should be encouraged to see themselves as members of the entire class, rather than as members of the subgroup.

— Fostering competition among subgroups is not appropriate.

— This grouping approach should not be used for more than two subjects in any classroom.

— Instruction and pace of presentation for the material must be adjusted to fit the specific and unique needs of the groups.

Creativity

Creativity is the ability to identify or prepare original, unique, and distinctive solutions to problems. People tend to be creative in specific areas rather than being generally creative in all aspects of their lives. Having a sufficient amount of knowledge and information about a particular task is one important requirement for creativity. However, a creative person must also **restructure** the information in a new and unique way that is imaginative and can solve a problem.

Creativity may be related to intelligence as measured on IQ tests, but it is not identical (Torrance, 1995). In general, though, people who score low on intelligence tests typically do not score high on measures of creativity. Yet getting a high score on an intelligence test does not necessarily mean that the person will score high on a test of creativity or that the person will, indeed, be creative. Creativity requires **divergent thinking**, which is the ability to present many different ideas, answers, or solution strategies to solve a problem.

Creativity seems to rely on at least three different types of intelligence (Sternberg & Lubart, 1995):

1. **Synthetic intelligence:** the ability to see problems in novel ways.

2. **Analytical intelligence:** the ability to understand the relationship between new ideas that could be productive and useful when applied to a specific problem area.

3. **Practical intelligence:** the ability to generate ideas and develop new ways of examining a problem because of feedback that others have provided about the situation.

There are several strategies that teachers can use in their classes to promote students' development of creative thinking. Through the use of **brainstorming**, children begin to create new ideas and perspectives about how to solve a specific problem (Baer, 1997). Initially, there are no correct or incorrect ideas and perspectives. The goal is simply to generate as many reasonable options as possible. The idea behind brainstorming is that one idea will encourage the development of other ideas that will be even more appropriate to a successful problem solution.

Sometimes allowing children to simply engage in play can lead to creative solutions. This play activity time can involve students being allowed to interact with the problem along a number of different sensory dimensions and being given time to reflect on or analyze the nature of the problem (Clements, 1991).

Finally, it is important for teachers to let students know that creative solutions and perspectives are appreciated. This means that teachers must have some flexibility in how they view solutions as well as tolerance for children who might have what seems to be a very different, or perhaps even odd, point of view about a situation.

ENVIRONMENTAL INFLUENCES ON INDIVIDUAL DEVELOPMENT

When examining environmental influences on individual and educational development, four areas must be considered: race, culture, socioeconomic status, and at-risk students. Each of these characteristics can interact with each other and have a powerful influence on how a child performs in school.

Race is a categorization of people who share the same visible, genetically determined physical characteristics. Yet it is important to be aware that physical racial characteristics among people *do not* necessarily mean that these people share the same culture or outlook toward life. Further, people of similar racial or even cultural backgrounds do not necessarily all share the same socioeconomic status or the same degree of being at risk for failure in school. A **minority group** represents either a racial or ethnic group of people who live within a larger society of people who are from a different race or ethnic background.

Culture represents the traditions, values, attitudes, and perceptions of reality that guide the behaviors of a group of people. Culture is created by the people within it. Within cultural groups, people communicate their traditions and values to each generation of new members. Children from different cultures learn to interact with adults in different ways. By the time a child enters school, the most important and common normative behaviors, traditions, language patterns, and expected ways of interacting socially have largely become absorbed and ingrained into their personalities as routine ways of functioning. These kinds of cultural differences can lead to misunderstanding and even conflict between a teacher and student unless the teacher is sensitive to and respectful of them.

Cultural differences influence the way in which children learn. For example, the following are some generalizations about culturally related learning differences that research has clarified:

— Mexican American children prefer to learn using concrete, social, and holistic approaches. Teaching that emphasizes abstract and analytical learning approaches typically causes these children to become unmotivated and have learning difficulties (Buenning & Tollefson, 1987).

— African American students prefer to learn using activities involving a visual or global approach rather than a verbal or analytical one. They enjoy focusing on people and relationships between people during learning and respond positively to teaching that is lively, energetic, and interactive. They also have been found to respond better to appropriate nonverbal cues and gestures, opportunities to interact verbally with teachers and peers, and engaging in hands-on contact involving movement and music (Hale-Benson, 1986).

— Native American children appear to respond better to a more global and visual style of learning. Some, such as Navajos, perform better when working independently with members of the same gender (Vasquez, 1990).

— Asian American children are more accustomed to being in a subordinate and compliant role in the classroom, where there is an emphasis on respecting teachers, doing hard work, and engaging in persistent effort that leads to attaining goals and succeeding academically. They tend to work better in a structured and quiet learning setting where goals are clear and concrete (Manning & Baruth, 1996).

— Some cultural groups do not emphasize the kind of individual initiative, competition, and responsibility that is implicit to most American public schools. Students from certain Native American groups and from Vietnam are not taught to compete with fellow students to get good grades. Consequently, they do not raise their hands during class discussion exercises in an effort to distinguish themselves from other students.

— Children of Chinese and Japanese heritage have been found to have families who are highly supportive of educational success and achievement. In general, these cultures emphasize independence, perseverance, and hard work. It is not uncommon to have many members of the family actually involved in assisting a child with their homework assignments.

IDENTIFYING AT-RISK CHILDREN

At-risk students are those who are in danger of failing to complete their education with the skills needed to function at a minimally successful level in society. Many of these children have learning, achievement, or social adjustment problems despite having the potential and capability to succeed in school. Those children most likely to be at-risk are males from lower SES backgrounds who have been retained in one or more grades. They have long-standing histories of low achievement, poor motivation, frequent suspensions from school, are seldom involved in school activities such as sports or clubs, and are often absent from school. They also frequently have behavior problems at school and engage in criminal activities in their communities. Substance use or abuse is also commonly seen.

These children offer a unique set of challenges to teachers. They require a great deal of constant and externally imposed support and structure regarding behavior and academic achievement standards. Frequent appropriate verbal feedback is needed as well as using quizzes and assignments to gradually shape their performance levels toward accepted standards. A strong success orientation in class work is also very important.

TEACHING STRATEGIES TO ACCOMMODATE BACKGROUND DIFFERENCES AMONG STUDENTS

Suggested general educational strategies when working with children from varying racial, cultural, SES, and at-risk backgrounds include:

— Take time to get to know each student as an individual and to appreciate and understand their views about the world, their reactions to life, and how they see themselves fitting in to a new cultural system.

— Teach students the essential skills for success both in school and life. These include reading, speaking, writing, thinking, and problem solving.

— Balance routine learning experiences with new and more complicated activities to encourage the child to grow and develop intellectually.

— Tell students why they are being taught the material given to them and how it will help them to be more successful.

— Keep redundancy in the educational curriculum to a minimum, unless redundancy provides students with the opportunity to practice and strengthen new skills and knowledge.

— Explicitly teach students, in a clear and respectful way, about how to be a good student in a classroom. This may require specifically teaching social conventions and courtesies, as well as how to be polite, whisper, and get help from someone when it is needed.

— Teach students specific study skills and strategies as related to a specific subject or content.

For students to be successful in school, it is important for them to know the practical aspects of classroom communication—specifically, how, when, and where to communicate their views or ask questions. Conflicts with other people can occur when the rules for communicating are unclear. Children should not be punished or criticized because they do not know the correct rules about successful communication in a new setting. They need to be taught these rules explicitly. Teachers should encourage students to express their thoughts fully and completely without interrupting or criticizing them. It is very important to be sensitive to how specific students from different background settings communicate both verbally and nonverbally in both structured and less structured settings.

EXCEPTIONAL LEARNERS

Exceptional learners are students who require specialized and/or additional educational assistance to reach their full academic and intellectual potentials. Some of these students have cognitive, intellectual, emotional, social, or physical impairments that interfere with their ability to function well in school. With the necessary and appropriate support, many of these children can perform reasonably well.

About 10 percent of children in the public schools receive some kind of special education services (U. S. Department of Education, 1994). About 52 percent of these children have some form of a learning disability, 22 percent have some kind of a speech disorder or language communication difficulty, 11 percent are mentally handicapped, 8 percent have some kind of emotional or behavioral disorder, 5 percent have some sort of physical or sensory impairment, and 2 percent have multiple disabilities.

Labeling and diagnosing exceptional learners has been a controversial issue for many years. Some professionals believe that using diagnostic labels to describe these children provides a common language so that teaching techniques and educational curricula can be used in a precise manner (Heward, 1996). Others, though, believe that categories are not useful because they encourage teachers to treat students as objects, implicitly set expectation levels for an individual child based on the diagnosis, and do not offer any kind of information about teaching methods or behavior management strategies.

This section reviews the important characteristics of seven exceptionalities. These are attention-deficit/hyperactivity disorder, behavior disorders, learning disabilities, mental retardation, speech and language communication disorders, visual and hearing impairments, and giftedness. The section concludes with a brief discussion of some general issues associated with exceptional learners.

Attention-Deficit/Hyperactivity Disorder

Attention-deficit/hyperactivity disorder (ADHD) is characterized by significant and rather constant difficulties in maintaining attention and concentration during learning. It is diagnosed in boys about three to nine times more frequently than in girls (American Psychiatric Association, 1994). There are three core symptoms of the disorder that must be present for at least six months or longer and at least some of which must have been apparent before the child reached the age of 7 years:

1. **Inattention:** The child is easily distracted, has difficulty focusing attention or keeping attention for more than a few seconds and may have problems remembering information.

2. **Impulsivity:** The child acts before thinking, shifts quickly and often from one activity to another without completing tasks, and engages in behaviors that may be dangerous or disturbing to others without regard for the consequences.

3. **Hyperactivity:** The child shows numerous inappropriate and excessive gross motor and fine motor body movements, such as shuffling the feet, tapping the hands or fingers, twisting the head around, or simply sitting up and down every few minutes.

Three types of ADHD exist:

1. **Predominantly hyperactive-impulsive type:** includes the symptoms of excessive motor movements and poor self-control.

2. **Predominately inattentive type:** does not include the symptoms of hyperactivity or impulsivity, but the child has difficulty maintaining attention and concentration for more than one or two minutes.

3. **Combined type:** includes all three core symptoms.

ADHD can also be associated with learning disabilities, which seem to magnify the effects of the ADHD. It has been estimated that as many as one-third of children who have learning disabilities also have an accompanying form of ADHD (Hallahan & Kauffman, 1994). Most interventions for children with ADHD require a combination of psychotropic medications, parent effectiveness training, behavior management programming in the schools, social skills and self-control training, and individual counseling for the child.

Behavior Disorders

A **behavior disorder**, sometimes referred to as an emotional handicap or an emotional disturbance, is a serious and persistent problem in getting along with either peers or teachers. Children with behavior disorders are often in conflict with other people, show inappropriate social behaviors, lack self-control, and typically (but not always) fail in school. Their behaviors are serious, occur across most settings, and may be seen several times throughout the school day. About one percent of school children have behavior disorders.

Two types of behavior disorders exist:

1. **Externalizing behavior disorders:** Children are defiant, angry, hostile, and verbally and/or physically aggressive toward other people. They may show hyperactivity and oppositional defiant conduct, even when asked to do relatively simple or easy tasks. They have tremendous difficulty responding to the rules that are typically used in classrooms and often fail to change their behavior because of the consequences they receive for inappropriate conduct. About three times as many males have externalizing behavior disorders as do females.

2. **Internalizing behavior disorders:** Children show feelings of depression and anxiety and may be socially withdrawn and fearful. They often lack confidence socially and academically. They tend to be socially withdrawn and prefer to remain alone and isolated from others.

Some behavior-disordered children also have learning disabilities that complicate their problems even further. The dropout rate for children with behavior disorders is roughly 40 percent, which is the highest of any group of exceptional learners (U.S. Department of Education, 1994).

Children with behavior disorders require a highly structured, consistent, and predictable educational program that emphasizes behavior modification procedures. Their teachers need to have some degree of sensitivity to their social, behavioral, and emotional needs and be able to respond in a professional manner that does not reflect anger when these children are noncompliant. It is important for these children to learn how to control their behaviors, understand how their behavior affects other people, and have an understanding of what is appropriate and inappropriate for specific situations.

Learning Disabilities

Children who are **learning disabled** have average or higher intelligence and show significant problems in their ability to read, express themselves in writing (although deficits in spelling skills are not included), perform mathematical computations and problem solving, listen, or speak (National Joint Committee on Learning Disabilities, 1994). Within the public school setting the most common areas of deficit are in reading, mathematics, and written expression. Learning-disabled students comprise the largest number of children who are identified as exceptional learners in the public schools—around 4 percent of the total school population. It is believed that learning disabilities may be associated with some kind of central nervous system dysfunction that interferes with students' ability to acquire, store, access, retrieve, or use information contained in either their short-term memory or long-term memory systems.

Students with learning disabilities may also develop emotional problems as they continue in school because of the failures they encounter. Many students fall progressively further behind in terms of achievement levels as they mature. In addition, many develop problems with their self-concept and self-image because of the frustration and challenges associated with learning and school success. Definitions of what a learning disability is differ significantly from one school district to the next, as do the requirements for eligibility in special classes. Once again, this disorder is seen at a much higher level of frequency in males than in females.

Mental Retardation

Mental retardation is a condition that is often present at birth or shortly thereafter and causes the child to have adaptive social behaviors and intellectual abilities that are well below average. It is believed that nearly 50 percent of children who are mentally retarded became this way because of preventable environmental situations involving neglect: poor prenatal care, inadequate nutrition by the mother or child during infancy, accidental trauma, ingestion of lead or some other kind of poison by the child, or alcohol abuse by the mother during pregnancy (Smith & Luckasson, 1995). It can also be caused by genetic disorders, diseases, and physical trauma during birth. Until recently, this exceptionality was most often defined by performance on a test of intelligence. The use of IQ test scores to make this diagnosis has been seriously criticized because people with similar IQ scores can vary widely in their ability to cope and be successful. Low IQ test scores can result from a number of factors, including social, cultural, and/or educational deprivation. Further, it is impossible to predict how a person will perform in the real world based on the score obtained on an IQ test.

Four levels of mental retardation exist (Luckasson et al., 1992):

1. **Intermittent:** Educational support services are provided to the child on an as-needed basis.

2. **Limited:** Educational support is provided consistently over a limited time span.

3. **Extensive:** Regular daily support is required for the child to progress in school.

4. **Pervasive:** High-intensity educational interventions and sometimes even life-sustaining supports are provided to help the child to progress in school.

This classification system is based on the amount of support needed for the child rather than using IQ scores to quantify a child's intellectual abilities. Prior to this system, children were categorized as having **mild** (IQ score of 50 to 69), **moderate** (IQ score of 35 to 49), or **severe and profound** (IQ score of 34 or lower) mental retardation. These categories are still used in many school systems.

Speech and Language Communication Disorders

Speech and language communication disorders reflect difficulties in the ability to either comprehend or express ideas using spoken language. **Expressive disorders** involve difficulty forming sounds or keeping sounds in the correct sequence when speaking. These disorders include stuttering and mispronouncing words such as "pasghetti" for *spaghetti* or "muthroom" for *mushroom*. **Receptive language disorders** represent problems in understanding language that is being communicated orally. Sometimes this disorder coexists with either a hearing impairment or a learning disability.

Three types of speech disorders exist:

1. **Articulation difficulties:** difficulty in pronouncing certain sounds or substituting, distorting, or omitting sounds during spoken language.

2. **Fluency disorders:** typically associated with stuttering.

3. **Voice disorders:** speaking in either a highly nasal or high-pitched voice because of some kind of disruption to the flow of air through the nose and/or throat.

In general, language disorders are more serious than speech disorders because language disorders reflect significant problems in the child's ability to understand spoken language or to express their ideas and thoughts using spoken language. Sometimes children with language disorders are reluctant to speak in a group or individually, use short words and phrases rather than complete sentences, speak in a soft tone of voice while avoiding eye contact, and use nonverbal gestures along with clichés such as "you know" or "like."

Speech and language communication disorders can create a great deal of difficulty for children both **academically and socially**. Teachers must remain sensitive to the effects of these kinds of disorders on the students' emotional functioning as well as on their academic performance. It is important that students not be ridiculed, berated, or penalized when they have difficulty either comprehending or expressing themselves using spoken language.

Visual and Hearing Impairments

A **visual impairment** is a disability related to a child's sight that is not correctable through lenses or surgery and has a significant negative effect on the child's ability to learn and achieve in general. Most visually impaired children have few or no intellectual or cognitive deficits as a result of their visual impairments, but they can have a great deal of difficulty with language development because they do not have the normal range and depth of visual experiences of other children. It is this lack of visual experience and exposure that can cause some visually impaired children to have difficulties with expressive or receptive language communications.

About 1 of every 1,000 children has a visual disability. They are typically diagnosed as either visually impaired or blind. A legally blind child has 20/200 vision or worse in the better eye with corrective devices. It is estimated that about 80 percent of legally blind children can read large print (Levin, 1996).

Some behaviors suggesting that a child may be having problems with their visual perception and acuity include reading with the head tilted to one side, having red eyes or eyes that water excessively, having difficulty reading small print, having difficulty being able to discriminate among letters with similar shapes (m, n, w; b, d, p, g), or complaining of dizziness or headaches after reading.

Hearing impairments have equally profound and negative effects on the child's ability to develop language and to understand the world using words and verbal concepts. Hearing impairments consist of either a partial impairment or complete deafness. Many hearing impairments are the result of diseases during pregnancy (rubella), trauma during pregnancy or birth, or early childhood diseases. Typical symptoms seen in children with hearing impairments include difficulty following oral directions, problems with articulating words or sound clusters, listening to audio tapes at a very high volume, or asking people to repeat what they have said to them.

The loss of either vision or hearing, to any degree, is a serious impediment to children in terms of academic, social, and psychological development. It is essential that teachers remain very supportive of these children and encourage them while using the appropriate instructional and curricular strategies to help them learn to the best of their abilities while minimizing or circumventing the negative effects from the sensory impairments. Sometimes these children will have problems with self-esteem or develop learned helplessness because of the tremendous difficulties imposed by the specific sensory impairment.

Gifted and Talented Children

Gifted and talented children comprise a unique group of learners who show outstanding intellectual ability or performance in an area such as science, mathematics, or theater. In the past, these children were almost exclusively identified on the basis of having a high IQ test score, 130 or higher. More contemporary definitions recognize that high intelligence is only one characteristic of this group and that qualities such as creativity, leadership ability, and the ability to perform in the visual arts are also equally valid indicators of gifted and talented functioning. As such, this broader definition recognizes students with extraordinary abilities in areas that are not necessarily restricted to the basic school curriculum.

Gifted and talented students are not necessarily or implicitly socially maladjusted, unable to get along with other people, or have very restricted interests in their world. Many gifted children have adequate social skills, are socially well adjusted and emotionally stable, and have numerous hobbies. Yet they also are high achievers and learn more easily than their peers. Davis and Rimm (1993) identified the following characteristics as typical of many gifted and talented children:

— Prefer to work alone

— Imaginative and enjoy pretending

— Show high levels of persistence

— Are highly verbal and often flexible in how they view problems

— Get bored quickly with routine tasks

— Are willing to work well beyond what is expected to achieve a satisfactory product

— Are sometimes impulsive and not interested in details

Because of these personality characteristics, gifted and talented students can be challenging for a teacher because they need to be constantly exposed to an enriched classroom experience that is flexible, maintains motivation and interest, and provides a sense of meaningfulness.

Educational programming for these children usually involves either:

— **accelerated programs**, in which children are taught information and then allowed to proceed at their own learning pace based on the degree of success they attain at each step in the process; or

— **enrichment programs**, where the child engages in independent study activities or works with an adult mentor on projects (e.g., sculpting, calculus, classical studies) in which they are highly interested.

Renzulli (1994) has proposed a model that emphasizes three types of general activities for all talented and gifted children:

1. **General exploratory activities** and projects that enable students to find out about topics on their own and begin to focus their interests and energies.

2. **Group training experiences**, using controlled learning experiences such as games and simulated activities, where the children are allowed to develop problem-solving skills for contrived dilemmas in creative and unique ways.

3. **Individual and small-group activities** that deal with real problems, such as putting together a classroom newspaper or interviewing people about historical periods (e.g., World War II, the Vietnam War) in which they lived.

READING ABILITY

Reading is the ability to translate written symbols into spoken language and ideas. It is a developmental process that expands on the child's background knowledge about the world as well as the child's increasing knowledge about the rules governing written and spoken language relationships. Learning to read occurs gradually and is related to the child's intellectual and social development. Spoken language communications also play an important role in learning to read.

There are presently two general perspectives of how a child learns to read: the meaning emphasis strategy and the code emphasis strategy.

The **meaning emphasis strategy** emphasizes the practical functions of script or written symbols. Script is seen to be a way to communicate ideas that the child can understand and comprehend. The most popular ways to achieve these goals are the language experience teaching strategy and the whole language approach.

The **language experience strategy** uses the child's own unique and specific spoken language system and daily life experiences to develop the content for stories the child dictates to an adult. The adult writes these words on paper, and the dictated stories become the content to teach the child how to read. Many believe that this strategy is highly effective because the content of the stories is information that the child is already familiar with and is contained in long-term memory.

The **whole language approach** views reading as one part of a total general program of literacy skill development. Speaking, listening, writing, and reading are taught as interrelated skills. Using combinations of videos, books, and student work projects is a common technique to emphasize the relationships among script, written and spoken vocabulary, and ideas. Language is simply a medium to describe experiences to others, as well as to oneself. Language skill development is applied across the curriculum.

The **code emphasis strategy** for reading instruction teaches children the rules about how to decode (read) and encode (spell) words. These rules typically involve learning the relationship between a letter and its corresponding sound as well as how groups of letters are put together. Perhaps the most well-known strategy is called the **phonics approach**, which teaches the child basic letter-sound relationships first and then applies these rules to words that are regular and consistent. It is believed that this approach develops and emphasizes the child's **phonemic awareness**, or the ability to understand that letters and letter combinations create different sounds in spoken language. A significant body of literature supports the role of phonemic awareness in reading competency (Spector, 1995). Phonics approaches teach about 40 sounds that are represented by a finite number of letter and letter combinations. The belief is that once the child learns these 40 sounds and their written symbol equivalents, they can sound out or decode any new word presented to them. The problem is that the English language often does not lend itself easily to this type of simple decoding process. For example, try saying the following words out loud: *dough, tough, bough, cough.*

During the latter portion of the third grade most reading instruction programs shift from learning how to read, using either a meaning emphasis or code emphasis strategy, to using reading as a means to acquire knowledge. **Data-driven models** of reading emphasize decoding where words are analyzed in a letter-by-letter approach. **Concept-driven models** are based on the belief that students derive meaning from text by relating the words to their individual experiences, knowledge base, and expectations. Most likely, it is some combination of these two viewpoints that accurately reflects reading and reading comprehension development specifically.

A great deal of controversy surrounds the issue of determining the most effective way to teach reading skills. It is generally agreed, though, that reading instruction needs to include both phonics skills and reading for meaning.

There are a number of activities and strategies teachers can use to help children improve their reading comprehension. One approach is to encourage students to summarize as they are reading a passage. In this strategy students read for meaning by identifying important information and then describing the information using their own words. Although this is an effective approach, it does require considerable time and effort from the child. Consequently, it can make reading a very difficult, unrewarding, and challenging activity.

Reciprocal teaching encourages children to monitor their own comprehension as they are reading by summarizing the passage using four specific steps (Palinscar, Brown, & Martin, 1987). In step one the children summarize the passage using their own words so the main idea is identified. During step two the children ask a question about the text that tries to capture the main point in the passage. At the third step the children go back and clarify any unclear points, ideas, or vocabulary presented in the passage. Finally, the children are asked to predict what the text might say in the next section or sections. This approach has been proven to be successful with many students at all achievement levels. Once again, though, it is a laborious approach that works most effectively with a maximum of only eight students being taught at any given time. It may also be difficult to implement this strategy in all subject areas taught in school. For example, in a class such as social studies or art history, it may not be appropriate to try to predict what is to occur next.

GENERAL ISSUES RELATED TO INDIVIDUAL LEARNING DIFFERENCES

Public Law 94-142 was enacted in 1975 to ensure that every individual who is an exceptional learner receives an appropriate educational program that meets his or her needs and helps the student reach his or her potential as a learner. As described in the following paragraphs, there are several important aspects to this law.

All exceptional learners must be educated in the *least restrictive environment* that allows them to participate in as normal a classroom setting as possible. This allows these children to experience being educated with other children who do not have exceptionalities and exposes them to the same kinds of social and learning experiences and knowledge.

Six types of delivery systems provide the least restrictive environment for a student:

1. Placing the student in a regular classroom setting with an individualized educational program (IEP) that requires minimal instructional or curricular modifications or support services.

2. Placing the student in a regular classroom setting in which they are provided with a specialist who consults with the regular teacher regarding the best and most effective ways to teach, motivate, and evaluate the student's learning progress.

3. Keeping the student in a regular classroom setting for most of the day and having the student attend a special education resource room for specific subjects.

4. Allowing the student to spend much of the school day in a special education classroom and to attend regular classes in subjects that the student is best able, academically and emotionally, to be successful, either with or without support services.

5. Placing the student in a full-time special education classroom located within a regular school setting.

6. Placing the student in a separate school designed specifically and uniquely for children with extraordinary and intense needs.

Inclusion is a process of educating exceptional students in a regular educational setting while providing the appropriate supportive and educational services so that the students' probability of success is maximized. Educational and supportive services can involve instructional modifications, curriculum adjustments, emotional support, as well as actual attention to specific physical or sensory limitations.

All children who are exceptional learners are guaranteed the *right to due process* under the law. Their *parents must be actively involved* throughout the entire process of diagnosing and developing an appropriate educational program for them. Parents are also guaranteed access to all school records on their children and the opportunity for *independent educational evaluations* if they are dissatisfied with the evaluations conducted by the school.

Each exceptional learner must be *evaluated* using testing procedures and personnel who speak the *child's native language*. No single test or criterion can be used to put a child into a special education program. This evaluation is conducted by a team of professionals from different disciplines and includes speech and language, psychology, special education, and the parents.

Once it is determined that a child needs special education, the school has a specific time frame in which to develop an **individualized educational program**, a legal document that defines the child's educational needs. This program, sometimes called an **IEP**, is a specific curriculum and instructional plan for both regular education and special education teachers and specialists to provide the most appropriate educational experiences in a continuous, active, and accountable way to help the child reach full intellectual and educational potential. The IEP consists of five components:

1   Assessment of the current level of functioning and performance.

2. Short-term and long-term educational objectives to be achieved by the child along with the specific teaching methods and strategies teachers will use to help the child reach the objectives.

3. Additional support services (e.g., counseling, speech and language services, adapted physical education) necessary to help the child meet the objectives in the IEP.

4. A timeline to implement the plan and monitor its effectiveness.

5. Specific criteria used to evaluate how successful the plan is in achieving the stated purposes and objectives.

The IEP is an extremely important and valuable document that provides the appropriate support for classroom teachers to deal with each exceptional child in their classrooms in unique and highly beneficial ways. It helps integrate regular teaching approaches with those used by specialists. Moreover, it allows parents to monitor the child's educational process and offers them a concrete guide about how to meet the child's needs.

In general, the following teaching practices and approaches may be useful with many different types of individual learners:

1. Provide children with meaningful learning tasks that allow them to spend more time actively working with the material and ample opportunity for drill, practice, and repetition of both concepts and skills.

2. Offer support to children so they feel comfortable in the class-room.

3. Provide corrective feedback gently and immediately so children do not learn facts or skills incorrectly that they must unlearn and then be taught new facts or skills.

4. Have a structured classroom setting that emphasizes a positive reinforcement approach for both work performance and conduct. Punishment approaches are seldom effective and often have negative effects for both the teachers and students.

REFERENCES

American Psychiatric Association. (1994). *Diagnostic and statistical manual of mental disorders: DSM-IV* (4 ed.). Washington, DC: Author.

Anastasi, A. (1988). *Psychological testing* (6th ed.). New York: Macmillan.

Baer, J. (1997). *Creative teachers, creative students*. Boston: Allyn & Bacon.

Berk, L. E. (2001). *Development through the lifespan* (2nd ed.). Boston: Allyn & Bacon.

Buenning, M., & Tollefson, N. (1987). The cultural gap hypothesis as an explanation for the achievement patterns of Mexican American students. *Psychology in the Schools, 14,* 264–271.

Capron, C., & Duyme, M. (1991). Children's IQ's and SES of biological and adoptive parents in a balanced cross-fostering study. *Cahiers de Psychologie Cognitive, II,* 323–348.

Cattell, R. (1971). *Abilities: Their structure, growth, and action*. Boston: Houghton Mifflin.

Catterall J., & Cota-Robles, E. (1988). *The educationally at-risk: What the numbers mean*. Palo Alto, CA: Stanford University Press.

Ceci, S. J. (1991). How much does schooling influence intelligence and its cognitive components? A reassessment of the evidence. *Developmental Psychology, 27,* 703–720.

Clements, D. H. (1991). Enhancement of creativity in computer environments. *American Educational Research Journal, 28,* 173–188.

Davis, G., & Rimm, S. (1993). *Education of the gifted and talented* (3rd ed.). Upper Saddle River, NJ: Prentice-Hall.

Gardner, H. (1983). *Frames of mind: The theory of multiple intelligences*. New York: Basic Books.

Gardner, H., & Hatch, T. (1989). Multiple intelligences go to school. *Educational Researcher, 18* (8), 4–10.

Garmon, A., Nystrand, M., Berends, M., & LePore, D. C. (1995). An organizational analysis of the effects of ability grouping. *American Educational Research Journal, 32,* 687–715.

Good, T. L., & Brophy, J. E. (1994). *Looking in classrooms* (6th ed.). New York: HarperCollins.

Guilford, J. (1967). *The nature of human intelligence*. New York: McGraw-Hill.

Hale-Benson, J. E. (1986). *Black children: Their roots, culture, and learning styles* (Rev. ed.). Baltimore: Johns Hopkins University Press.

Hallahan, D., & Kauffman, J. (1994). *Exceptional children* (6th ed.). Needham Heights, MA: Allyn & Bacon.

Herrnstein, R., & Murray, C. (1994). *The bell curve*. New York: Free Press.

Heward, W. (1996). *Exceptional children* (5th ed.). Upper Saddle River, NJ: Merrill/ Prentice-Hall.

Hilliard, A. G. (1994). Misunderstanding and testing intelligence. In J. I. Goodlad & P. Keating (Eds.), *Access to knowledge*: *The continuing agenda for our nation's schools* (pp. 145–157). New York: College Entrance Examination Board.

Levin, A. V. (1996). Common visual problems in the classroom. In R. H. A. Haslam & P. J. Valletutti (Eds.), *Medical problems in the classroom*: *The teacher's role in diagnosis and management* (pp. 161–180). Austin, TX: Pro-Ed.

Luckasson, R., Coulter, D., Pollaway, E., Reiss, A., Shalock, R., Snell, M., et al. (1992). *Mental retardation: Definition, classification, and systems of supports*. Washington, DC: American Association on Mental Retardation.

Macionis, J. (1994). *Sociology* (4th ed.). Upper Saddle River, NJ: Prentice-Hall.

Manning, M. L., & Baroth, L. G. (1996). *Multicultural education of children and adolescents* (2nd ed.). Boston: Allison & Bacon.

McCall, R., Appelbaum, M., & Hogarty, P. (1973). Developmental changes in mental performance. *Monographs of the Society for Research in Child Development, 38*.

National Joint Committee on Learning Disabilities. (1994). Learning Disabilities: Issues on definition. In *Collective perspectives on issues affecting learning disability: Position papers and statements*. Austin, TX: Pro-Ed.

Palinscar, A., Brown, A., & Martin, S. (1987). Peer interaction in reading comprehension instruction. *Educational Psychologist, 22,* 231–253.

Renzulli, J. S. (1994). *Schools for talent development: A practical plan for total school improvements*. Mansfield Center, CT: Creative Learning Press.

Rifkin, J. (1998). The sociology of the gene. *Phi Delta Kappan, 79*(9), 649–657.

Slavin, R. E. (1990). Achievement effects of ability grouping in secondary schools: A best-evidence synthesis. *Review of Educational Research, 60,* 471–500.

Smith, D. D., & Luckasson, R. (1995). *Introduction to special education* (2nd ed.). Boston: Allyn & Bacon.

Spector, J. (1995). Phonemic awareness training: Application of principles of direct instruction. *Reading and Writing Quarterly, 11,* 37–51.

Sternberg, R. (1990). *Metaphors of mind*: *Conceptions of the nature of intelligence*. New York: Cambridge University Press.

Sternberg, R., & Lubart, T. I. (1995). *Defying the crowd: Cultivating creativity in a culture of conformity.* New York: Free Press.

Torrance, E. (1995). Insights about creativity: Questioned, rejected, ridiculed, ignored. *Educational Psychology Review, 7*(3), 313–322.

U.S. Department of Education. (1994). *Sixteenth annual report to Congress on the implementation of the Individuals with Disabilities Act.* Washington, DC: Government Printing Office.

Vasquez, J. A. (1990). Teaching to the distinctive traits of minority students. *The Clearing House, 63,* 299–304.

CHAPTER 7
Testing

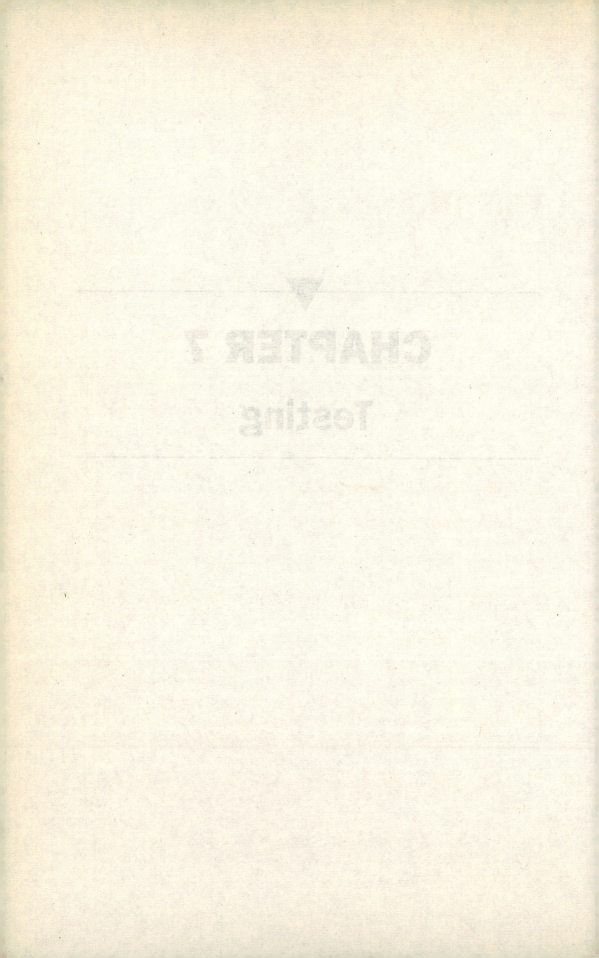

CHAPTER 7

TESTING

Effective teaching requires that teachers collect data about how well students are learning, understanding, applying, and retaining the material presented in class. The primary way this information is collected is by using a variety of testing strategies to measure accumulated knowledge and skills. This chapter addresses the various testing strategies and approaches that can be used to meet this goal. It begins with the development and use of instructional objects and mastery learning. The various types of teacher-developed tests and how these can be used most effectively to orient instruction are then reviewed. The chapter concludes with an examination of reliability, validity, and interpretation of norm-referenced tests.

INSTRUCTIONAL OBJECTIVES

Instructional objectives are an extremely important component of instruction because they directly integrate teaching with student evaluation and assessment. Objectives provide a plan that enables the teacher to present important information systematically and logically to bring a program of study to an effective conclusion. Instructional objectives also help teachers develop specific daily lessons and focus on the key contents and skills students need to master the objectives.

Objectives are much more specific and concrete than goals. **Educational goals** tend to be general statements about the desired outcomes of a teaching-learning experience. Instructional objectives, on the other hand, present the specific, observable, measurable, and concrete skills that students are expected to achieve related to the educational goals. Objectives provide focus and direction for both students and teachers.

For students, objectives also offer ongoing and clear feedback about how they are progressing in a course. Regardless of their grade level, students can see when they are making satisfactory progress in acquiring important skills and information. Because students can make changes in their study habits as a result of this feedback, they are in greater control of the academic outcomes.

For teachers, objectives give feedback about how effective their teaching programs are and when they should modify their programs to enhance student performance. Objectives also provide an accountability system so teachers can justify their professional efforts as well as assist parents in understanding their child's quality of performance in the classroom.

Students benefit from getting feedback about how well they are meeting instructional objectives. Positive feedback increases students' levels of motivation and effort, especially when they receive recognition in the form of good grades or awards for outstanding performance (Dempster, 1991).

A comprehensive classification system, called a **taxonomy**, was developed to guide teachers in organizing goals and objectives in a logical and sequenced hierarchy. Teachers can use it as a reference guide to be sure they are teaching a broad range of skills and content and not overlooking skills.

Three types of taxonomies exist:

1. **Cognitive objectives:** emphasize the development of intellectual skills and acquiring knowledge.

2. **Affective objectives:** deal with values and attitudes about important issues in life.

3. **Psychomotor objectives:** focus on development of physical abilities and competencies.

There are two general viewpoints about how objectives should be developed. One approach was developed by Mager (1997) and a second was developed by Gronlund (2000). Mager believes that instructional objectives must consist of three components. The teacher must tell students clearly what they are expected to do and indicate how the teacher will know if they are meeting those expectations. Next, the teacher must identify, clearly and concretely, the specific behaviors necessary to demonstrate achievement so the students and the teacher can recognize them. Finally, the teacher must communicate, clearly and specifically, the conditions under which the necessary behaviors are to occur and the specific criteria for acceptable performance levels. Separate objectives must be prepared for each learning task or activity.

Gronlund (2000) recommends that the best way to develop instructional objectives is for the teacher to write general teaching objectives that outline what students are expected to learn. These teaching objectives are further clarified into learning objectives, which are the specific behaviors students are expected to show at the end of a lesson or unit. Test questions for the unit should be made before teaching the material so that instruction can emphasize the contents to be tested.

Gronlund is not concerned about the conditions and criteria for achievement as is Mager. Gronlund believes that using **general objectives** (related to concepts such as knowing, understanding, or being able to or apply learned information) that are further clarified by **specific learning outcomes** (define operationally what students need to know, understand, and/or apply) is more realistic in reflecting what teachers actually do during instruction.

Regardless of which perspective the teacher takes, it is important that instructional objectives be *clear, meaningful, specific, and measurable*. Sometimes it is important for teachers to **task analyze** an instructional objective by breaking down the objective into the sequence of steps or basic subskills that lead to mastery (Gagne, 1977). When doing a task analysis the teacher must identify the prerequisite skills the student needs to meet the objectives. For example, a student who is reading disabled cannot be expected to do a library research paper on astral physics. Task analysis also requires that the teacher identify the skills needed to teach students effectively before the teacher actually begins working on the specific instructional objective. Finally, the teacher must organize the subskills to be taught into the appropriate sequence so students can use them effectively when learning.

Bloom (1968) proposed a mastery learning approach as an effective teaching strategy to use with instructional objectives. **Mastery learning** presumes that all students are able to achieve most instructional objectives if they are given enough on-task learning time and the appropriate teaching and learning experiences. Corrective instruction is provided to students who need more help, while those who reach the mastery level quickly can become involved in enrichment activities such as independent or small-group assignments, including research projects or more difficult and complex problem solving.

Other important benefits from using instructional objectives include:

1. **Focusing** student attention on the most important material to be learned.

2. **Alerting** students about the specific performance-based criteria to meet the objectives.

3. **Increasing** the probability of student success because students have greater control over their learning outcomes.

Instructional objectives may not be as effective when students are being asked to read and understand lengthy narrative passages or transfer information from one setting to another. With these learning experiences it may be better to give students a list of questions to focus their attention on the meaning of the passage before actually reading it (Hamilton, 1985).

TEACHER-DEVELOPED TESTS IN THE CLASSROOM

Using tests and quizzes as a regular part of the teaching program is important because it allows the teacher to monitor student performance and give students specific feedback about their progress, strengths, weaknesses, and levels of competency. If developed appropriately, tests and quizzes can also become an important motivator for many students.

The specific kind of test a teacher uses depends on what the teacher hopes students will accomplish. Students are either required to know factual information about an area or demonstrate the ability to perform some series of behaviors or skills leading to the solution of a problem.

There are several kinds of tests for teachers to use: essay, multiple-choice, true-false, fill-in-the blank, matching-item, short answer, and performance-based. Each type is described in the following paragraphs.

Essay tests require students to develop, generate, and communicate their ideas in writing. Most essay tests require a rather lengthy response that reflects how well students can recall, organize, and integrate information and concepts. These tests also typically require high-level cognitive skills, such as analysis, synthesis, organization, and evaluation of concepts, in addition to recall of information and the ability to express ideas in writing. The major problem with essay tests is inconsistent grading by the teacher. Indirectly related variables, such as a student's penmanship, grammar, level of vocabulary, spelling ability, writing style, or phrasing, can detract from the ideas the student presents, even if those ideas have merit. Essay tests are also time consuming to evaluate, and teacher fatigue or boredom can become another source of grading bias. The advantage of essay tests is that they allow the teacher to evaluate how much knowledge a student has about a topic and how well they can express it.

Multiple-choice tests are widely used in the classroom. The questions can be worded in such a way that they test both factual knowledge as well as more sophisticated kinds of analysis and synthesis. Multiple-choice tests are used to measure how much information students know about a particular subject area. The tests are easy to administer and can be very efficient because a large number of questions can be asked and accurately scored. The challenge in writing good multiple-choice questions is that the stem of the item must be worded clearly and the choices to the question must be written so there are clearly distinguishable alternatives.

A **true-false test** asks students to read and compare information presented in a group of sentences and determine whether the information is correct or incorrect. Each sentence must be written clearly, express only one factual concept, and not be an opinion. Words such as *always* or *never* should be avoided as much as possible. True-false tests are easy to use, can be scored reliably, and do not require a large amount of the teacher's time.

Fill-in-the-blank tests have many of the advantages described for multiple-choice tests, although it is very important that the items are not ambiguous or presented in a confusing manner.

In a **matching-item test** students are presented with two lists of terms or phrases. One item (e.g., a word, phrase, date, or name) in the first list is matched with an item in the second list. This test strategy measures information recall and recognition. It also offers the teacher a reliable and objective assessment of student performance and is easily scored.

Short-answer tests can take the form of a brief essay; students are provided with a stem and asked to complete the stem by forming a complete sentence containing important points. These tests are useful because they test students' knowledge of facts as well as comprehension.

Finally, the teacher can use numerous **performance-based test strategies** to determine how much information students have learned or the degree of success they have gained with a particular skill. These strategies are usually longer-term projects that are completed over several days or even months. In general, there are three types of performance-based testing strategies:

1. **Portfolios** contain several pieces of student work reflecting their progress and competency at various stages in a project. Using portfolios allows the teacher to assess how well the student is progressing at various stages in the learning experience and determine the degree of growth that is occurring.

2. **Exhibitions** require students to work over a long period to produce a finished product. Although exhibitions are commonly used in subjects such as music and art, they can also be used in other subject areas. Typical exhibitions involve various types of artwork, videotapes, photograph collections, or completed science projects. They can also be used in history classes.

3. **Demonstrations** show how well knowledge learned in one setting can be applied to a new setting or problem. Demonstrations typically require a combination of knowledge and skill in practical or novel ways.

Each of the performance-based evaluation strategies can be very useful in monitoring and identifying student achievement levels as well as offering interesting activities that provide meaning and energy to learning. As a general rule, multiple-choice, true-false, and short-answer tests are used to assess facts and knowledge. Essay tests are more often used to evaluate students' comprehension of material as well as their ability to organize, integrate, and summarize at a conceptual level. Performance-based evaluations examine the student's ability to work tenaciously over a sustained period and apply knowledge and skills to realistic problems in concrete and even complicated ways.

FORMATIVE EVALUATION

A **formative evaluation** is a strategy that enables the teacher to determine how well students in the class are learning and comprehending the material being taught. It is a form of ongoing diagnosis that can help to identify why a student is having difficulty keeping pace with the rest of the class. The teacher can determine which students are misunderstanding certain concepts, are not learning skills correctly, or would benefit from remedial instruction. Formative evaluation can also help the teacher decide if the class needs to be divided into smaller groups based on ability and comprehension levels for certain topics.

A formative evaluation is different from a **summative evaluation**, which is primarily used to determine a student's overall level of achievement so a grade can be assigned to reflect the student's level of competence and knowledge. Grades are not given on formative tests and quizzes.

Formative evaluations can be done in several different ways, depending on the preference of the teacher, the composition of students in the class, and the specific content being covered. The use of a **dynamic assessment** strategy allows students to work independently on assignments while the teacher examines how much external direction, guidance, and support they require to solve the problem (Shepard, 2000). The teacher gives students both direct and indirect feedback to guide them in identifying and understanding what is important to learn and how to integrate that information to achieve a positive outcome. This type of strategy can increase motivation because students can come to see themselves as being knowledgeable and competent in problem solving. It can also help students improve their studying methods and prepare more effectively for summative assessments. Finally, many students learn information and skills better because the learning and evaluation feedback experiences provided by the dynamic assessment help them to consolidate knowledge in a meaningful way (Crooks, 1988).

Formative evaluation can be conducted before beginning a unit as well as systematically throughout the teaching process as a guide for the teacher. Quizzes give students specific and direct feedback about how well they are progressing and identify areas where they need to apply more effort. Pretests can help establish the beginning knowledge base of students so the teacher can orient instruction more precisely based on real-life characteristics and needs.

Students' performance on formative tests does not count toward their final grades. In this respect, students who are anxious may find this repeated test-taking practice useful to reduce test-taking anxiety during a summative assessment.

CLASSROOM GRADING APPROACHES

One of the most difficult, challenging, and controversial tasks teachers face is how to evaluate the quality of work produced by students. In general, specific grading criteria are usually set by the individual teacher, and standards can vary significantly from one teacher to the next. In some school systems the administration may have some general criteria about what the grades represent, but it is the responsibility of the teacher to assign grades based on their personal judgments about the quality of students' work.

Most school systems continue to use report cards that are given every six or nine weeks. The grades on a report card usually reflect a summative evaluation of a student's performance based on some combination of scores from quizzes and tests, in-class assignments and projects, homework assignments, seat work assignments, classroom conduct and attitude, the amount of effort the student seems to have put forth, and the amount of participation in class discussion and activities.

Six different grading approaches exist:

1. **Letter grading approaches** use the letters of the alphabet to designate the student's level of performance and competency. The letter grades typically reflect five levels of achievement: outstanding (A); above average (B); average, indicating that the student is competent but not exceptional (C); below average in competency but passing (D); and failure to achieve even minimal competency in the particular subject or content area (F).

2. **Absolute grading standards** use either a 10-point or 7-point grading scale. These numerical scores may be reported as an overall summative arithmetic average or they may be translated

into letter grades. For example, in a 10-point grading system a letter grade of A would reflect performance of 90 and higher. In a 7-point grading system a letter grade of A would correspond to an average of 93 and higher.

3. **Relative grading scales** compare individual student performance with the performance of other students in that same class or grade. Sometimes this grading approach is referred to as **curving** because students are assigned grades on the basis of their position according to a predetermined distribution of school grades. A major problem with this approach is that there are a limited number of students who can achieve grades of B and above because these numbers are fixed on the curve distribution. Consequently, students who are high achievers and in high-achieving classes must constantly get higher scores on tests to earn the higher grades. Students who are in low-achieving classes may not have to score as high to get the same grade. Further, it is possible that some teachers give better grades to students in high-achieving classes than those in low-achieving classes if the curve is based on an entire grade level of students rather than an individual classroom of children. Finally, this grading approach often fosters a great deal of competition among students because when one student earns a good grade it lowers the probability of others earning a good grade.

4. **Descriptive grading scales** use terms such as *outstanding, satisfactory,* and *unsatisfactory* or *exceeds expectations, meets expectations,* and *fails to meet expectations* to describe student performance levels. These descriptive terms are often difficult for parents to understand and do not offer a great deal of detail about how the student is doing precisely except as compared with other students in the class.

5. **Performance grading scales** use work samples from class and homework assignments compiled into a portfolio for each student (Wiggins, 1994). The teacher compares assignments done early in the school year with later work assignments. Performance grading emphasizes a student's growth over time, but it also compares the student's individual performance to that of others in the class. Grades are assigned based on the teacher's judgment about each of these variables as representing student growth and competency.

6. **Mastery grading scales** establish a predetermined standard for children to meet. Students who fail to achieve this criterion, for example 90 percent or 95 percent correct on a test, receive additional corrective instruction and then retake the test. All students

who achieve the predetermined criterion earn a grade of A, whether they meet it on the first or second testing. Some teachers will assign grades based on a student's improvement over the course of the year, rather than on meeting a predetermined criterion (Tomlinson, 2001). These teachers believe that using this approach will motivate students to perform better in school.

CRITERION-REFERENCED TESTING

With **criterion-referenced testing** the teacher establishes a certain level of **performance for mastery** for each student. Performance is specified using an instructional objective. The student's performance is evaluated using the objective as the target goal.

The student's performance is not compared with that of others in the class. The focus of this strategy is to determine how much gain the student makes following a certain period of instruction. This testing approach uses very specific objectives to identify what the student can and cannot do under certain conditions. It can be a useful procedure to measure a student's level of basic skills development, determine if the student has the prerequisite skills to begin a new instructional unit, and group students with similar strengths and weaknesses for specific lessons.

There are two primary advantages to using criterion-referenced tests. First, the teacher receives precise feedback about which objectives the student can achieve on the way to attaining a goal and mastering a particular subject area. Second, because of the highly individualized nature of the objectives, competition among students for grades is reduced (Stipek, 1996).

Criterion-referenced tests may not be appropriate in every school subject. It is sometimes difficult to task-analyze some lessons into specific objectives. This could occur in subjects like English, calculus, organic chemistry, and theoretical physics. Further, the criterion for mastery sometimes can be arbitrary rather than objective. For example, a child can correctly add 17 out of 20 arithmetic problems that use three two-digit numbers, but the objective specifies that 18 correct out of 20 problems meets the criterion. Has the child failed to master this skill and needs to receive more instruction?

NORM-REFERENCED TESTING

A **norm-referenced test** is a type of **standardized test** in which the performance of an individual student can be compared with that of a larger group of students who took the same test earlier and have characteristics that are similar, such as age and other important demographic variables. These tests are usually used to determine how much knowledge students have learned, identify cognitive strengths and weaknesses, and select students for educational programs.

There are four types of standardized or norm-referenced tests:

1. **Achievement tests** measure how much knowledge students have acquired in a specific subject area. Some achievement tests are designed to test one specific area, such as reading or mathematics, while other test formats group several different content areas to form an **achievement test battery**.

2. **Aptitude tests** evaluate students' ability and potential to develop advanced skills and knowledge. The most commonly used aptitude test involves measuring intelligence to determine eligibility to participate in programs for gifted children. Aptitude tests may also be used for admission to a private high school and are routinely used for college admission.

3. **Competency tests**, sometimes described as **end-of-grade tests**, are used to determine if students have the required skills necessary to certify that they have completed a minimal educational program of study.

4. **Diagnostic achievement tests** are used to diagnose specific content strengths and weaknesses. These tests are most frequently used to determine if students need some kind of remedial or special education services.

INTERPRETING NORM-REFERENCED TEST SCORES

This section examines how norm-referenced tests are interpreted and important psychometric characteristics (validity and reliability) that can impact the meaning of a students' test scores. For the results from standardized or norm-referenced tests to be useful and meaningful, the number of items answered correctly on the test must be summarized into a total raw score. This total raw score is then transformed into a **derived score** that allows a student's performance to be evaluated by comparing it with other students who have taken the same test. This large group of other students is called the **norm group**.

When developing a test, large numbers of students are tested and their raw scores organized and analyzed using **descriptive statistics**. This group of students is referred to as a **sample** and is considered to be representative of all students in a particular age group. The sample is drawn randomly and is presumed to be representative of all students, or the **population**, in that age group.

Raw scores from the sample are mathematically analyzed according to the **normal distribution**. Three measures of central tendency and two measures of dispersion are calculated for the sample. Collectively, these five statistical procedures allow the test user to interpret a specific student's performance level in comparison with other students who have taken the same test.

Following are the three measures of central tendency:

1. **Mean:** the arithmetic average or midpoint of the distribution sample. It is computed by adding up all the raw scores from the sample and dividing by the number of students who took the test. The mean can be influenced by extreme scores but is considered to represent the exact arithmetic average for the sample.

2. **Median:** the score in the sample at which exactly half the sample falls above and half the sample falls below. It is determined by rank ordering the scores from lowest to highest and then dividing the total number of scores by two. If there is an odd number of students in the sample, the middle score is used as the median. If there is an even number of students in the sample, the median must be interpolated.

3. **Mode:** the score that occurs with greatest frequency in the sample distribution. This is considered to be the weakest of the three measures of central tendency.

Under ideal circumstances all three of these scores will be nearly identical.

Following are the two measures of dispersion:

1. **Range:** calculated by subtracting the lowest score from the highest score in the distribution. This difference reflects the range of scores.

2. **Standard deviation:** reflects how far away from the mean individual scores lie.

These transformed scores (derived from analysis of the raw scores) are based on the **normal distribution**, or bell-shaped curve. The use of the normal curve allows test scores to be interpreted easily and consistently without bias. Using IQ tests as an example, where the mean has been determined to be 100 and the standard deviaiton is 15 points, a score of 100 is interpreted to be exactly average. The higher the score, the better the student performed compared with the norm group. The **standard deviation** describes how scores **differ from the mean score** on the standardized test.

Theoretically, 68.26 percent of scores fall within plus or minus 1 standard deviation; 95.44 percent fall within plus or minus 2 standard deviations; and 99.72 percent fall within plus or minus 3 standard deviations.

Five other kinds of transformed (or derived) scores are used to interpret standardized testing and performance:

1. **Stanines,** with a mean of 5 and standard deviation of 2. This transformed score was developed to reduce the tendency of people to misinterpret small differences between scores. Stanines divide the norm group's performance into ninths. The first stanine usually reflects performance that falls 2 standard deviations below the mean, and the ninth stanine reflects performance falling 2 standard deviations above the mean. A student's score is ranked on a scale from 1 to 9 and reported as a whole number.

2. **Z-scores** have a mean of 0 and standard deviation of 1.

3. **T-scores** have a mean of 50 and standard deviation of 10.

4. **Percentile scores** describe the percentage of students with scores falling at or below the student's score. For example, a student who scores at the 90th percentile on an intelligence test has scored better than 90 percent of the norm group.

5. **Grade-level equivalent scores** describe students' performance in terms of the grade level at which they are functioning. The score is reported using grade and month in the grade. If a student has a grade-level equivalent score of 5.3 on a standardized reading test, it means that the student's performance was at the level of fifth grade, third month. Grade-level equivalent scores can be deceptive because the meaning of the score can vary from one test to the next. It is also not clear what a 5.3 grade-level equivalent score means in terms of the exact academic skills and competencies of the student.

VALIDITY

Validity is a measure of the relationship between test performance and the actual behavior, trait, or construct that the test claims to measure. It addresses three primary questions:

1. How representative of the person's overall ability in an area is the sample of behavior taken by the test (content validity)?

2. What does the test behavior mean about the degree to which the person actually possesses the trait that the test measures (construct validity)?

3. How well can test performance predict the person's future real-life performance (predictive validity)?

Six types of test validity exist:

1. **Content validity:** describes the degree to which the contents, or information contained in the test items, represent the broad content domain that the test claims to measure. This type of validity is most relevant for achievement tests or tests that measure skill mastery and development. Test contents should reflect facts, application of principles, and interpretation of facts.

2. **Face validity:** describes the physical appearance of a test to the person taking it. Test items that are silly, irrelevant, inappropriate to the person's age, or appear to be illogical can destroy the usefulness of the test.

3. **Criterion-related validity:** describes how well a test correlates with a direct and independent measure of what the test is designed to evaluate. An example of this would be correlating performance on a reading achievement test with actual reading levels of students in school as indicated by teacher judgments and measurements. The difference between criterion-related validity and predictive validity is the time span between when the testing occurs and when the results are used to make decisions.

4. **Predictive validity:** describes how accurately a test can predict a person's future behavior several months or even years in advance. This type of validity is especially important in aptitude tests used for making student selections (e.g., college admissions), business or military specialties.

5. **Construct validity:** describes how well a test measures the trait or construct it is designed to measure. Many psychological tests measure constructs, or hypothetical entities, that are difficult to define operationally. Construct validity is established by statistical studies using factor analysis that show that test items are measuring the same trait and correlations with other tests that claim to measure the same characteristic.

6. **Concurrent validity:** involves administering two tests to the same group of people and correlating how well performance on one test predicts performance on the second test. This type of validity is often used to support the appropriateness of new intelligence tests.

The specific type of validity needed depends on the use and purpose of the test. Most standardized psychological tests (e.g., intelligence tests, reasoning tests) must demonstrate acceptable levels of content, criterion-related, and construct validity. Interestingly, the predictive validity of these tests is seldom of interest, even through the tests are often used to make decisions that have long-range implications for people's lives.

RELIABILITY

Reliability is a measure of the consistency in the scores achieved on the same test for the same people who take the test on two or more different occasions. It reflects the degree to which individual differences in test scores occur because of error associated with the test used. Reliability is important because it tells the person or group administering the test the degree to which people's performance on the test will be stable over time. Scores for the first test administration are correlated with scores for the second test administration, and the closer the correlation approaches 1.0, the more reliable the test is because the rankings of people within the group based on their test scores remain about the same.

A reliable test gives a stable and consistent assessment of a student's ability over time and repeated test administrations. The presumption here, though, is that the student's trait also remains stable during this period. In general, the greater the number of items making up a test, the higher its reliability.

Four types of reliability procedures are used:

1. **Test-retest reliability:** The same test is given to the same group of people on two occasions separated by several weeks or months. Scores from the first test are correlated with scores from the second test to determine if the rankings of the test takers remain about the same or change greatly. This type of reliability reflects how stable the test results are over time. In general, a correlation coefficient of around .80 is considered very good for this type of reliability with norm-referenced tests.

2. **Alternate, or parallel, forms reliability:** Two different tests are administered, each of which were developed to measure the same construct or skill. The two tests are administered to the same group of people and the scores from both sets of tests are correlated with each other.

3. **Split-half reliability**, sometimes known as Spearman-Brown reliability: To measure the internal consistency of the contents of a test, a group of people is given one test. The individual items on that test are divided into two subtests, typically using the odd numbers to

make up one subtest and the even numbers to make up the second subtest. The total scores for the odd-numbered and even-numbered items are correlated with each other to determine how well the test items measure the construct or skill that the test claims it measures. An acceptable correlation is considered to be .90 and higher for this type of reliability with norm-referenced tests.

4. **Kuder–Richardson reliability:** A single administration of the test provides a measure of internal consistency using a different theoretical perspective than that used for split-half reliability.

The reliability of a test is affected by a number of characteristics of the people taking the test. Some characteristics that are influential include having a variety of people of different intellectual abilities and different educational abilities included in the sample. When either of these variables is limited or restricted then the reliability of the test will be lower.

TEST BIAS

Test bias exists when a test consistently provides an inaccurate assessment because of the test taker's gender, socioeconomic status, ethnic background, or race. A biased test does not measure objectively a student's ability in the trait that the test claims it measures. Instead, the test gives an unfair advantage to people who are from one particular category or have one particular set of background characteristics. The standardized tests administered in most public schools have been seriously criticized because they tend to generate lower scores for students from minority cultural backgrounds and lower SES families (Suzuki, Ponterotto, & Meller, 2000). In general, students from each of these backgrounds score lower than children who come from middle-class white families. Some research indicates that performance on standardized tests predicts school achievement equally well for all groups of students, regardless of cultural or ethnic background.

Specific criticisms about testing and test bias include the following:

— Correct answers are awarded more points when they reflect middle-class values.

— Students who are more verbally skilled have an advantage on many widely used intelligence tests because many of these tests are highly verbally loaded.

— Many of the questions focus on experiences and information that are more commonly experienced by the dominant culture.

— The wording and vocabulary used in tests is sometimes quite different from that which the student from a minority or disadvantaged background is accustomed to using.

Several attempts have been made to develop culture-fair or culture-free tests, but these efforts have met with limited success. Federal law mandates that any tests used to place children into special programs must be conducted in the student's native language by a qualified professional who can communicate well in that language. No single test score can be relied on to place the student in a special program or to diagnose a student with a disability. It is extremely important to include information about the student's actual performance in the classroom as well as the student's general social behaviors at home and in school when making any kind of determination about placement in an educational program.

USING TESTS APPROPRIATELY

No test, especially a norm-referenced test, provides a completely accurate description of a student's abilities, deficits, and strengths. It is important to remember that the test provides a small sample of the student's behavior under very specific, well-defined conditions. Test performance is affected by many variables that can interact with each other and cloud an interpretation of the score. Among these variables are the following:

— The **reliability** of the test.

— The **validity** of the test.

— The **standard error of measurement,** which is an estimate of how variable the student's observed score can be because of the unreliability of the test. The standard error of measurement provides a **confidence interval,** or range of scores, that the student's observed test score could fall within if the student were to take the same test several times on different days. It mathematically identifies the amount of error associated with the imperfect reliability of the test, as well as measurement error associated with the personal characteristics of the student that can vary from day to day (e.g., feelings, mood, level of alertness, stress associated with specific situations).

— The **standard error of estimate** reflects the imperfect validity of the test and describes the range of scores that a student's observed score could fall within if the test were repeatedly administered to the student over several consecutive days.

Students should never be placed into special or remedial programs solely on the basis of the observed score they obtain on a test. The standard error of measurement and standard error of estimate must be carefully considered when interpreting the student's observed score. The confidence intervals associated with each of these sources of error should be relied on more than the observed score, because this interval identifies the lower and upper limits that the student could attain on the test. Therefore, it reflects the lower and upper limits of the student's abilities in the area being tested.

It is also important to remember that the purpose of testing and assessment is to identify what the student has learned, evaluate how well the teaching program is working for that student, and use these data to make changes in the educational program so the student can achieve the highest level of capability and potential. Test data should not be used to label or categorize students or place them in educational programs that are inappropriate in meeting their needs.

There are several legal issues involved in testing students to maintain and ensure that all students are treated in an accurate, objective, and fair manner that does not misuse the testing data. First, parents must be involved in the decision to test a student initially and kept informed about the student's performance on the tests.

Second, a student must be tested by qualified personnel in the child's native language. A student of Hispanic origin would be severely penalized if given a test that was developed for English-speaking students. That student's test score would not reflect his or her ability or lack of ability; rather, it would reflect the student's difficulty caused by language differences.

Finally, the results from tests should be linked directly to the teaching program. Goals and objectives should be developed from the test results so teaching strategies and approaches can be adapted more precisely to the student's learning needs and characteristics.

REFERENCES

Bloom, B. S. (1968). Learning for mastery. *Evaluation Comment, 1*(2). Los Angeles: University of California, Center for the Study of Evaluation of Instructional Programs.

Crooks, T. J. (1988). The impact of classroom evaluation practices on students. *Review of Educational Research, 58*(4), 438–481.

Dempster, F. N. (1991). Synthesis of research on reviews and tests. *Educational Leadership, 48*(7), 71–76.

Gagne, R. (1977). *The conditions of learning* (3rd ed.). New York: Holt, Rinehart, & Winston.

Gronlund, N. E. (2000). *How to write and use instructional objectives* (6th ed.). Upper Saddle River, NJ: Merrill.

Hamilton, R. J. (1985). A framework for the evaluation of the effectiveness of adjunct questions and objectives. *Review of Educational Research, 55,* 47–86.

Mager, R. F. (1997). *Preparing instructional objectives* (3rd ed.). Atlanta, GA: Center for Effective Performance.

Shepard, L. A. (2000). The role of assessment in a learning culture. *Educational Researcher, 29*(7), 4–14.

Stipek, D. (1996). Motivation and instruction. In D. Berliner & R. Calfee (Eds.), *Handbook of Educational Psychology* (pp. 85–113). New York: Macmillan.

Suzuki, L. A., Ponterotto, J. G., & Meller, P. J. (Eds.). (2000). *Handbook of multicultural assessment* (2nd ed.). San Francisco: Jossey-Bass.

Tomlinson, C. A. (2001). Grading for success. *Educational Leadership, 58*(6), 12–15.

Wiggins, G. (1994). Toward better report cards. *Educational Leadership, 52*(2), 28–37.

CHAPTER 8
Pedagogy

CHAPTER 8

PEDAGOGY

Pedagogy is the science and practice of teaching. This chapter discusses a number of proven techniques and strategies to make teaching more effective and meaningful for students. The chapter concludes with a discussion of technology in the classroom and how to develop and implement behavior management systems for an individual student and an entire class of students.

EXPOSITORY TEACHING AND DISCOVERY LEARNING

Expository teaching is instruction that involves students in organizing relationships between ideas, concepts, and verbal information in a meaningful manner to facilitate comprehension and retention (Ausubel, 1963, 1977). Expository teaching does not consider rote memorization as meaningful learning because it is not connected to preexisting knowledge that the student possesses.

Using the expository teaching model the teacher first presents information in a general overview. Once students are oriented to the overall perspective and sequence of the new material, the teacher then begins to teach more specific concepts with greater detail and depth. It is believed that this strategy allows students to understand the increasingly detailed explanations of the information and link those explanations to information that was presented previously as part of the general overview.

Expository teaching is most effective in highlighting the relationships among concepts and ideas. It requires students to have some previous knowledge about the concepts before the teacher presents the interrelationships, similarities, and underlying commonalities. The challenge for the teacher is to organize the lesson in a precisely sequenced manner so students are presented with basic facts and concepts efficiently and effectively. Teachers may actually have to tell students specifically what is important to know and where they should focus their attention during the lesson. Further, the teacher may need to highlight similarities and differences existing between the new material and what students were taught earlier in the unit. Students are encouraged to ask questions with the goal of clarifying these relationships and to have an active role during learning. Questioning also provides students with a personal frame of reference using their own vocabulary as well as repetition of the information.

Expository teaching is a rather sophisticated instructional strategy. The teacher must consider both the intellectual maturity and the cognitive developmental status of children in the class when using this approach. The approach emphasizes an abstract representation of information. It requires students to manipulate ideas mentally, even if those ideas tend to be concrete and relatively simple. The approach is recommended with students at a fifth or sixth grade level and higher. It is important to remember, however, that many students at these grade levels will not have the cognitive developmental maturity to be able to mentally manipulate and process all types of subject matter in this way.

Discovery learning challenges students to take a highly active role in their educational experience by formulating hypotheses and guesses based on incomplete data. The teacher then encourages the students to either confirm or disprove the hypotheses using a systematic and logical approach that will require them to show an in-depth level of understanding about the problem and the data given to them. This approach is based on the work of Bruner, Goodman, and Austin (1956), who believed that understanding and active learning are essential for students to truly learn, comprehend, and remember new information.

To engage students in a discovery learning experience, the teacher must organize the classroom in such a way that students are given some degree of independence, within a structured environment. The teacher assumes the role of guide for the students, giving them direction and focus as they attempt to confirm or disprove the concepts. The process used by the teacher in a discovery learning environment is called **guided discovery**. The challenge for the teacher using a guided discovery approach is to present stimulating questions, interesting problems, or real-life situations that have the appearance of being confusing or highly complex. The teacher then must help students compile data, arrive at rules or patterns based on the data they collect during the problem-solving phase, develop hypotheses or strategies on the basis of what they have observed, and then develop procedures to test the validity of the hypotheses they developed. It is important for the teacher to give appropriate feedback when the students need to use a new hypothesis for the problem or may be unsure of what they are doing, even though they are progressing in the correct direction.

The inquiry process used by students during the discovery learning process usually consists of five steps (Kauchak & Eggen, 1998):

1. Identify the question or problem to be solved.

2. Develop a hypothesis or strategy to begin to answer the question or solve the problem.

3. Collect data to test the hypothesis or solution strategy.

4. Develop logical conclusions based on the data collected.

5. Make generalizations from these conclusions that are based on the data and not opinions.

Throughout this process the teacher can use small- and large-group discussions to stimulate thinking, challenge the beliefs or strategies being developed, and teach the students how to interact in socially appropriate ways with each other when dealing with conflicted or contradictory information. Discovery learning is believed to help students become more accepting of different viewpoints, learn how to critically examine their own ways of thinking and viewing the world, learn how to critically examine the views of other people about the world, and learn through active engagement with various concepts, ideas, and principles.

Research has demonstrated that discovery learning produces greater transfer of information and more effective long-term memory of science concepts and facts than does direct instruction (Bay, Staver, Bryan & Hale, 1992). This learning approach can be used in many subject areas, including both the social sciences and hard sciences.

Yet the approach is not without limitations. Discovery learning can become an inefficient and impractical way to teach students, especially if the students are not socially or intellectually capable of responding positively to this kind of intuitive and constructivist teaching approach. The teacher must be sensitive to the cognitive developmental levels of the students and their potential to engage in independent thinking, their capacity to formulate abstract ideas and concepts, and their willingness to interact in socially mature ways with other class members.

ADVANCE ORGANIZERS

In addition to being well organized and well prepared, a teacher should begin every lesson by emphasizing for students the practical application and interest of the material they are about to learn. When the teacher specifically and explicitly relates classroom learning activities to real life, the students are more likely to approach the lesson with a heightened degree of motivation and energy (Ames, 1992). **Advance organizers**, first proposed by Ausubel (1963), are designed to introduce students clearly and practically to the relationship between what they are about to learn and the information they have already learned. A second purpose is to help students remember previously learned information so they can integrate it with the new material. Advance organizers are provided at the beginning of a lesson and contain enough information to guide students toward the focus of their learning efforts and studying activities.

An advance organizer generally accomplishes three purposes:

1. **Focus** students' attention on what is important to learn.

2. **Highlight** relationships among the ideas that will be taught during the lesson.

3. **Relate** information students learned in the past to the new learning experience to make it easier and more relevant.

There are two types of advanced organizers (Joyce & Weil, 1996):

1. **Comparative advance organizers** provide a foundation of information the students have already learned but may not be aware is relevant to what will be taught in the new lesson.

2. **Expository advance organizers** give students new information that is necessary to understand concepts, skills, and patterns that will emerge throughout the new material.

Research on advance organizers has shown them to be particularly useful when the material being taught is complex or unfamiliar to students (Corkill, 1992). They are especially useful when the content has a clear and sequenced structure in which previous concepts build on earlier ones that might not be immediately apparent to the students.

Advance organizers may not be as useful or effective when students are learning factual information that lacks organization or a pattern. They also may not be useful in subjects in which many different and basically unrelated or separate topics are presented (Corkill, 1992). Yet even with these subjects advance organizers are useful to alert students to what they need to know at the end of an individual lesson or unit of information.

COOPERATIVE LEARNING

An effective alternative strategy to classroom lecturing involves putting students together into small groups to work on problems and assignments. This approach, called **cooperative learning**, can have many positive effects on both the social and academic achievement levels of children, if it is implemented correctly. It is believed that working together in small, heterogeneous groups of four to five helps students master the various aspects of the assignment and learn more than if they were to work independently. Cooperative learning also improves students' motivation and increases comprehension and retention of the information.

Individual students in the group are held personally accountable to reach a specific level of performance. Outstanding performance by one student does not compensate for another student being unable to achieve the established criterion. Rewards can be given in one of three ways:

— All the teams can have access to all the available rewards.

— Only some of the teams can have access to the rewards available; for example, awards for first, second, and third place.

— Only one of the teams is able to earn the rewards available based on the team's performance in reaching a preestablished standard more quickly and successfully than other teams in the class.

Two specific approaches have been developed to focus cooperative learning activities:

1. **Student Team Achievement Decisions** (STAD; Slavin, 1995) begins with direct instruction to the students. Next the teacher gives the student teams the opportunity to practice the skills presented. The teacher provides consultation to the teams only if the team members cannot resolve disagreements about answers or approaches to the correct solution. The unit is complete when all members of the team understand and can explain the problem solution approach and skills necessary to reach the solution. Quizzes can be given and points awarded on the basis of group performance and improvements.

2. **Jigsaw II** requires each team member to become an expert on a subsection of the overall topic. Each student then must teach that area of expertise to other students in the group. This strategy can be particularly effective in subject areas like social studies or English. Each student is held personally accountable for the content of each area. For example, a unit on the Civil War could have one student researching the northern army from a military perspective, another student researching the southern army from a military perspective, a third student analyzing the terrain of the battlefields on which the two armies clashed, and the fourth student studying the personalities and strategies used by the generals on each side.

The discussions occurring within each team encourage students to rehearse, expand, and elaborate on their knowledge base in the area. If conducted correctly, these discussions can also generate questioning and explaining to help students organize knowledge, comprehend key issues better, develop connections among contents and information, and provide an opportunity to review the information using multimodal learning experiences. The teacher's primary role is to be a facilitator or guide for the group so that they achieve the established goal.

Cooperative learning approaches are in sharp contrast with competitive and individualized learning strategies. Yet this approach has several potential disadvantages, depending on the specific students in the class where the strategy is to be used. Students can get off task easily because of distractions caused by their peers in the group and engage in silly or inappropriate behavior or conversation. Some students may not focus on the topic because they misperceive or misinterpret the appropriate way to reach the goal, or they lose sight of the goal altogether; this can generate conflict among team members. Finally, an unfair division of workload among the team members can occur. It is possible to minimize some of these limitations by assigning each team member a specific role to maintain the group dynamic. One student could be identified as the taskmaster to ensure that all students have essentially equal workloads, while another could serve the role of monitor to keep the group focused on its purpose and progress.

ORGANIZING INFORMATION

The organization of the information presented during learning improves students' ability to comprehend and retain the information, enables them to see relationships among concepts and facts, and helps them to create a knowledge base on which they can add more new information. Organization also helps students apply the information later on in other classes or real-life situations. Many of the strategies to organize information have been identified by research clarifying how people learn cognitively. Several of these strategies were discussed in Chapter 2 and the more important ones discussed again to emphasize their significance and effectiveness.

There are three ways in which a teacher can organize information so that it is presented in an integrated, meaningful, and logical order:

1. **Clustering** organizes information on the basis of categories, patterns, or sequences. Using graphic aids such as hierarchy trees, charts, or matrices can be a very effective way to present a great

deal of information in a meaningful and useful manner. These strategies have been shown to enhance comprehension, memory, and transfer of information (Shah, Mayer, & Hegarty, 1999).

2. **Providing models** for students is a second effective way to represent relationships among concepts using visual representations such as written outlines, which give an overall structure for the information; maps; flowcharts; and tables. Each of these visual aids can help students develop a mental picture, or visual image, of what they are being taught. The use of visual imagery has been shown to be a very effective way to increase memory and retention (Clark & Paivio, 1991).

3. **Elaboration** can make information more meaningful by relating the new information to preexisting knowledge of the students. With elaboration the teacher explicitly links newly presented information to information and skills students have already learned during earlier stages of instruction. Some techniques to help elaborate information include using analogies to emphasize similarities between apparently dissimilar constructs and mnemonic devices so students form associations between ideas and content that may not naturally exist. One common mnemonic strategy is the use of acronyms. These techniques have been discussed earlier in Chapter 2.

Having a clear and well-organized lesson has been found to increase achievement and help students see teachers in a more positive light. Many studies have shown that effective teachers are well organized when they present their lessons (Berliner, 1987). They try to plan for questions that students may ask, as well as anticipate problem areas with the material to be taught. They use precise, concrete words and concepts that students are familiar with when explaining new concepts during instruction. They try to emphasize relationships to preexisting knowledge stores.

Many well-organized teachers use **questioning techniques** that challenge students to evaluate their understanding of what they have heard during lectures or read in assignments. Sometimes presenting these questions prior to teaching the information helps focus the students' attention and mental energy in a more effective and efficient manner.

INSTRUCTIONAL DESIGN AND TECHNOLOGY

The development of the computer and the Internet has had significant implications for education. These technologies give teachers and students the opportunity to tap a nearly unlimited collection of information, accessing resources throughout the entire world. Students and teachers can now examine complex problems using this vast reservoir of information from sources that range from incredibly simple to highly complex.

Computers can be very effective learning mechanisms that provide students with feedback about the quality of their performance, self-paced instruction, and opportunities to engage in drill, practice, and repetition until they achieve a predetermined level of performance. Students are afforded these opportunities privately so that their learning characteristics are not publicly revealed to other students in the class. The computer can be compared to a personal tutor that presents information and provides as much instruction as is necessary. This tutor, though, can also provide multisensory and multimedia presentations that can tap into the preferred learning styles of students to reinforce comprehension and retention of information. Such experiences can increase students' motivation and challenge them without generating the negative emotional reactions that can arise in reaction to verbal or nonverbal feedback given by the teacher.

Using **simulations**, computers can present highly complex concepts and ideas that may be difficult to represent or describe through lecture or other common teaching approaches. For example, simulations can be used in various science classes to demonstrate the steps of a chemical reaction or dissect a frog without exposing students to an actual frog dissection—a process that generates negative emotional responses from many students. These learning experiences are presented on a **videodisc**, which is an interactive technology that uses films, pictures, music, and actual visual representations that are structured and logically sequenced. Students can go through the exact sequence and order of the videodisc as many times as they need to learn the information.

Educationally appropriate computer games can teach students how to solve problems in a logical and systematic way. As part of this problem solving, students will also learn facts and important information, as well as the algorithms necessary in problem-solving activities. The problems presented on computer games are oriented toward real-life, real-world situations, which makes the educational experience personally relevant and meaningful for students. Computers are especially useful in helping students develop problem-solving abilities for situations that are not necessarily clearly defined. These kinds of problem-solving situations are typically seen in most real-life experiences. As such, students have the opportunity to engage in realistic learning experiences that they can take with them and apply in their own lives outside the school setting.

PSYCHOLOGY OF CONTENT AREAS

An important component of effective teaching is the amount of material covered by the teacher during each lesson. Teachers who cover more information in their classes have students who learn more (Barr, 1987). This is not to imply that a teacher should present volumes of information quickly and to the point that students fail to learn important facts and skills. Rather, the teaching pace must be balanced with the students' ability to understand and learn the skills needed for success in that subject area. Having a relatively rapid pace of instruction can sometimes prevent students from becoming bored or engaging in distractions that then present management problems for the teacher.

Two primary factors involved in teaching are the *teacher's knowledge* of the content and material to be taught and *using multiple representations* and modes of instruction. A teacher must know the subject matter well, understand the key facts and skills necessary for students' success, and be able to communicate these to students in a comprehensible and meaningful way. If the teacher is unsure of the material or does not have a full understanding of it, it will be impossible for the teacher to communicate the information.

The teacher must also know which aspects of the subject matter will be easy for students to learn and which topics will be difficult (Shulman, 1986). Further, the teacher needs to understand students' learning styles and characteristics and be creative in developing alternative instructional presentations.

Sometimes **multimodal instruction**—using visual, auditory, tactile, kinesthetic, and various simultaneous combinations of these sensory modalities—can tap into a student's preferred learning style and enhance learning and retention as well as comprehension. Multimodal instruction can be supplemented with analogies, personalized learning experiences with guided instruction, guided discovery, and other forms of examples so students can fully appreciate the content being taught and encode it for long-term retention and later use.

BILINGUAL EDUCATION AND ENGLISH AS A SECOND LANGUAGE PROGRAMS

Rapidly increasing numbers of students enrolled in the public schools have limited proficiency or no ability to speak English. It has been estimated that the number of non-English-speaking children in the schools is growing at about 4 percent each year (Catterall & Cota-Robles, 1988), with nearly half the children in California schools speaking English as a second language (Fitzgerald, 1995). Further, bilingual education has become a highly emotional topic with significant sociopolitical implications.

Two basic viewpoints exist about the relationship between culture and education. **Cultural deficit theories** argue that the language, cultural, and/or social backgrounds of minority children negatively affect their ability to perform successfully in school (Villegas, 1991). **Cultural differences theories** view children's language, cultural, and/or social backgrounds as strengths that can enhance education and learning. Teaching should attempt to build upon these strengths.

Providing a culturally responsive educational program recognizes and respects the different cultural backgrounds of students while actively trying to accommodate for those differences using appropriate teaching practices. For example, knowing that many Asian-American children feel uncomfortable and confused in classrooms that lack organization and structure is an important piece of information for a teacher. By keeping the classroom a more organized and quiet setting, it is possible to help these students learn more effectively.

There are three basic types of bilingual education programs used in the schools:

1. **Maintenance bilingual programs** are used mainly in the elementary grade levels and have the goal of helping students to be truly competent in both their native language and English. These programs maintain respect for the child's language, cultural traditions, and heritage. They are difficult to implement, however, because they require several students who share the same native language and cultural backgrounds as well as bilingual teachers who can speak the language and understand the traditions.

2. **Transitional bilingual programs** use students' native language as part of the instructional approach until they become competent in English. Over time the students typically become less proficient in their native language and sometimes lose the ability to speak it altogether. The school program does not recognize family cultural values as part of the educational process.

3. **English as a second language (ESL) programs** emphasize mastery of English as the primary goal. These programs try to integrate children into regular English-speaking classes as quickly as possible, a process that typically requires about two years in a language-rich setting before students develop sufficient social communications skills (Cummins, 1991).

SOCIOECONOMIC STATUS AND SCHOOL PERFORMANCE

Research has consistently shown a strong positive relationship between socioeconomic status (SES) and school performance (Goleman, 1988). The research has been consistent in showing that high-SES students from all ethnic or cultural groups have higher average levels of achievement and stay in school longer than low-SES students. A number of factors contribute to the educational failure of lower-SES children. Typically, these families lack adequate health care for mothers and children, they are often under a great deal of rather constant psychological and social stress as a family unit, they have limited financial and emotional resources to help them deal with the stresses of living, many work in low-paying jobs that have poor or no benefits, and they are often discriminated against by others.

Low-SES students may wear old clothes, speak using inappropriate language, and be less familiar with the experiences, books, and information than other children in their grade levels. It is not unusual for some teachers and peers to make assumptions about the intellectual levels and learning potential of these children on the basis of their physical appearance. Some teachers may conclude that the students are not motivated or capable of learning. Teachers may not call on them during class discussions and may sometimes respond inappropriately to their perspectives. Over time in school many of these children come to believe that they are simply not competent intellectually and cannot succeed with schoolwork.

SES is based on family annual income, the educational level of parents, the occupation of parents, and the family's status in society (see Chapter 6). Collectively, these characteristics typically have a significant impact on how a child performs in school. Within contemporary U.S. society five SES levels are usually identified (Levine & Levine 1996): the **upper class**, consisting of 3 percent of the population; the **upper-middle class**, 22 percent; the **lower-middle class**, 34 percent; the **upper working class**, 28 percent; and the **lower working class**, 13 percent. In addition, research has shown that each social class is characterized by a rather pervasive set of views about reality, behaviors, expectations, and attitudes. In general, it has been found that students from working-class and lower-class backgrounds are less likely than middle- and upper-class students to enter school knowing how to count, knowing the names and sounds of the letters of the alphabet, being able to manipulate scissors, and correctly name colors. The working-class and lower-class students are also more likely to have behavior problems in school (Duncan & Brooks–Gunn,

1997; McLloyd, 1998). Of course, it is important to keep in mind that these statistics reflect generalities and that there are people within each of these socioeconomic groups who do not fit these generalities derived from research.

TEACHER EXPECTATIONS

Teachers have a highly influential role with their students. Many students are very sensitive to how their teacher reacts to them and what their opinion is of them. Several studies have shown that teachers' opinions and expectations about students are influenced by test scores, physical appearance, race, ability, gender, and SES (Jones, 1990; Jussim, 1989).

Rosenthal and Jacobsen (1968) conducted an experiment using teachers of grades one through six who were led to believe that certain students in their classes had higher intellectual abilities than those students' class work actually showed. The teachers were also told that these students would be making higher intellectual gains during the coming school year based on their scores on a new type of ability test the authors had developed. In fact, the test was simply composed of standard items that gave it the appearance of an intelligence test. The students designated to make high intellectual gains during the coming year were randomly chosen by the researchers. It was found that those students performed at levels throughout the school year that were consistent with their teachers' expectations.

On the basis of these data the authors proposed the existence of a **self-fulfilling prophecy**—the idea that a teacher's expectations about a student come true, even when there is no actual data on which to base these expectations of student performance. The self-fulfilling prophecy can have one of two effects. It can cause teachers to inflate their evaluations of student performance because they expect students to perform well. It can also cause teachers who develop accurate assessments of students' capability levels early in the school year to ignore any significant improvements shown by students; in other words, teacher expectations remain stable. It is believed that the second type of teacher expectancy effect is more common than the first (Cooper & Good, 1983).

Nonetheless, it is also important to know that numerous studies indicate that many teachers base their expectations about students on actual student performance and learning in class as well as tests and assignments (Good & Brophy, 1997). Several studies have also suggested that *teacher viewpoints about students are far more accurate* than testing-data predictions (Helmke & Schrader, 1987; Short, 1985).

The effects of teacher expectations can be subtle, with teachers often unaware of how they are interacting with their students. Teachers tend to expect more from students whom they see as being high achievers. They tend to interact with these students more frequently, smile at them more often, make more direct eye contact with them, be more positive in verbal and nonverbal interactions with them, provide clear expectations and explanations for them, give them more praise and less criticism, call on them more often and give them more time to respond, encourage them more and provide them with prompts to help them answer questions, and use more follow-up questions (Good & Brophy, 1997).

Several factors have been identified that could influence how teachers form expectations about students (McLloyd, 1998; Nieto, 2000):

— Attractive children are more often perceived to be brighter and more socially skilled.

— Teachers are more approving of girls' behaviors than boys' behaviors.

— Teachers tend to be more influenced by negative information about a student than neutral or positive information.

— Teachers see children from poor homes as being less able to follow instructions, generally being unable to work independently, and overall showing less maturity.

— African Americans students often get less attention and are expected to learn less than Caucasian students, even when both groups of children have the same ability levels.

— Middle-class children are often expected to get higher grades than lower-SES children, even when their IQ and achievement test scores are similar.

One strategy that a teacher can use to encourage all students is providing a longer period of waiting time after asking a question, allowing the student to think. In most classes teachers wait less than 1 second before moving on to another student (Rowe, 1986). Increasing the waiting time from 1 to about 5 seconds can facilitate student learning and invite greater participation. Teachers should also provide clear expectations about student performance levels, offer clear feedback so students can improve their performance in a concrete way, and give immediate and frequent feedback so students do not practice skills incorrectly or feel confused because they do not know precisely what is being asked of them.

CLASSROOM MANAGEMENT

Using appropriate teaching strategies matched to the cognitive and emotional characteristics of students is very important in helping to maintain a controlled classroom setting. Yet it is necessary for teachers to understand and be able to implement effective behavior management interventions for an individual student and the entire class. These interventions can be motivating to students and enhance achievement. They also help teachers deal with students who simply are not mature enough to appreciate the significance and relevance of what they are being taught.

There are three general ways to approach classroom management:

1. **Authoritarian approach:** The teacher makes the rules for student behavior and expects those rules to be obeyed. The rules are not explained, nor are students involved in making them. The teacher gives rewards and punishments based on student compliance or failure to comply with the rules.

2. **Permissive approach:** The teacher imposes few external rules and a minimal structure for the class. Students are permitted to make many of the decisions regarding appropriate and unacceptable conduct. Sometimes the class becomes involved in meting out rewards and punishments to noncompliant students. The teacher provides advice or assistance but does not actively lead or control the class.

3. **Authoritative approach:** The teacher provides rules for the students but also discusses with them the reasons for the rules. Children are taught how to meet the rules. The teacher gives rewards to children who show appropriate compliance.

Each of the approaches has its merits and limits. Regardless of which general approach to classroom management a teacher takes, it is essential for the teacher to establish specific procedures and routines for the children to follow daily. These include how to make transitions from one activity to another, how to ask for permission, how to hand in papers, and how to sharpen their pencils. By giving students the specific way in which the teacher wants these kinds of frequently occurring behaviors to be conducted, the teacher provides students with a clear pattern for what is acceptable and what is unacceptable in the classroom. This knowledge will increase the students' ability to take control and be responsible for their behaviors.

Successful rules typically have a reason underlying them. This reason should be explained to the children so they understand why the rule was developed, how it protects everyone in the class, and how to behave in the appropriate way. Depending on the intellectual maturity and emotional stability of students, it may be appropriate to allow students to have some input in the rule-making process. It is believed that by including students in making rules they will see the value to having rules and have an increased sense of personal ownership that will encourage them to obey the rules.

Classroom rules should have the following characteristics:

— They should be clearly stated so there is no confusion about what is meant by the rule. A neutral observer in the classroom should be able to tell whether a student is following the rule or not.

— Rules should be expressed in positive terms that encourage prosocial behaviors.

— The list of rules should be short, concrete, and reasonable, and they should protect the rights and safety of everyone in the class.

— Classroom rules should be presented during the first few days of school. The teacher should clearly orient students to the rules several times during the first week or two, because most student behavior patterns for the school year are established during the first few days of school. The teacher might want students to practice the rules and receive corrective feedback.

— Classroom rules should be consistently followed, with the teacher implementing rewards and punishments based on how well students meet the standards. The key element is consistency in implementing the classroom management system.

— The teacher should be clear with students about what is expected from them in terms of behavior, levels of self-control, and academic performance.

— The teacher should establish contact and communication with parents early on in the school year, preferably within the first two weeks. It is essential for parents to know how their children are adjusting in school and for the teacher to maintain accurate data about students' social and behavioral functioning in the classroom setting.

— The teacher should try to create a classroom setting in which students feel free to express their ideas in socially acceptable ways that respect the rights and feelings of other students and the teacher.

— The teacher's verbal communications with students should be consistent with the nonverbal behaviors accompanying those statements. Consistency between verbal and nonverbal communications will minimize students' receiving confusing feedback about their behavior. The teacher should be aware of his or her stimulus impact value, which includes facial expressions, gestures, tone of voice, loudness when speaking, and body posture.

— The teacher should avoid arguing with students and try to keep interventions short and effective so that the instructional program is not significantly disrupted by a noncompliant student. If the teacher takes too much time to discipline a student, the student is being given an inordinate amount of power and control over the teacher and the teaching program.

The teacher needs to **actively monitor** the classroom dynamics and understand how students are interacting with and treating each other. Kounin (1970) describes this kind of active monitoring as "withitness." **Withitness** describes when the teacher knows what is going on in the classroom nearly all the time and communicates this knowledge verbally and nonverbally to students as a way of letting them know that the teacher is in control of the classroom dynamic.

Weinstein (1996) outlined the following **general routine areas** where teachers should develop specific procedures to maintain classroom structure and organization:

— **Administrative routines**, such as taking attendance

— **Student movement patterns**, such as getting permission to go to the bathroom or getting a drink of water

— **Housekeeping activities,** such as watering plants or storing personal items

— **Specific routines** to accomplish lessons, collect assignments, and return homework assignments to students

— **Attracting the teacher's attention** properly when students need help

— **Communicating with each other** during class time when students work on team assignments or give help to a classmate.

Evertson, Emmer, Clements, and Worsham (1997) suggest these rules for students in the elementary grade levels:

— Be polite and helpful with adults and peers.

— Respect other people's property.

— Listen quietly when others are speaking.

— Do not hit, shove, or hurt others (the teacher needs to clearly explain what each of these words means in terms of behaviors).

— Obey all school rules related to chewing gum, cell phones, listening to the radio, or playing video games during class time.

Emmer, Evertson, Clements, and Worsham (1997) suggest these rules as important for secondary-level students:

— Bring all needed **materials** to class (the teacher should be specific about what exactly is needed).

— Be **in your seat** and ready to work when the bell rings.

— **Respect others** and be polite to everyone (the teacher should include specific rules about verbal arguments, physical fighting, verbal abuse, and general trouble making).

— Respect other people's **property**.

— **Listen and stay seated** when someone else is speaking, whether it is the teacher or another student.

— **Obey all school rules**.

Four other systematic and structured classroom management systems exist and have been reviewed in Chapter 3:

1. **Group consequences:** Rewards or punishments are given to an entire class based on their compliance or violation of rules.

2. **Token economy reinforcement:** Students are awarded tokens (e.g., checkmarks, plastic tokens, colored paper clips) for acceptable academic performance and positive conduct in class. Students accumulate these tokens and exchange them for some desired reward, such as a small toy or free time playing an educational game on the computer.

3. **Contingency contracting:** The teacher and an individual student enter into a written agreement that specifies what the student must do to earn a particular reward or privilege. The written contract is signed by both teacher and student and is usually jointly developed by them.

4. **Assertive discipline** (Canter & Canter, 1992): The teacher clearly identifies expectations for student conduct. Students are given clear, firm, and calm verbal feedback for their inappropriate behavior. The teacher does not argue with the students and often

follows up his or her verbal feedback with behavioral consequences that are implemented consistently. This approach has been controversial and many questions have been raised about its effectiveness.

Regardless of the approach taken, it is essential that there be some kind of effective behavior management system operating daily in class. This system should be used consistently and have consequences that are immediate and meaningful to the students. After identifyng the consequences the teacher should not continually refer to the previous incident so that a subsequent violation of the rules is treated as an independent incident. It is inadvisable to repeatedly threaten to impose consequences and do so only after the student has been warned several times. Some commonly used individual consequences for students who are not cooperative include the following:

— **Ignoring** inappropriate behaviors, although some students interpret being ignored as approval of their behavior

— **Praising** positive behaviors

— Using **I-messages**, in which the teacher focuses on the impact of the child's behavior rather than on their personal characteristics

— **Telling** the child directly to stop a behavior or a consequence will be implemented

— **Rewarding** other students for appropriate conduct so they serve as models for the noncompliant student.

Each of these techniques may be effective for some students but not for others, depending on the emotional and intellectual characteristics of the student.

REFERENCES

Ames, C. (1992). Classrooms: Goals, structures, and student motivation. *Journal of Educational Psychology, 84,* 261–271.

Ausubel, D. P. (1963). *The psychology of meaningful verbal learning.* New York: Grune & Stratton.

Ausubel, D. P. (1977). The facilitation of meaningful verbal learning in the classroom. *Educational Psychologist, 12,* 162–178.

Barr, R. (1987). Content coverage. In M. J. Dunkin (Ed.), *International encyclopedia of teaching and teacher education* (pp. 19–33). New York: Pergamon.

Bay, M., Staver, J., Bryan, T., & Hale, J. (1992). Science instruction for the mildly handicapped: Direct instruction versus discovery teaching. *Journal of Research in Science Teaching, 29,* 555–570.

Berliner, D. (1987). But do they understand? In V. Richardson-Koehler (Ed.), *Education handbook: A research perspective* (pp. 259–293). New York: Longman.

Bruner, J. S., Goodman, J. J., & Austin, G. A. (1956). *A study of thinking.* New York: Wiley.

Canter, L., & Canter, M. (1992). *Lee Canter's assertive discipline: Positive behavior management for today's classroom.* Santa Monica: Lee Canter.

Catterall, J., & Cota-Robles, E. (1988). *The educationally at-risk: What the numbers mean.* Palo Alto, CA: Stanford University Press.

Clark, J., & Paivio, A. (1991). Dual coding theory and education. *Educational Psychology Review, 3,* 149–210.

Cooper, H. M., & Good, T. (1983). *Pygmalion grows up: Studies in the expectation communication process.* New York: Longman.

Corkill, A. J. (1992). Advance organizers: Facilitators of recall. *Educational Psychology Review, 4,* 33–67.

Cummins, J. (1991). Interdependence of first and second-language proficiency in bilingual children. In E. Bialystol (Ed.), *Language processing in bilingual children* (pp. 70–89). New York: Cambridge University Press.

Duncan, G., & Brooks-Gunn, J. (Eds.). (1997). *Consequences of growing up poor.* New York: Russell Sage Foundation.

Emmer, E. T., Evertson, C. M., Clements, B. S., & Worsham, M. E. (1997). *Classroom management for secondary teachers* (4th ed.). Boston: Allyn & Bacon.

Evertson, C. M., Emmer, E. T., Clements, B. S., & Worsham, M. E. (1997). *Classroom management for elementary teachers* (4th ed.). Boston: Allyn & Bacon.

Fitzgerald, J. (1995). English-as-a-second-language learners' cognitive reading processes: A review of research in the United States. *Review of Educational Research, 65*(2), 145–190.

Goleman, D. (1988). An emerging theory on blacks' I.Q. scores. *New York Times* (Education Section), pp. 22–24.

Good, T. L., & Brophy, J. E. (1997). *Looking in classrooms.* New York: HarperCollins.

Helmke, A., & Schrader, F. (1987). Interactional effects of instructional quality and teacher judgment accuracy on achievement. *Teaching and teacher education, 3,* 91–98.

Jones, E. (1990). *Interpersonal perception.* New York: Freeman.

Joyce, B., & Weil, M. (1996). *Models of teaching* (5th ed.). Boston: Allyn & Bacon.

Jussim, L. (1989). Teacher expectations: Self-fulfilling prophecies, perceptual biases, and accuracy. *Journal of Personality and Social Psychology, 57,* 469–480.

Kauchak, D., & Eggen, P. (1998). *Learning and teaching: Research-based methods* (3rd ed.). Needham Heights, MA: Allyn & Bacon.

Kounin, J. (1970). *Discipline and group management in classrooms.* New York: Holt, Rinehart & Winston.

Levine, D. U., & Levine, R. F. (1996). *Society and education* (9th ed.). Boston: Allyn & Bacon.

McLloyd, V. C. (1998). Economic disadvantage and child development. *American Psychologist, 53*(2), 185–204.

Nieto, S. (2000). *Affirming diversity: The sociopolitical context of multicultural education* (3rd ed.). New York: Addison Wesley Longman.

Rosenthal, R., & Jacobsen, L. (1968). *Pygmalion in the classroom.* New York: Holt, Rinehart & Winston.

Rowe, M. (1986). Wait-time: Slowing down may be a way of speeding up. *Journal of Teacher Education, 37*(1), 43–50.

Shah, P., Mayer, R., & Hegarty, M. (1999). Graphs as aids to knowledge construction: Signaling techniques for guiding the process of graph comprehension. *Journal of Educational Psychology, 91*(4), 690–702.

Short, G. (1985). Teacher expectation and West Indian underachievement. *Educational Researcher, 63,* 95–101.

Shulman, L. (1986). Those who understand: Knowledge growth in teaching. *Educational Researcher, 15*(2), 4–14.

Slavin, R. E. (1995). *Cooperative learning: Theory, research, and practice* (2nd ed.). Boston: Allyn & Bacon.

Villegas, A. (1991). *Culturally responsive pedagogy for the 1990s and beyond.* Princeton, NJ: Educational Testing Service.

Weinstein, C. S. (1996). *Secondary classroom management: Lessons from research and practice.* New York: McGraw-Hill.

CHAPTER 9

Psychological Research and Methods

CHAPTER 9

PSYCHOLOGICAL RESEARCH AND METHODS

Psychological research clarifies the nature of problems that affect people. By analyzing these problems, researchers attempt to find solutions that will improve the quality of life for all people. The findings of psychological research are published so that other researchers can confirm or dispute the findings and determine the validity and reliability of the results. **Validity** is the degree of accuracy with which the findings correspond with reality, and **reliability** is the consistency of the results across multiple administrations of the same test or experiment. Acceptable studies use representative samples of participants who are randomly selected. The data collected are subjected to statistical analyses that indicate their level of significance to accept or reject the null hypothesis.

All research is directed by the scientific method, which provides a clear framework about how to conduct an experiment. The scientific method consists of five steps:

1. Define the problem operationally in a concrete and measurable way.

2. Develop hypotheses about what might occur.

3. Create a problem-solving strategy to test the hypotheses.

4. Run the experiments to collect data.

5. Analyze the data objectively using statistical procedures to determine if the hypotheses are accepted or rejected.

The goals of all research are to *describe* the nature of the problem, *explain* why the problem exists, *predict* what will likely happen in the future, and *control* how one set of variables influences or affects another set of variables. **Null hypotheses** are proposed with the basic presumption that there is no difference in performance between participants in the various groups in the study and/or that no relationships exist among the variables being studied.

RESEARCH DESIGNS

Four basic types of research design have been developed. The first type is the **case study**, in which an individual is studied in detail, often over a relatively long period. This approach relies on interviews and sometimes questionnaires to collect the data. A case study is time-consuming and it may be difficult to draw inferences from its results because much of the information is about unique personal experiences that are not easily quantified. Yet this approach does provide in-depth information about the participants and helps in understanding aspects of individual human development that may suggest future, more rigorous, research studies.

The second research approach is the **field study**, or **naturalistic observations**. In this type of study people are observed interacting and behaving in their usual social environment. The advantage of this approach is that it allows the researcher to study behaviors as they occur naturally and realistically. Its results may be limited by the researcher's overlooking important information because of a personal bias or lack of knowledge about what to identify as significant.

With **survey studies**, researchers administer tests and questionnaires to large groups of people to gain their perceptions, beliefs, or attitudes about a particular topic. Although the researchers can collect large amounts of data easily and quickly, the information is limited to the contents of the instruments. There is no an opportunity to clarify what participants were thinking or how they interpreted the question when responding.

The final type of research approach is the **experiment**, which is a highly controlled study done in a restricted setting with a researcher regulating or manipulating situational variables, or selecting study participants with specific, measurable characteristics, to determine their impact on one or more experimental outcomes.

An experiment has two types of variables. The **independent variable** is one that the researcher manipulates or selects carefully to investigate how changes to this variable may affect people's performance on another variable that is being measured. The second variable is called the **dependent variable**, and its values are intended to reflect the effects of the independent variable on the participants in the study. Typical independent variables in psychological studies include group membership, gender, or personality type. Commonly used dependent variables are memory capacity, attitudes about a topic, and achievement levels. An experimental design is the only approach that allows the researcher

Table 9.1: Summary of the Advantages and Disadvantages of Three Experimental Designs

Design	*Advantages*	*Disadvantages*
Correlational	Convenient to do Easy to get many participants	No cause-effect relationships defined Question of generalizability of results
Quasi-Experimental	Convenient to do Done in natural settings so the results may be more accurate	Participants are not randomly selected May not have a control group No cause-effect relationships defined
Experimental	Randomly assigns participants Defines cause and effect Controls variables well so can see effects	Sample may not represent population Questions about generalizability May have ethical concerns

greater opportunity to identify cause-and-effect relationships between the independent variable and the dependent variable, depending on how well other possible influences on the dependent variable have been controlled by the research design.

Three types of experimental design exist: correlational, quasi-experimental, and experimental. **Correlational** designs are used to identify the relationship between two preexisting events or traits. This type of study can be done in either a laboratory or a real-life setting, but they do not give information about cause-and-effect relationships between the two traits or events. Correlational experiments usually correlate scores on one test with those from another test. **Quasi-experimental** designs are similar to experimental designs in many ways. However, in the quasi-experimental design the researcher cannot control some of the variables of interest in the study, randomly assign participants to treatment conditions, or both. The quasi-experimental design is commonly used in educational psychology because it is highly useful to do applied research that examines the learning, achievement, or social difficulties of children in real-life situations.

The **experimental** design is the most efficient and effective way to do research because it can suggest cause-and-effect relationships among variables depending, in part, on the statistical methods used for data analysis. This design will have an independent variable that the researcher manipulates in a controlled manner while holding other influences constant. The effects of the independent variable are then observed on a second variable called the dependent variable. The dependent variable is what is being studied to see how the independent variable influences it.

Table 9.1 summarizes the advantages and disadvantages of each design type.

SAMPLING

A group participating in a study is called a **sample**. The sample of a study is presumed to be representative of the **population**, or the entire group of individuals who have characteristics similar to those of the people in the sample. There are five kinds of sampling procedures: random, stratified, biased, clustered, and convenience.

Random sampling is the most appropriate way to choose people for a study. In this technique each person in the population has an equal and independent chance of being chosen to participate in the study. It is believed that random sampling provides a subgroup of people who adequately and truly reflect characteristics of people in the population. This process provides a **representative sample**, which is a valid and reliable description of the population's characteristics. **Stratified random sampling** is used when the population is made of two or more distinct subpopulations, such as sixth- and seventh-graders in a study about the learning characteristics of middle school children. A predetermined number of sixth- and seventh-graders would be randomly selected and the statistical analyses done separately for each grade level. This approach offers a higher degree of precision in describing learning characteristics of middle school children.

When researchers use a certain subgroup of participants in a study because those particular individuals are readily available and easy to evaluate, the study comprises a **convenience sample**. Many psychology experiments conducted at universities use convenience samples because introductory psychology courses often require students to be involved as research participants. The limitation of this sampling approach is that any conclusions made using a convenience sample may not be true for the larger population, even if that population is college freshman students.

A **clustered sampling** approach is typically used with survey research, in which researchers collect data across a specifically defined geographical area. This can be a time- and cost-efficient way to gather a great deal of information among various locations in a community or state.

The final sampling strategy is **biased sampling**, in which a researcher systematically and intentionally includes only persons who meet specific predetermined characteristics. People without these characteristics are excluded from the study.

Most studies have at least two groups of participants. The **experimental group** comprises participants who are exposed to a prescribed set of circumstances or treatments being studied. The **control group** usually is not exposed to these treatments so that the effects of the treatment can be compared with the performance of the experimental group. Some studies have more than one experimental group as well as a control group.

STATISTICAL ANALYSES

Once researchers have selected a sample, they can begin testing or assessing each participant with respect to the independent variables chosen for the study. When they have tested all participants, the researchers organize the data for analysis using various statistical methods. Statistical analyses describe whether the independent variables meaningfully co-vary with the dependent variable. **Inferential statistics**—such as the t-test, analysis of variance (ANOVA), and multivariate analysis of variance (MANOVA)—allow the researcher to make educated guesses about a possible cause-and-effect relationship. This type of statistics shows the degree to which researchers would expect to find the same results with a different sample from the same population using the same procedures and variables. These statistics provide a level of significance that specifies this probability. The most commonly accepted levels of significance are $p < .05$ and $p < .01$. These levels indicate that the probability of the findings being the result of chance factors only and not due to a causal relationship are less than 5 out of 100 and 1 out of 100, respectively. The minimal acceptable level of significance is $p < .05$.

Nonparametric statistics are used when the sample does not have the characteristics needed to use inferential procedures. Unlike inferential statistics, nonparametric statistics do not require that the sample be normally distributed. Some types of nonparametric statistics are the Kruskal-Wallace test and chi-square. Their purpose is identical to that of inferential statistics.

RESEARCH IN CHILD DEVELOPMENT

The study of child development presents a unique challenge to researchers. The most common areas of interest are difficulties, influences, development, maturation, and patterns of social growth. Studies can be done using different time frames. Many studies involve testing several groups of children who are at different ages or stages and then analyzing the results. This type of study, referred to as a **cross-sectional design**, measures several samples at about the same time. This is a highly time- and cost-efficient way to collect a good deal of data. However, its limits are that developmental, cultural, and historical experiences affecting participants are not well controlled. A cross-sectional design also does not show precisely how age or social experiences alter development.

Researchers use a **longitudinal design** to study developmental trends and patterns of growth by measuring the same participants several times over a long period. This approach can provide valuable information about the influence and effects of age, history, and life experiences. Each person serves as his or her own baseline by which change is compared. This design is limited by its costliness, need for extensive record keeping and tracking of participants, and the loss of participants over time (called **attrition**).

ETHICAL CONSIDERATIONS IN RESEARCH

Doing psychological research can pose a number of ethical challenges. Sometimes participants must be kept unaware of the true purpose of the study until it is completed so the results are not influenced intentionally by their attitudes or responses. The practice of withholding information about the purpose of a study is called **deception**. Deception can be done only when its benefits clearly and obviously outweigh its liabilities, which cannot always be clearly determined, and if it does, not violate other ethical standards.

Procedures have been developed to protect the emotional and physical safety of people participating in studies. All research must be approved by an **Internal Review Board** (IRB) before any data are collected. An IRB is intended to ensure that the methods used in the study are reasonable and appropriate and will not cause any kind of psychological or physical distress to participants. Following IRB approval of the research, each participant, or a parent if a participant is under the age of 18 years, must give informed consent before becoming involved. **Informed consent** explains the activities used, what may be asked of the participant, and what situations may arise during the course of the study. A participant may withdraw from the study at any time and for any reason without risk of penalty or negative repercussions.

After participants have completed the study they must be **debriefed**. The exact purpose of the study and information about any deceptions used and why they were necessary are disclosed and explained to the satisfaction of the participants. All responses provided by individual participants are maintained in strict confidentiality, and any references to their identities are destroyed so that later examination of the data cannot reveal any person's identity or performance levels.

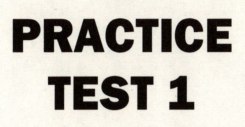

PRACTICE
TEST 1

CLEP INTRODUCTION TO EDUCATIONAL PSYCHOLOGY

Practice Test 1

(Answer sheets appear in the back of this book.)

TIME: 90 Minutes
100 Questions

DIRECTIONS: Each of the questions or incomplete statements below is followed by five possible answers or completions. Select the best choice in each case and fill in the corresponding oval on the answer sheet.

1. Which of the following variables has been shown to have a highly significant influence on the educational achievement of children?

   (A) the neighborhood in which they live

   (B) the number of students in their classes

   (C) growing up in a two-parent family

   (D) parents' occupations

   (E) parents' level of education

2. _____ describes the process in which information is learned so well that the person can perform the task without thinking.

   (A) automaticity   (D) perception

   (B) encoding   (E) decoding

   (C) retrieval

3. A ratio category for reinforcement relies on:

    (A) the amount of time that has passed before giving the reinforcement

    (B) the child attaining a predetermined level of functioning based on the proportion of target behaviors to the total number of behaviors shown

    (C) the use of primary reinforcers to focus the child's attention on the reinforcing stimulus

    (D) the number of target behaviors that have been shown by the child before reinforcement is given

    (E) the teacher being consistent in rewarding behaviors according to a predetermined schedule

The following three questions apply to Piaget's theory of cognitive development.

4. A 13-year-old child is studying Einstein's theory of relativity. On the basis of her readings she begins to form hypotheses about the implications of this theory for the meaning of time. This child is most likely in which of the following stages of cognitive development:

    (A) sensorimotor   (D) formal operational

    (B) preoperational   (E) preconcrete operational

    (C) concrete operational

5. A young child places every object given to him in his mouth. The child rolls the object around inside his mouth while feeling it with his fingers. This child is most likely in which of the following stages of cognitive development:

    (A) sensorimotor   (D) formal operational

    (B) preoperational   (E) preconcrete operational

    (C) concrete operational

6. A third-grade child begins to recognize that a hammer, screwdriver, and wrench are all related to each other because they are tools. The child is most likely in which of the following stages of cognitive development:

   (A) sensorimotor

   (B) preoperational

   (C) concrete operational

   (D) formal operational

   (E) preconcrete operational

7. Ms. Jones, a seventh-grade teacher, believes that the use of points, which can be traded in for material objects earned for good school-work, is the best way to motivate children. Her view of motivation is based on which of the following perspectives:

   (A) behavioral theory

   (B) human needs theory

   (C) attribution theory

   (D) expectancy theory

   (E) prosocial behavioral theory

8. One of the most important variables affecting a child's performance in school is:

   (A) the family's socioeconomic status (SES)

   (B) the father's occupational status

   (C) the educational philosophy of the school

   (D) the child's genetically based characteristics

   (E) whether the mother works outside the home setting

9. Mr. Jones has developed this instructional objective for students in his mathematics class: "Given 40 arithmetic problems involving division of three-digit numbers by one-digit numbers, students will be able to perform successfully." This objective lacks which of the following criteria?

   (A) the actual behavior required

   (B) statements about how students will be motivated

   (C) a criterion for success

   (D) how feedback will be given to the students

   (E) how the teacher will actually teach this information to students

10. A major emphasis of expository teaching is:

    (A) lecturing followed by small-group discussions

    (B) drill, practice, and repetition of information to enhance comprehension and retention

    (C) emphasizing relationships between concepts and ideas

    (D) rote learning and knowledge

    (E) lecturing accompanied by audio-visual materials to enhance retention of the material

11. Linda and Fred attend a weekly required class at their school on decision making and values clarification. In this class they discuss what they should do when dealing with various kinds of social issues and personal problems. This kind of educational experience is best described as:

    (A) character education

    (B) community-based education

    (C) citizenship education

    (D) simple moral education

    (E) civics

12. Angela is told to memorize the following list of items: five, horse, tree, two, nine, camel, flower, lion, and grass. Angela memorizes the list according to animals, numbers, and plants. The learning strategy she uses is:

    (A) outlining   (D) clustering

    (B) encoding   (E) mnemonics

    (C) chaining

13. Variable schedules of reinforcement have which of the following characteristics:

    (A) are less resistant to extinction than fixed categories

    (B) have a closely similar pattern of behavior when the reinforcement ceases

    (C) are more resistant to extinction than fixed categories

(D) are more appealing to use because children enjoy receiving a variety of reinforcers

(E) give the teacher greater flexibility in giving reinforcements to the children

14. Maria is in the second grade. She has a brother one year older whom she admires greatly. Her brother failed the second grade. Maria told her teacher that she will also fail the second grade because she is not as smart as her brother. Which of the following describes Maria's beliefs about herself?

(A) she has a negative attitude about learning

(B) she has a high level of self-efficacy

(C) rewarding her for school success will change her attitude

(D) she has a low level of self-efficacy

(E) her parents have communicated to her that she is not academically oriented

15. All of the following characteristics are typical of high-SES families EXCEPT:

(A) their children are more involved in athletic activities outside school

(B) parents are more directive with their children and use commands to manage them

(C) they have more access to technology

(D) verbal communication is an important activity

(E) parents tend to provide a number of cultural and educational experiences for their children

16. Mr. Sawyer has just completed a unit on World War I in his history course. He intends to give students a test about the social and economic conditions leading up to the war. The most effective way to test student knowledge about these conditions would be through a(n):

(A) matching-item test   (D) essay test

(B) true-false test   (E) fill-in-the-blank test

(C) multiple-choice test

17. Mr. Andrews teaches science to sixth-graders. His main instructional approach is to give the students various experiments to conduct so they can compile data. Once the data are collected, the students are encouraged to form hypotheses and arrive at general conclusions. Mr. Andrews' role becomes that of a consultant for the students during this process. His teaching approach is best described as:

    (A) expository   (D) small-group processing

    (B) guided discovery   (E) nondirective

    (C) direct

Questions 18 through 21 relate to the following:

A researcher believes that learning-disabled children do not remember as much information in their short-term memories (STMs) as children without learning disabilities. The target group is sixth-graders. To test this hypothesis, the researcher randomly selects two groups of students from five different school systems where there is a total of 12, 284 sixth-graders, with 1,939 diagnosed as learning disabled. One group is made up of 200 sixth-grade students who have been diagnosed as learning disabled. The second group is made up of 200 sixth-grade students who are performing at or above grade level in school. Each student is tested individually. They are asked to recall lists of nonrhyming consonants presented to them visually and orally. The total number of letters correctly recalled by participants in each group is statistically analyzed using a t-test. The learning-disabled children are found to recall less information than the children without learning disabilities, whether the information is presented orally or visually.

18. The children in the learning disabled group are referred to as:

    (A) the control group   (D) the population

    (B) the sampling group   (E) the standardization group

    (C) the experimental group

19. The dependent variable in this study is:

    (A) the lists of nonrhyming consonants

    (B) the group membership for each student

    (C) the t-test

    (D) the grade level in school

    (E) the school attended by the children

20. This study is most accurately described as a(n):

    (A) case study   (D) quasi-experimental study

    (B) experimental study   (E) developmental study

    (C) longitudinal study

21. Which of the following would be the null hypothesis for this study?

    (A) the non-learning-disabled children have larger short-term memory spans than the learning disabled children

    (B) the learning-disabled children have larger short-term memory spans than the non-learning-disabled children

    (C) the non-learning-disabled and learning-disabled children have short-term memory spans that are consistent with those of sixth-graders in general

    (D) there is no difference in the short-term memory spans of learning-disabled and non-learning-disabled children.

    (E) non-learning-disabled children learn better than learning-disabled children

22. William is enrolled in a class that meets once a week to discuss topics such as justice, freedom, voting, and diversity in society. This class is best described as:

    (A) character education

    (B) community-based education

    (C) citizenship education

    (D) simple moral education

    (E) civics

23. The most common reason for forgetting in the working memory is:

    (A) decay

    (B) interference

    (C) failure to have sufficient recall cues

    (D) ineffective modality tagging

    (E) failure to rehearse the information

24. The law of effect predicts that a behavior:

    (A) is more likely to occur if there is a positive outcome for it

    (B) will occur more often if the child understands its benefits

    (C) reflects the effects of the environment

    (D) is suppressed by punishment

    (E) the child performs naturally will be shown with greater frequency

25. Philip, a tenth-grade student, has decided to try out for the school track team as a miler because he wants to earn his varsity letter. He believes that having this letter will make him a more attractive candidate for colleges. His motivation for running is best described as:

    (A) extrinsic   (D) internal

    (B) intrinsic   (E) compensation

    (C) external

26. Linda is an eighth-grader who has average grades in all her academic subjects. She shows an extraordinary ability to understand how other people are feeling and can be very compassionate and kind toward them. According to Gardner, Linda is showing which type of intelligence?

    (A) linguistic   (D) interpersonal

    (B) bodily kinesthetic (E) prosocial

    (C) naturalist

27. Ms. Philips teaches a freshman honors writing course and requires that the 28 students in the class take one essay test each week. She recently realized that she grades test responses lower and offers less positive corrective feedback when she reads the essays in one session rather than reading a maximum of four essays and then taking a substantial break. This tendency to grade the essay tests harder when she reads them in one sitting may be the result of:

    (A) poor penmanship by the students

    (B) the vocabulary and grammatical structure used by students

    (C) students' writing styles

    (D) fatigue and boredom

    (E) anger because of the quality of the students' work

28. Ms. June begins each lesson by listing on the chalkboard the five key points or facts that each student should know by the end of the day's lesson. She usually shows how each point is related to some concept or skill the students have learned earlier. This technique is known as:

    (A) cuing

    (B) an advance organizer

    (C) highlighting

    (D) guided learning

    (E) brainstorming

29. The length of time that information and knowledge remain in the long-term memory is:

    (A) 30 seconds

    (B) 4 weeks

    (C) permanently

    (D) 6 months

    (E) 2 years

30. Lin is at the grocery store with her mother and wants her mother to buy her a doll. Lin's mother refuses, and Lin begins crying loudly, embarrassing her mother. Lin's mother wants this behavior to stop, so she buys Lin a doll and some candy. Lin's mother is _____ this behavior.

    (A) punishing

    (B) extinguishing

    (C) negatively reinforcing

    (D) reinforcing

    (E) selectively reinforcing

31. Which of the following statements is true about maturation?

    (A) genetics dictate maturational processes

    (B) the environment molds physical characteristics that are genetically determined

    (C) genetic qualities exist and evolve independent of the environment

    (D) genetic characteristics interact with the environment, and the environment influences how genetic characteristics are shown

    (E) the role of genetics is much more powerful than that of the environment

32. Research has indicated that girls generally see themselves as being:

    (A) as competent as boys

    (B) more competent than boys

    (C) less competent than boys

    (D) better students who will achieve better grades

    (E) more socially oriented with higher levels of self-control

33. William has taken an intelligence test and was found to have achieved a score of 117. This score places him in which range of intelligence?

    (A) average   (D) below average

    (B) above average   (E) superior

    (C) high average

34. The main reason to use taxonomies is to:

    (A) save time when planning lessons

    (B) cover all the skills needed for success

    (C) treat each student fairly and accountably

    (D) create effective assessment procedures and strategies

    (E) comply with state-required curriculum standards for performance

35. Mr. Bradfield teaches a unit on World War II by having students assigned to small groups consisting of four students. Student A in each group is responsible for collecting biographical information about a specific general and presenting it to the other group members. Student B is responsible for researching the role played by a unit led by that general. Student C discusses significant battles involving the unit, while student D shares specific feats of heroism by men in the unit. This teaching approach is described as:

    (A) discovery teaching   (D) cooperative learning

    (B) guided learning   (E) group think

    (C) experiential learning

36. Patrick is in the first grade and has learned to use a ruler to draw straight lines. He is now given the same ruler and asked to measure

the length of a line he has drawn. He becomes upset and tells the teacher that he cannot use the ruler to measure lines because it is only used to draw lines. This is an example of:

(A) response set

(D) functional fixedness

(B) specialization

(E) accommodation

(C) poor teaching

37. Sara is at the department store with her mother and wants her mother to buy her a doll. Sara's mother refuses, and Sara begins crying loudly, embarrassing her mother. Sara's mother wants this behavior to stop, so she buys Sara a doll and some candy. From Sara's perspective she is _____ her mother's behavior.

(A) punishing

(D) reinforcing

(B) extinguishing

(E) selectively reinforcing

(C) negatively reinforcing

38. Which of the following theorists believed that language is an extremely important experience for human beings in their cognitive development?

(A) Piaget

(D) Vygotsky

(B) Erikson

(E) Bruner

(C) Kohlberg

39. Mr. Bean relies heavily on a reinforcement-and-reward approach to motivate students in his classes. He believes that giving material reward is the most effective way to motivate all children. Which of the following is very important for Mr. Bean to use as part of this program?

(A) having clear expectations about student performance

(B) using edible rewards as part of the approach so student physiological needs are addressed

(C) remaining detached emotionally when rewarding the students

(D) using varied teaching strategies to keep students on task and motivated

(E) accompanying concrete rewards with the appropriate verbal comments and feedback

40. Achievement tests are designed to measure:

    (A) a particular academic area

    (B) a specific intellectual ability

    (C) the final performance levels in a course

    (D) aptitudes

    (E) basic skills development

41. The main difference between formative and summative evaluations is that the:

    (A) results from a formative evaluation count toward the final grade, whereas results from a summative evaluation do not

    (B) formative evaluation is done on a weekly basis, whereas a summative evaluation occurs daily

    (C) summative evaluation is done on a weekly basis, whereas a formative is reported on the report card

    (D) results from a summative evaluation count toward the final grade, whereas results from a formative evaluation do not

    (E) formative evaluation is more meaningful to parents

42. Using flowcharts, maps, and tables for student instruction is an example of which of these methods of organization?

    (A) clustering   (D) mnemonics

    (B) models   (E) visual imagery

    (C) elaboration

43. In a study about the effects of multimodal teaching approaches on achievement, statistical analyses indicated that the experimental group showed significantly higher achievement ($p < .01$) than the control group. This finding means that:

    (A) these results would occur only 1 percent of the time

    (B) these results would occur only 1 percent of the time if chance factors were causing the findings

    (C) these results fail to occur 1 percent of the time

    (D) the control group would be expected to learn better than the experimental group 99 times out of 100

    (E) the experimental group would be expected to learn better than the control group 99 times out of 100

44. Which of the following describes the primary components involved in the two-store model of memory?

    (A) short-term memory and long-term memory

    (B) sensory register, working memory, and long-term memory

    (C) sensory register, working memory, and short-term memory

    (D) sensory register, episodic memory, and semantic memory

    (E) working memory, episodic memory, and semantic memory

45. A father and his five-year-old son are working together in their yard. The father begins raking leaves into a pile so they can be burned. His son picks up another rake and begins doing the same thing. This is an example of:

    (A) reinforcement   (D) symbolic modeling

    (B) imprinting behaviors   (E) rote imitation

    (C) direct modeling

46. Joanne is in the second grade. She has a great deal of difficulty getting along with her peers and often accuses them of trying to hurt her. When her teacher tries to find out more about these conflicts, Joanne becomes angry and accuses him of trying to hurt her and siding with the other children. According to Erikson, at which of the following stages of development might Joanne have an unresolved issue?

    (A) trust versus mistrust   (D) industry versus inferiority

    (B) autonomy versus shame   (E) intimacy versus isolation

    (C) initiative versus guilt

47. A 12-year-old child sits and waits for the teacher before beginning each assignment that is given to the entire class of students. The child makes no effort to work individually until the teacher comes to her desk and helps her begin. This child is likely showing a behavior associated with:

    (A) decreased self-efficacy

    (B) the effects of an extrinsic reward system in the class

    (C) depression

    (D) learned helplessness

    (E) attention-deficit/hyperactivity disorder

48. Juan is applying to a private college and is required to take a test that the school specifically developed to determine who is likely to be a successful student. This test is most likely a(n):

    (A) achievement test   (D) aptitude test

    (B) intelligence test   (E) speed test

    (C) norm-referenced test

49. Which of the following teaching strategies may be helpful to students who are anxious during test taking?

    (A) formative evaluation

    (B) summative evaluation

    (C) mastery learning approach

    (D) overlearning and a supportive teaching approach

    (E) teaching the student how to relax using meditation and relaxation techniques

50. In general, teachers who cover more content and information in their classes:

    (A) rely on computer technology for drill and repetition for students

    (B) use simulations of real-life problems to engage student interest and motivation

    (C) have students who learn more

(D) are rated as better teachers by students in their classes

(E) tend to frustrate students and have more students who get lower grades

51. A quasi-experimental design:

(A) uses no statistics to analyze data

(B) produces results that are less valid than experimental designs

(C) has no control over any of the variables being studied

(D) controls all the variables being studied

(E) is not able to control some of the variables being studied

52. The iconic storage register has a storage capacity of _____ , while the echoic storage register has a storage capacity of _____ .

(A) 4 seconds, 10 seconds

(B) 1 second, 10 seconds

(C) 5 seconds, 10 seconds

(D) 1 second, 4 seconds

(E) each retains information for 1 second

53. According to cognitive learning theory, all human behaviors are:

(A) self-regulated

(B) reinforced by others

(C) taught to a child by their social living situation

(D) lawful, regular, and follow the law of effect

(E) the result of genetic factors interacting with situational variables

54. Philip is very concerned about how society treats people who are underprivileged. He has started an organization at school to help less educated people become more socially empowered. He believes that all people are entitled to the same set of basic rights from the larger society. He is most likely in which stage of moral development?

    (A) preconventional reasoning, stage 2

    (B) conventional reasoning, stage 3

    (C) postconventional reasoning, stage 5

    (D) postconventional reasoning, stage 6

    (E) postconventional reasoning, stage 4

55. According to Maslow, the highest level of human need is:

    (A) self-actualization   (D) altruism

    (B) intellectual achievement   (E) wisdom

    (C) aesthetic appreciation

56. Ms. Figuera encourages students in her sixth-grade science class to express their views about each problem they study. She encourages them to offer new or different ways of analyzing the problem. This teaching technique is an example of:

    (A) creative engagement   (D) top-down analysis

    (B) brainstorming   (E) convergent instruction

    (C) group think

57. An honors-level science teacher has received a grant to send the three best science students to a national competition in applied research science. The teacher tells the class about this opportunity and challenges the class of 10 students to develop a project that meets the criteria for the grant. Students with the three best projects will be selected to attend the competition. What type of testing procedure would best be applied to this assignment?

    (A) diagnostic   (D) aptitude

    (B) standardized   (E) achievement

    (C) criterion-referenced

58. Children from backgrounds of low socioeconomic status (SES) are more likely to:

    (A) perform as well as children from high-SES backgrounds

    (B) enter school with fewer basic academic skills and knowledge

    (C) be as well behaved as other children in school

    (D) have as much parental support and involvement as other children

    (E) have essentially the same level of intelligence on standardized intelligence tests as children from high-SES backgrounds

59. For a person to use information that has been stored in long-term memory, the information must be _____ the long-term memory and _____ the working memory.

    (A) retrieved from, transferred to

    (B) encoded in, stored in

    (C) perceived in, retrieved from

    (D) rehearsed in, stored in

    (E) decoded in, encoded in

60. In positive punishment the person:

    (A) gives the child something positive for unacceptable behavior

    (B) takes away something positive for unacceptable behavior

    (C) gives the child something negative for unacceptable behavior

    (D) takes away something desirable for unacceptable behavior

    (E) takes something desirable away from the child while being verbally reassuring with him or her

61. David is in the eleventh grade and plays on the school basketball team. He believes that his real father is a professional athlete and that the man living with him now is not his real father. He tells people that his real father will be coming to visit soon and help him get a position as a professional athlete. David is showing which of the following characteristics of an adolescent?

    (A) imaginary audience fallacy

    (B) invincibility fallacy

    (C) athletic self-concept

    (D) personal fable

    (E) narcissism

62. All of the following variables affect a child's sense of self-efficacy EXCEPT:

    (A) past experiences

    (B) social persuasion

    (C) emotional feedback from significant adults

    (D) external rewards and punishments earned by their behavior

    (E) peer verbal feedback

63. Culture reflects:

    (A) the visible physical characteristics of people

    (B) the patterns of language used by people

    (C) how people behave in certain social situations

    (D) the traditions, values, attitudes, and perceptions that a group of people hold

    (E) how genetics, environment, and society impact each other

64. A psychology instructor administered a group multiple-choice examination to the 80 students in her class. The lowest grade achieved was a 44, and the highest grade achieved was a 91. The following distribution of scores was obtained using letter grades:

Grade	Students Who Achieved This Grade
A	2
B	12
C	25
D	31
F	10

The modal letter grade for the class is:

(A) A   (D) D

(B) B   (E) F

(C) C

65. Which of the following statements has been supported by research?

(A) teachers tend to base their judgments of students on the basis of information in cumulative school records

(B) teacher judgments are not as accurate as testing data to predict student behavior

(C) teacher judgments are often more accurate than testing data to predict student behavior

(D) many teachers evaluate students based on the self-fulfilling prophecy

(E) in the elementary grades, teachers grade students based more on the student's personal interactions with the teacher than on objective test performance

66. The process of combining pieces of information into larger and interrelated pieces of information is referred to as:

(A) elaborative encoding   (D) chunking

(B) rehearsal   (E) clustering

(C) rote rehearsal

67. Reinforcement is designed to:

    (A) decrease behavior

    (B) increase behavior

    (C) suppress behavior

    (D) teach the child how to self-regulate behavior

    (E) reward the child for socially appropriate conduct

68. One of the best predictors of school failure and becoming a high school dropout is:

    (A) the presence of an eating disorder

    (B) social rejection from peers

    (C) dominating parents

    (D) having a part-time job after school

    (E) parents' values and attitudes about education

69. Individualistic cultures tend to have:

    (A) lower crime rates

    (B) more high achievers in school who contribute more to the society as adults

    (C) a greater incidence of alcoholism

    (D) higher levels of physical and emotional abuse of children

    (E) higher levels of technological development

70. Which of the following educational strategies is NOT appropriate when working with children from different cultural backgrounds?

    (A) teaching the essential skills for success in school and life

    (B) explaining to students why they need to learn the material they are being taught

    (C) understanding how the child views the school environment and reacts to it

    (D) speaking loudly and slowly to students beginning to use English so they learn how to speak correctly

    (E) allowing the child to use English in the class setting

71. Sarah recently took the Miller Analogies Test and earned a score that placed her at the 65th percentile. This means that Sarah:

    (A) scored equal to or better than 65 percent of the students who have taken the test

    (B) had 65 questions correct out of 100 total questions

    (C) placed in the bottom half of students who have took the test

    (D) achieved an average score

    (E) scored equal to or higher than 65 percent of the students who took the test at the same time she did

72. Contingency contracting requires the teacher to:

    (A) make a contract with an individual student about behavior or academic standards

    (B) make a contract with the whole class about behavior or academic standards

    (C) make group contracts with each class taught

    (D) set up a token economy system in which the rewards are clearly identified in the contract

    (E) make a contract with the parents of a problem student so that home-based contingencies are used when the student does not perform at acceptable levels in school

73. Matthew is having difficulty remembering the meaning and purpose of the echoic storage register. After much study he begins to picture in his mind someone shouting in a canyon and the echo bouncing off the canyon walls. This image reminds him about the function of the echoic storage register. This memory technique is an example of:

    (A) elaborative encoding   (D) maintenance rehearsal

    (B) imagery   (E) encoding

    (C) elaborative rehearsal

74. A teacher has been giving students a homework pass for every ten points they earn for good behavior at school. The teacher has stopped using this approach because the children were earning too many homework passes. The behavior of the class has gotten much worse, and many children are being verbally reprimanded and criticized by the teacher. These three situations are examples of:

    (A) positive reinforcement, satiation, and positive punishment

    (B) positive reinforcement, satiation, and negative punishment

    (C) satiation, extinction, and positive punishment

    (D) positive reinforcement, extinction, and positive punishment

    (E) satiation and negative punishment

75. Many television programs show women as being:

    (A) concerned about their physical appearance

    (B) rewarded for assertive behavior

    (C) equal to men in the kind of roles they have

    (D) independent and career oriented

    (E) having difficulty making decisions independently

76. In most school learning, it is important for teachers to:

    (A) show students the value of what they are being taught

    (B) encourage the development of intrinsic rewards as the basis of learning

    (C) help students who are misunderstood by others

    (D) address students' basic human needs, especially those that are growth oriented

    (E) use extrinsic rewards to prepare students for how adult society functions

77. An internalizing behavior disorder is one where the child:

    (A) shows feelings of anxiety, depression, and may be socially withdrawn

    (B) is angry, hostile, and verbally or physically aggressive toward others

(C) is impulsive and has difficulty paying attention

(D) shows periods of having difficulty understanding what is being said

(E) often has unusual sensory experiences that affect school learning

78. Concurrent validity is established by:

(A) examining the physical appearance of the test to be sure it looks appropriate

(B) determining how well the test corresponds with accepted theory

(C) correlating one test with another that claims to measure the same traits

(D) correlating a test with real-life performance

(E) determining how well the test discriminates between extreme groups on the traits tested

79. Which of the following must be considered when ignoring inappropriate behaviors?

(A) it is a type of punishment that may hurt the child's feelings

(B) the child may not be aware of the teacher's ignoring

(C) the child may begin to ignore the teacher as a retaliatory reaction

(D) the child may see being ignored as the teacher approving the behavior

(E) other children will also start to ignore the child's inappropriate behaviors

80. The dual coding hypothesis predicts that:

(A) pairing verbal and visual images enhances learning and retention

(B) human beings use two types of encoding strategies in long-term memory

(C) color coding and auditory cues are effective teaching strategies for young children

(D) some children learn better visually while others learn more effectively with auditory input

(E) multimodal instruction is the best approach for children with learning problems

81. During the preschool years one of the best predictors of later reading achievement level is:

    (A) visual motor coordination

    (B) gross motor coordination

    (C) intelligence test performance

    (D) alphabet recognition and letter naming

    (E) the ability to count correctly from 1 to 50

82. A problem in which of the following areas does NOT qualify as a disability within the public schools?

    (A) reading   (D) spelling

    (B) written expression   (E) speech and language deficits

    (C) mathematics

83. Performance on a learning test using memory for sequences of letters has been shown consistently to identify students in medical school who are likely to have academic problems during their first year and be put on academic probation. This test has which of the following types of validity?

    (A) construct   (D) predictive

    (B) concurrent   (E) face

    (C) content

84. Children in a third-grade class are being taught the principles involved in long division. These principles represent which of the following types of problems?

    (A) a working forward strategy

    (B) specific transfer

    (C) a nonroutine problem

    (D) a routine problem

    (E) a working backward strategy

85. Social success in school during the preschool and kindergarten years is reflected by a child's:

    (A) socioeconomic status

    (B) degree of self-control

    (C) parents' educational levels

    (D) athletic ability and motor coordination skills

    (E) verbal communication skills

86. Which of the following environmental conditions is related to an increased incidence of mental retardation in babies?

    (A) low SES of the mother

    (B) alcohol use by the mother during pregnancy

    (C) single-parent family

    (D) alcohol use by the father during pregnancy

    (E) mother exposed to domestic violence during her pregnancy

87. Tests that are used to predict future behavior and performance are:

    (A) achievement tests

    (B) diagnostic tests

    (C) aptitude tests

    (D) end-of-grade tests

    (E) projective tests

88. Teaching children algorithms is most appropriate in subject areas such as:

    (A) chemistry

    (B) English

    (C) social studies

    (D) foreign languages

    (E) vocational education courses

89. Syntax describes which of the following aspects of human language?

    (A) meanings of words

    (B) social aspect of language

    (C) grammatical structure of language

    (D) smallest meaningful units of human language

    (E) nonverbal messages that accompany all verbal communications

90. Amy has a great deal of difficulty keeping sounds in the correct order when she is saying words that have three or more syllables. She mispronounces these words and sometimes stutters. Her disability is best described as a(n):

    (A) expressive language disorder

    (B) receptive language disorder

    (C) articulation disorder

    (D) voice disorder

    (E) processing disorder

91. Linda has studied biology for two years. She has decided to change her major area of study to organic chemistry. She finds that the foundation of knowledge learned in biology has made it much easier to learn organic chemistry. This is an example of:

    (A) zero transfer of learning

    (B) insightful learning

    (C) positive transfer of learning

    (D) negative transfer of learning

    (E) generalization of specific information

92. Most children learn the basic essentials of adult spoken language syntax by age:

    (A) 4   (D) 10

    (B) 5   (E) 8

    (C) 6

93. Allen strongly dislikes reading. When he is forced to read he will tilt his head from one side to the other. His eyes will also water, and he often complains about having headaches. It is possible that Allen has a(n):

    (A) learning disability

    (B) receptive language disorder

    (C) intermittent mental retardation

    (D) visual impairment

    (E) information-processing disorder

94. General problem-solving strategies that only sometimes lead to correct answers are referred to as:

    (A) insightful learning

    (B) working backward strategies

    (C) focused verbalizations

    (D) heuristics

    (E) trial-and-error learning

95. According to Piaget, intelligence is:

    (A) the set of behaviors that allows people to deal effectively with their world

    (B) mental schemata that represent information and reality in the memory system

    (C) verbal ability and language competence

    (D) genetically determined and cannot be altered by the environment

    (E) the result of parent involvement and teaching during the first 5 years of the child's life

96. Tanya, a fifth-grader, is a highly verbal and academically successful student who prefers to work alone on problems that are especially challenging to other students in the class. She gets bored quickly when required to do class assignments that are routine or repetitious. She is beginning to have difficulty paying attention and complains about being bored. Her teacher might begin to suspect that Tanya is:

    (A) gifted and talented   (D) troubled

    (B) ADHD   (E) unmotivated and lazy

    (C) learning disabled

97. A language experience approach to teaching reading:

    (A) uses reading as one component of a total program of literacy skill development

    (B) uses the child's life experiences as core material to teach reading

    (C) emphasizes decoding and encoding words

    (D) focuses on phonemic awareness skills development

    (E) relies heavily on a combined visual and auditory teaching approach

98. The right to due process for all exceptional children means that:

    (A) professional educators will work diligently to provide the best educational program for a child

    (B) parents can rely on educators' opinions about their child's needs and abilities

    (C) a child can be tested by the school as soon as a teacher suspects that a problem might exist

    (D) parents can request an independent educational evaluation if they disagree with the school's findings

    (E) parents should consult an educational attorney before agreeing to any program changes offered by the school

99. In general, research has shown that children with high-achieving parents are likely to:

    (A) be lower achieving than their parents

    (B) enter school with the same skills as children from lower-achieving parents

    (C) have higher demands placed on them by their parents

    (D) drop out of school because their physical needs have been met by their parents

    (E) be high achievers

100. What that two types of intelligences did Cattell (1971) propose?

    (A) verbal and performance   (D) global and fluid

    (B) verbal and full scale   (E) fluid and crystallized

    (C) global and crystallized

CLEP INTRODUCTION TO EDUCATIONAL PSYCHOLOGY PRACTICE TEST 1

1.	(A)	26.	(D)	51.	(E)	76.	(A)
2.	(A)	27.	(D)	52.	(D)	77.	(A)
3.	(D)	28.	(B)	53.	(A)	78.	(C)
4.	(D)	29.	(C)	54.	(C)	79.	(D)
5.	(A)	30.	(D)	55.	(A)	80.	(A)
6.	(C)	31.	(D)	56.	(B)	81.	(D)
7.	(A)	32.	(C)	57.	(C)	82.	(D)
8.	(A)	33.	(B)	58.	(B)	83.	(D)
9.	(C)	34.	(B)	59.	(A)	84.	(D)
10.	(C)	35.	(D)	60.	(C)	85.	(B)
11.	(D)	36.	(D)	61.	(D)	86.	(B)
12.	(D)	37.	(C)	62.	(D)	87.	(C)
13.	(C)	38.	(D)	63.	(D)	88.	(A)
14.	(D)	39.	(A)	64.	(D)	89.	(C)
15.	(B)	40.	(C)	65.	(C)	90.	(A)
16.	(D)	41.	(D)	66.	(D)	91.	(C)
17.	(B)	42.	(B)	67.	(B)	92.	(B)
18.	(C)	43.	(B)	68.	(B)	93.	(D)
19.	(A)	44.	(B)	69.	(C)	94.	(D)
20.	(B)	45.	(C)	70.	(D)	95.	(A)
21.	(D)	46.	(A)	71.	(A)	96.	(A)
22.	(C)	47.	(D)	72.	(A)	97.	(B)
23.	(B)	48.	(D)	73.	(B)	98.	(D)
24.	(A)	49.	(A)	74.	(D)	99.	(E)
25.	(A)	50.	(C)	75.	(A)	100.	(E)

DETAILED EXPLANATIONS OF ANSWERS

PRACTICE TEST 1

1. **(A)** The kind of neighborhood in which a child lives significantly shapes the kind of adult role models they are exposed to outside their homes, the quality of the schools they attend, and the quality of the educators teaching in their schools.

2. **(A)** Automaticity involves learning information to the point that the skill or task can be performed with very little conscious effort. An essential for skills such as reading and mathematics, automaticity enables the learner to devote more mental energy and effort to comprehension and problem solving.

3. **(D)** Ratio categories of reinforcement always refer to the number of target behaviors shown by the child before reinforcement is given. The child is reinforced only when a prespecified number of target behaviors have been shown.

4. **(D)** During the formal operational stage of cognitive development, adolescents begin to think and reason abstractly. They are also able to examine information and develop hypotheses and insights about the relevance of the information to other areas.

5. **(A)** The sensorimotor stage is the first stage of development according to Piaget. It is the time of development when children interact with their world mainly through sensory and motor functions, such as crying, breathing, and mouthing and touching objects.

6. **(C)** One of the major characteristics of the child in the concrete operational stage of cognitive development is developing the capacity to understand and see interrelationships among objects based on the similarity of their characteristics. This is referred to as class inclusion, and it allows the child to process large amounts of information simultaneously.

7. **(A)** Behavioral theories of motivation emphasize the use of externally given rewards and material objects as incentives to encourage children to perform well.

8. **(A)** Research has demonstrated consistently that the socioeconomic status (SES) of the child is one of the most important variables affecting school performance. SES reflects how much money the parents earn annually, their level of educational achievement, and the kinds of jobs in which they are employed.

9. **(C)** Every instructional objective must have a specified criterion for success. Without this criterion neither the teacher nor the student can determine if the objective has been met.

10. **(C)** Expository teaching involves students developing an understanding of the underlying relationships and commonalities among ideas to enhance their comprehension, retention, and ability to apply this knowledge in appropriate situations.

11. **(D)** Simple moral education programs typically occur in a classroom setting and discuss topics that adults believe are important to children. These programs tend to be instructional in focus and have limited success in truly influencing a child's moral or character development over a sustained period.

12. **(D)** Clustering is a learning strategy that requires a child to organize information into common categories or clusters. The category names can be cues to help the child recall the specific items in the category.

13. **(C)** Variable ratio and variable interval reinforcement categories show the greatest resistance to extinction effects, meaning that the child continues to show the target behaviors for a much longer time even though the behaviors are not being reinforced. Fixed categories of reinforcement are seriously and negatively affected when the reinforcement ceases, and the child often will resume old, unacceptable behaviors quickly.

14. **(D)** A child's sense of self-efficacy is influenced by several factors, including vicarious experiences. Often a child selects another child to observe based on whether that child appears to have similar characteristics. Decisions about the probability of success or failure are made by observing whether the target child is successful or fails in the same task or area.

15. **(B)** Research indicates that low-SES families are more likely to use verbal commands and direct statements when speaking to their children, provide vague directions and instructions, and fail to encourage their children to engage in independent thinking.

16. **(D)** Essay tests require students to demonstrate their ability to analyze and integrate information in a systematic and comprehensive way. These tests also require students to show their level of comprehension as well as recall of specific acts and sequences of information.

17. **(B)** Mr. Andrews is using a guided discovery, or discovery learning, approach in which he guides the students to discover patterns, solve problems, and make generalizations from the data. This approach is also called constructivist.

18. **(C)** The experimental group in this study is the learning-disabled children because their memory spans are being compared with children who have no learning problems. The presence or absence of a learning disability is also the variable that the researcher is carefully controlling to determine how having a learning disability affects memory span.

19. **(A)** The lists of nonrhyming consonants are being used to measure short-term memory span. The researcher is interested in determining if the memory span is impaired compared with the memory spans of non-learning-disabled children. It is the memory span that changes as a function of the manipulation of the independent variable (group membership).

20. **(B)** In an experimental study the researcher is able to manipulate the independent variable (group membership) and assess its effects on memory span while using a random sample. If the study were quasi-experimental, the researcher would not have been able to randomly select the children in each group.

21. **(D)** The null hypothesis is always expressed in a form that states there is no difference expected between the groups on the dependent variable.

22. **(C)** Citizenship education increases a student's knowledge about how the government and the various mechanisms making up government operate. These programs educate children about the core values of society, including justice, authority, participation in the governing process, freedom, personal privacy, and due process.

23. **(B)** Interference of newly acquired knowledge has been shown to be the most influential cause of forgetting in the working memory because the working memory is a limited-capacity mechanism consisting of a span of about seven items (bits) at any one time.

24. **(A)** Thorndike's law of effect was the first law that predicted how humans would perform based on whether the behavior led to a positive experience.

25. **(A)** Extrinsic motivators are rewards and material reinforcements a person works to earn, with the primary goal of achieving the reward. The reward is given to the person by someone else, who also decides the standards to earn it.

26. **(D)** Interpersonal intelligence is the ability to be aware of and understand other people's feelings and the impact those feelings have on people's behavior.

27. **(D)** One of the major difficulties teachers have in grading essay tests is remaining objective across tests. Reading 28 essay tests in one sitting can lead a teacher to become bored and tired, which could lead to increased irritability and criticism.

28. **(B)** An advance organizer introduces students to important concepts and information they must know if they are to be successful in a given lesson. This introduction occurs before the actual lesson begins so that students can focus their attention effectively and link new information with information previously learned.

29. **(C)** All knowledge contained in the long-term memory is permanent. Failure to retrieve information is the result of an insufficient number of cues being available to locate the target. The greater the number of cues available during original learning and stored in the long-term memory, the more likely that the information will be recalled later.

30. **(D)** The mother's behavior increases the likelihood that the child will cry and misbehave in the future when she wants her mother to buy her something. Reinforcement always increases the probability of a behavior occurring again.

31. **(D)** Genetics provides the plan for a person's development, and the environment influences how genetic characteristics become visible during

the person's lifetime. It is the interaction between genetics and the environment that impacts maturation. Extreme environmental conditions, such as a head injury or sexual abuse, can interfere with genetically programmed characteristics.

32. **(C)** Juvonen and Weiner (1993) found that girls generally see themselves as being less competent than boys and will set much lower expectations and personal standards for achievement.

33. **(B)** Intelligence test scores falling above 109 and below 119 lie within the above average range. Scores between 90 and 109 are considered average, while scores above 119 are considered superior.

34. **(B)** Taxonomies help teachers present a lesson in a comprehensive and systematic manner so that a broad range of skills and content are taught.

35. **(D)** Cooperative learning uses small groups of students working together on a common project. Each student is assigned a specific task to gather information and is expected to become an expert about this area and to share the information with other group members. The contribution of each member leads to the overall success of the group with the project.

36. **(D)** Functional fixedness describes the inability of a person to use a tool or object in ways that are creatively different from the way the person has learned to use it. This characteristic limits the person's ability to solve problems that require complicated or new methods.

37. **(C)** The child is removing an undesirable stimulus (crying), which increases the probability in the future that the mother will continue to buy her what she wants. This is negative reinforcement.

38. **(D)** Vygotsky believed that human language encourages the child to develop an inner private speech system. This speech system enables the child to represent the world using verbal symbols in the form of self-talk. Self-talk guides patterns of thinking and behaving.

39. **(A)** All reinforcement/reward-oriented programs require clear expectations so that all students know how to focus their efforts to meet the defined expectations, or standards. Clear expectations also reduce the chances of rewards being given out according to variables other than meeting expectations.

40. **(C)** Achievement tests are norm-referenced instruments that reflect or measure the amount of learning that a student has gained. They are typically used to measure the final performance level in a course.

41. **(D)** The main purpose of formative evaluation is to assess how well students are learning and comprehending information and skills so that instruction can be modified to help students achieve mastery. Summative evaluation reflects the student's overall achievement level in the form of a grade presented on a report card.

42. **(B)** Models are visual graphic organizers that provide an overall structure that can help students form visual representations of how information is interrelated.

43. **(B)** The value of p, or the level of significance, always specifies the probability of the results being due to chance factors; in this case chance factors are likely to have caused these findings less than 1 out of 100 times.

44. **(B)** The two-store model of memory developed by Atkinson and Shiffrin (1968) has three components: the sensory register, the working memory, and the long-term memory. The model is referred to as the two-store model of memory because information used by the person is stored, processed, and organized within the working memory and the long-term memory.

45. **(C)** Direct modeling is when a person imitates the behavior of the model in a direct way, even if the person does not understand why he or she is imitating the behavior.

46. **(A)** The life experiences children have during infancy with their primary caregivers leads to the development of trust or mistrust of others. If an infant has a caregiver who does not meet the infant's need for an emotionally warm and secure relationship, then it is likely the infant will see the social world as a hostile place and feel that no support or resources can be relied on.

47. **(D)** A child with learned helplessness believes he or she has no power to change things in life or to be successful on his or her own. It can undermine the child's ability to put forth any energy or effort in school because the child believes failure is inevitable regardless of what he or she does.

48. **(D)**   Aptitude tests are usually used to predict how successful a person will be in a particular program or occupation.

49. **(A)**   When used systematically as a routine part of the teaching program, formative evaluation using frequent quizzes that do not count toward the final grade can provide a student with a high degree of success, help reduce anxiety, and help the student feel more comfortable when the summative evaluation occurs.

50. **(C)**   Barr (1987) found that teachers who present more information and content have students who learn and achieve at higher levels. This does not mean that a teacher should overwhelm students with content. Rather, the teaching pace must be balanced relative to the learning abilities of students in the class.

51. **(E)**   Quasi-experimental designs are similar to experimental designs in many ways. However, the quasi-experimental design does not control some of the variables of interest in the study and does not randomly assign participants to treatment conditions. It is a very commonly used research design in educational psychology that provides valid and useful information about students and the variables that affect their learning and adjustment in school.

52. **(D)**   Research has demonstrated that information is stored within the iconic (or visual) storage register for about 1 second before it is lost from the system. The echoic storage register, which stores heard information, has a maximum storage capacity of 4 seconds, after which the information is lost permanently through decay.

53. **(A)**   Cognitive learning views all human behavior as self-regulated—under the control of the person rather than others who use reinforcement and punishment to manipulate behavior.

54. **(C)**   At stage 5 of moral development people begin to see themselves as members of a larger society, with each member of the society having an implicit contract with the larger group. They believe that group standards must be maintained and that all individuals have implicit rights and values. Among these are the right to liberty, equal opportunity, and an appropriate education.

55. **(A)**   Maslow's highest level of human need is self-actualization, which is a person's desire to reach the maximum level of development in ability and potential.

56. **(B)** Brainstorming (Baer, 1997) is a technique to stimulate creative thinking with the goal of generating as many new ideas and reasonable viewpoints as possible about how to solve a problem.

57. **(C)** Criterion-referenced testing is most appropriate because it evaluates the student's performance relative to prescribed standards of functioning with a certain level of mastery specified.

58. **(B)** Children from low-SES backgrounds often enter school not knowing the letters and sounds of the alphabet and lacking other basic skills such as counting, fine motor coordination, and knowing color names.

59. **(A)** Information is stored in the long-term memory permanently. However, the key to making this information available for use in the present is for the person to retrieve the information from the appropriate storage file and transfer the information to the working memory, where it becomes consciously available for the person to use.

60. **(C)** Positive punishment involves giving something negative to the child for an inappropriate behavior.

61. **(D)** A personal fable is a belief in which an adolescent sees that their destiny is for fortune and fame.

62. **(D)** Experiences related to past success and failure, the amount of social support and encouragement a child receives from important people, the emotional reactions of significant adults and peer feedback provide the child with a clear view about whether he or she is seen as competent and successful or inept and a failure.

63. **(D)** Culture describes the traditions, values, attitudes, and perceptions of reality that guide and influence behaviors for a group of people. It is created by the people who make up the culture. These traditions and values are communicated across each generation.

64. **(D)** The mode represents the score or grade that occurs with greatest frequency in a distribution.

65. **(C)** Several studies have shown that teacher judgments about student learning and achievement are more accurate than predictions made on the basis of educational testing data (Helmke & Schrader, 1987; Short, 1985).

66. **(D)**   With chunking, smaller units of information are enhanced and combined into larger and more integrated units, or bits. Increasing the size or amount of information contained in a bit increases the amount of information that is being actively used and processed in the working memory.

67. **(B)**   Both positive and negative reinforcement increase a desirable behavior in the child.

68. **(B)**   An adolescent who does not feel part of a larger peer group often develops a sense of loneliness and alienation. The more actively that peers reject an adolescent, the greater these feelings and the higher the probability that the adolescent will drop out of high school.

69. **(C)**   Cultures in which people have a greater commitment to individual achievement, even at the expense of the larger group, have greater numbers of people who have alcohol abuse problems.

70. **(D)**   Speaking loudly and slowly to non-English-speaking students is likely to embarrass them in front of their peers. This kind of embarrassment can create other kinds of personal and social difficulties that interfere with the students' ability to adjust to their new cultural setting.

71. **(A)**   Percentile scores indicate the percentage of students who had scores that fell at or below the student's score on a given test.

72. **(A)**   Contingency contracts are made between a teacher and a student to enhance the student's academic performance and/or personal conduct.

73. **(B)**   Imagery occurs when a person forms an internal picture or image that triggers the correct meaning and recall of information. For people who prefer visual experiences imagery can involve generating visual pictures; it can also involve auditory images and sounds for people who rely on auditory cues.

74. **(D)**   The teacher began by using a positive reinforcement program that was highly effective. When the teacher stopped using the program and no longer reinforced good behavior, the teacher was using an extinction program. Finally, criticizing students is an example of positive punishment because the teacher is adding something undesirable to the situation to suppress inappropriate behaviors.

75. **(A)** The media have a significant influence on gender role stereotyping and gender bias. Television programs often depict women as being concerned about their physical appearance, taking care of their families, and performing household chores. Women typically serve in supporting roles to males.

76. **(A)** School learning tends to be implicitly uninteresting to many students. It is often difficult for students to understand the relevance or usefulness of the material to their lives or futures. To focus and motivate students, teachers should explicitly teach students the value, relevance, and usefulness of the instructional material.

77. **(A)** Internalizing disorders are often characterized by a lack of confidence socially and academically, social retreat and a tendency to remain alone, anxiety, and depression.

78. **(C)** Concurrent validity involves administering two separate tests to the same group of children to see how well performance on each test correlates with each other. Usually one of the tests is already accepted by professionals as being valid, and the second test is being used to establish its validity in measuring the same traits.

79. **(D)** Some children interpret a lack of reaction from an authority figure as approval for what they are doing. Ignoring can actually reinforce negative behaviors in these children.

80. **(A)** The dual coding hypothesis (Clark & Paivio, 1991) proposes that linking verbal and visual imagery produces a more vivid and distinct representation in the mind because it involves pairing both a concrete image (visual) with an abstract image (verbal). Concrete words can be better recalled than abstract words because of this dual elaborative encoding process.

81. **(D)** The ability to name letters and recognize the alphabet has been found to be a consistent predictor of how well a child will read in the upper-grade levels. Knowledge about how letters operate allows the child to focus mental energy on comprehending what is being read rather than on trying to decode words.

82. **(D)** In most school systems students can be identified as having a learning disability in either reading, written language, or mathematics. Students who have only spelling problems are generally not considered learning disabled.

83. **(D)**   Predictive validity reflects the ability of a test to predict a student's future behavior based on earlier testing performance.

84. **(D)**   A routine problem has a ready-made and consistent solution. They are well defined and highly structured so that the solution strategy is known or easily developed.

85. **(B)**   A child's level of self-control in preschool and kindergarten has been found to be highly predictive of later social success. Behavioral self-control and the ability to restrain emotions are very important skills that can increase a child's ability to be accepted by peers and viewed as socially acceptable and competent.

86. **(B)**   The use of alcohol during pregnancy is associated with fetal alcohol syndrome, one symptom of which is mental retardation. It is preventable by the mother abstaining from alcohol use throughout pregnancy.

87. **(C)**   Aptitude tests evaluate a child's potential to succeed and are often used to select students for various programs or school admissions.

88. **(A)**   An algorithm is a step-by-step process that leads to a specific answer or outcome each time the algorithm is used correctly. Algorithms form the basis of knowledge in content areas such as mathematics, statistics, and many of the physical sciences.

89. **(C)**   Syntax, or grammatical structure, is the set of rules that determines how words are organized to create phrases and sentences. Syntactic structure defines the relationship of nouns to verbs, verbs to adverbs, and the kinds of punctuation used during written communication.

90. **(A)**   Children with expressive language disorders have difficulty forming sounds or keeping sounds in the correct sequence when speaking. These children can have significant communication problems because they often distort or mispronounce words.

91. **(C)**   Positive transfer of learning is one of the three types of transfer that exist. Positive transfer involves a learner using information acquired in one setting to solve problems in a new setting. The information learned in the previous setting enhances performance and achievement in the new area.

92. **(B)** Most children within the United States have acquired the basics of adult spoken language syntax by the time they are 5 years old. By age 10 many children have developed spoken language competency that is essentially the same as that of adults.

93. **(D)** Characteristics of a child who has difficulty seeing include tilting the head from one side to the other when reading; having eyes that are red and water excessively, especially when reading; complaining of having difficulty reading small print; misidentifying letters of similar shapes; and complaining of headaches or feeling dizzy after reading.

94. **(D)** Heuristics are general problem-solving strategies typically used when problems are poorly defined. Poorly defined problems have no specific algorithms or clear and concrete solution approaches available. Heuristic procedures are typically useful in content areas such as geometry and English because they guide students toward a specific outcome or solution.

95. **(A)** Piaget emphasized the strong interrelationship between genetics and the world in which people live. He defined intelligence as the set of behaviors that a person takes on to deal successfully and optimally with their surroundings.

96. **(A)** Gifted and talented children are typically high achievers who learn more easily and quickly than their peers. They prefer to work alone, enjoy challenging or difficult problems, and get bored with routine tasks and activities. If the educational program is not sufficiently stimulating, these children sometimes begin to daydream or not pay attention during class.

97. **(B)** Language experience approaches use the child's own spoken language system and daily life experiences as content for stories that the child dictates to an adult. The adult writes these stories on paper, and these dictated stories become the text to develop the child's reading skills.

98. **(D)** All children who are exceptional learners are guaranteed the right to due process under federal and state laws. Parents must be actively involved throughout the entire process of identifying and diagnosing their child's needs. Parents are guaranteed access to all school records and can request an independent educational evaluation, at the full financial expense of the school, if they are dissatisfied or disagree with the findings compiled by the school team.

99. **(E)**   Children whose parents are high achievers are more likely to model the behavior of their parents and be high achievers throughout their educational experiences.

100. **(E)**   The two types of intelligence that Cattell proposed are fluid and crystallized. Fluid intelligence represents a person's general ability to solve new problems and tasks. Crystallized intelligence represents the amount of education and knowledge a person has acquired throughout his or her lifetime.

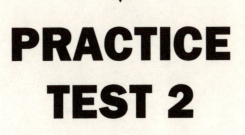

PRACTICE
TEST 2

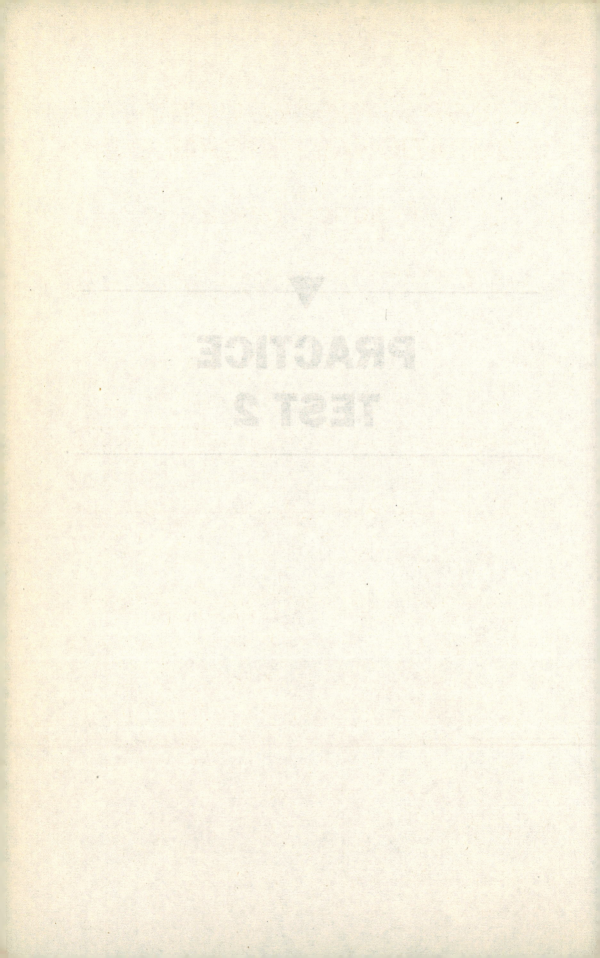

PRACTICE
TEST 2

CLEP INTRODUCTION TO EDUCATIONAL PSYCHOLOGY

Practice Test 2

(Answer sheets appear in the back of this book.)

TIME: 90 Minutes
100 Questions

DIRECTIONS: Each of the questions or incomplete statements below is followed by five possible answers or completions. Select the best choice in each case and fill in the corresponding oval on the answer sheet.

---

1. The tendency of a person to behave in ways that reflect honesty, responsibility, and respect for the rights of others is called:

    (A) dignity

    (D) courage

    (B) character

    (E) maturity

    (C) integrity

2. NATO is an example of a(n) _____ memory strategy.

    (A) acronym

    (D) imagery

    (B) acrostic

    (E) locus

    (C) keyword

3. Shaping is used to:

   (A) reinforce an established behavior in a cost-efficient way

   (B) encourage a child to accept reinforcement using an intermittent schedule

   (C) strengthen a behavior that is often shown at the wrong time

   (D) teach a desired behavior that occurs at low levels

   (E) encourage a child to accept reinforcement using a fixed schedule

4. A young child is shown a toy. The toy is removed so the child can no longer see it. The child responds by losing interest in pursuing the toy. According to Piaget, the child lacks:

   (A) assimilation   (D) object permanence

   (B) goal orientation   (E) reality permanence

   (C) egocentricity

5. Ms. Smith teaches third graders. She often tells students they are in control of their success in her class and that if they use proper study habits and practice what they have been taught in class they will do well. She is relying on which theory of motivation with these children?

   (A) behavioral theory   (D) expectancy theory

   (B) human needs theory   (E) social learning theory

   (C) attribution theory

6. Dropout rates for children who come from families with low socio-economic status (SES) are:

   (A) the same as those for the general population

   (B) lower than those for the general population

   (C) twice as high as those for the general population

   (D) lower if the child is in special education programs

   (E) the same as those for the general population if both biological parents live in the home

7. Ms. Green teaches a course in values clarification. Many of the instructional objectives in this course come from which of the following taxonomic domains:

    (A) affective   (D) application

    (B) cognitive   (E) social skills

    (C) psychomotor

8. Mr. Martinez challenges students in his junior-level advanced course on culture and society to identify the similarities among various cultures. His purpose is to highlight how societies tend to be more alike than dissimilar. The most effective teaching approach would be:

    (A) expository teaching

    (B) didactic instruction

    (C) lecture coupled with independent student projects

    (D) lecture followed by small-group projects

    (E) independent student papers and projects

9. A group of college students is administered two self-report questionnaires as part of a research study. The questionnaires are given to the students while they are eating lunch in the cafeteria. One questionnaire measures depression, and the other measures how much exercise students have on a daily basis. What type of study is this research likely to be?

    (A) quasi-experimental   (D) cross-sectional case study

    (B) naturalistic   (E) experimental

    (C) correlational

10. The most effective way for a child to learn positive moral values is by:

    (A) participating with other people who encourage the development of positive moral values

    (B) having role models who regularly visit their schools and conduct assemblies about appropriate social and moral conduct

    (C) exposing children to adults who have been convicted of crimes and spent time in prison for inappropriate behaviors and tell the children about these experiences to "frighten them"

    (D) telling children repeatedly what is correct and what is inappropriate behavior

    (E) being taught using positive reinforcement and punishment

11. The episodic memory file contains knowledge and information about:

    (A) abstract information and concepts

    (B) poorly formed schemata

    (C) well-formed schemata

    (D) personal experiences and events

    (E) specific and concrete factual information

12. Which of the following statements reflects the Premack principle?

    (A) if you do your homework correctly you can stay up later tonight

    (B) if you finish your class work you will not go to the time-out room

    (C) you will receive two points each time you complete your spelling test with a grade of 75 percent correct or higher

    (D) do your homework or you will get a spanking

    (E) each time you fail to complete your homework you will be put in time-out for 20 minutes

13. A four-year-old child is shown a ball that is made of clay. An adult takes the ball and shapes it into a long round tube. The child is asked which form has more clay in it and responds that the second one does. The child is NOT showing the characteristic of:

    (A) assimilation   (D) accommodation

    (B) conservation   (E) object permanence

    (C) centration

14. Teachers who have a high sense of self-efficacy have been found to:

    (A) be more successful with high-achieving students

    (B) work harder and persist longer with difficult students

    (C) be more motivated and enthusiastic about their jobs

    (D) become more tired and frustrated than those with a moderate level of self-efficacy

    (E) provide more academically interesting lessons that apply directly to skills students can use in real life situations

15. The longer children stay in school:

    (A) the higher the probability they will get high grades

    (B) the better they are when interacting socially with other people

    (C) the higher their level of motivation to be successful and remain in school

    (D) the higher their scores on intelligence tests

    (E) the more likely they will continue their education at the postsecondary level

16. Mr. Sawyer has just completed a unit on World War I in his history class. He is interested in giving students a test about the time frame in which the most important events and battles occurred during this war. The most effective way to test student knowledge of this information would be through a(n):

    (A) matching test   (D) essay test

    (B) true-false test   (E) short-answer test

    (C) multiple-choice test

17. Which of the following teaching approaches has been shown to lead to greater retention of information in the long-term memory?

    (A) direct   (D) guided discovery

    (B) expository   (E) experiential learning

    (C) small-group processing

18. A psychologist interested in studying how one group of 35 mothers and their children bond from infancy through early adolescence would most likely use which of these research designs:

    (A) longitudinal design   (D) case study design

    (B) cross-sectional design   (E) experimental

    (C) correlational design

19. Nine students in a high school biology class were found by their teacher to have submitted research papers that were copied directly from various Internet sources. When the teacher confronted each student individually about this plagiarism, none of them believed he or she had done anything wrong. In fact, nearly every student told the teacher that all their friends did similar kinds of things in this class and in other classes. Several actually challenged why the teacher was "picking on them." The reasoning of these students reflects the belief that:

    (A) cheating is acceptable as long as you do not get caught

    (B) the assignment was too difficult and challenging and should not have been assigned

    (C) the behavior was moral because it was effective in completing the required task

    (D) the teacher was discriminating against them but not against other students who plagiarized

    (E) the teacher's values were not realistic and consistent with the values of contemporary society

20. Timothy has to learn the names of the capitals for the New England states. He is doing this by saying the capital names and states out loud repeatedly and in order. This is an example of:

    (A) elaborative encoding   (D) elaborative rehearsal

    (B) chunking   (E) imagery

    (C) maintenance rehearsal

21. Which of the following behavior management techniques is an example of negative punishment?

    (A) spanking

    (B) losing points for bad behavior

    (C) time-out

    (D) standing up while holding several books in outstretched arms

    (E) contingency contracting

22. According to Vygotsky, the main development of cognitive and mental structures in children is influenced primarily by:

    (A) social interactions

    (B) the zone of proximal development

    (C) the language acquisition device

    (D) private speech

    (E) selective attention and perception

23. Philip earned three varsity letters in track and got into the college of his choice after graduating from high school. He has decided not to continue running track competitively in college but still runs three miles every day. He experiences a sense of inner peace and focus from running. His motivation for running is best described as:

    (A) extrinsic   (D) internal

    (B) intrinsic   (E) conditioned relaxation

    (C) external

24. Jamal has an incredible ability to look at a problem and solve it immediately. He is especially talented at being able to assemble complicated items (bookcases, mechanical equipment) without using instructions. Yet his vocabulary development and academic skills are all in the average range. Jamal is demonstrating which of the following kinds of intelligence:

    (A) crystallized   (D) fluid

    (B) logical-mathematical (E) spatial-perceptual

    (C) linguistic

25. One of the challenges in developing multiple-choice questions is:

    (A) the stems for each question must be clearly worded

    (B) students tend to misinterpret the choices

    (C) they restrict students to demonstrating knowledge

    (D) students who are test-wise often do very well on them

    (E) important information is often not included in the options

26. Advance organizers are most effective when used to present material that is:

    (A) complex or unfamiliar to the students

    (B) factually based and will require a good degree of rote memorization by the students

    (C) more logical and scientifically or mathematically focused

    (D) poorly organized and lacks a specific sequence or interrelationships among various concepts

    (E) complex, unfamiliar, factually based, or logically organized

27. Reliability describes:

    (A) the consistency of the results across time

    (B) how accurately the results represent those found in the sample

    (C) how accurately the results represent those found in the population

    (D) how well the researcher complies with ethical practices

    (E) the degree of confidence the researcher has in the findings from the study

28. Using the sentence "Every good boy does fine" to recall the names of the lines in music is an example of:

    (A) visual imagery   (D) an acronym

    (B) a keyword approach   (E) maintenance rehearsal

    (C) an acrostic device

29. An unconditioned stimulus is one in which:

   (A) prior learning experiences are very important to shaping the response

   (B) no prior learning is necessary to bring forth a response

   (C) extinction occurs when the neutral stimulus is removed

   (D) a continuous schedule of reinforcement has been used to associate it with the response

   (E) an intermittent schedule of reinforcement has been used to associate it with the response

30. Susan is in the tenth grade. Her dress and behaviors vary widely from day to day. One day she went to school dressed all in black, including black lipstick and nail polish, and behaved assertively and verbally offended others. Another day she came to school dressed in a business suit and interacted with others in a very dignified way. According to Erikson's theory of development, which stage is Susan most likely to be in at this time?

   (A) industry versus inferiority

   (B) identity versus role confusion

   (C) intimacy versus isolation

   (D) autonomy versus shame

   (E) trust versus distrust

31. A child's school performance can be improved most by:

   (A) verbal support and encouragement

   (B) a structured teaching approach that emphasizes rewards and punishments

   (C) a positive self-efficacy on the part of the teacher

   (D) developing clearly identifiable goals

   (E) using positive and negative punishment as routine parts of the management program

32. An IQ test score really reflects which of the following ratios?

   (A) Mental age divided by chronological age multiplied by 100

   (B) Chronological age divided by mental age multiplied by 100

   (C) Mental age divided by chronological age plus 100

   (D) Chronological age divided by mental age plus 100

   (E) Mental age divided by chronological age

33. "Being ready to perform a particular kind of physical skill" would most likely be an example of which of the following taxonomic domains?

   (A) cognitive   (D) application

   (B) affective   (E) concepts

   (C) psychomotor

34. Which of the following is NOT usually a disadvantage of a cooperative learning strategy?

   (A) students can easily get off task because of distractions from others in the group

   (B) the group can lose its focus

   (C) the teacher may spend more time working with one group

   (D) the workload can be unevenly distributed

   (E) effective behavior management of students can become a problem

35. Deception is:

   (A) an important aspect of psychological research that allows the researcher to study real-life problems

   (B) usually accepted by Internal Review Boards as an acceptable practice

   (C) never appropriate in psychological research, regardless of the importance of the research

   (D) sometimes permissible if its benefits outweigh its limitations and no other ethical standards are violated

   (E) the primary manner in which studies of human behavior can attain valid results

36. Which of the following perspectives views human beings as having a constructive role in the perception and interpretation of reality?

    (A) sociobiological psychology

    (B) behaviorism

    (C) humanism

    (D) cognitive psychology

    (E) radical behaviorism

37. A secondary reinforcer is:

    (A) a neutral stimulus that has been paired with a primary reinforcer

    (B) a primary reinforcer that has been paired with a negative reinforcer

    (C) another reinforcer used to strengthen the effects of a primary reinforcer

    (D) food or water

    (E) a conditioned stimulus that has been paired with a primary reinforcer

38. Preconventional moral reasoning is guided primarily by:

    (A) making decisions that benefit the interests of others and oneself

    (B) group conformity

    (C) mutual expectations

    (D) reward and punishment

    (E) fair and just treatment for all people

39. In general, the reinforcing value of many extrinsic rewards:

    (A) remains constant as the child gets older

    (B) increases as the child learns how to manipulate the system to acquire them

    (C) diminishes as the child gets older

    (D) is related to the educational status of the child's family

    (E) interferes with the development of the child's moral set of values and personal motivation

40. Aptitude tests have sometimes been used to:

    (A) group students according to capability levels

    (B) measure final performance in a course or subject area

    (C) develop teaching goals and strategies

    (D) measure achievement levels

    (E) evaluate how well teachers are meeting the goals on the individualized education program (IEP)

41. William's performance in algebra has improved since the teacher began evaluating his daily class and homework assignments and giving him specific corrective feedback and assistance to master the contents taught. His teacher is most likely using which of the following strategies:

    (A) mastery learning   (D) instructional objectives

    (B) summative evaluation   (E) guided corrective instruction

    (C) formative evaluation

42. Students in a human anatomy course are routinely presented with individual words that represent various systems of the body. For example, the lobes in the brain are represented by FLOPT, which is pronounced "flopped." This teaching/learning technique is known as a(n):

    (A) acronym   (D) visual image

    (B) acrostic   (E) metacognition

    (C) analogy

43. If a person decides not to continue participating in an experiment after having given their informed consent, the researcher can:

    (A) seek punitive damages through the court system because this person's leaving places the results of the study in jeopardy

    (B) coerce the person to continue because he or she entered into a contract by giving written informed consent to complete the experiment

    (C) inform others about the person quitting so that this person is not allowed to participate in other studies

(D) do nothing but allow the person to end his or her involvement

(E) inform the person's employer or professor about the refusal to fulfill the agreement

44. The two types of information files contained within the long-term memory are:

(A) semantic memory and episodic memory

(B) sensory memory and semantic memory

(C) episodic memory and coding memory

(D) experiential memory and social memory

(E) spatial memory and visual memory

45. Interval categories of reinforcement depend on:

(A) the number of behaviors shown by the child before reinforcement is given

(B) the shaping procedure used to reach the target behavior

(C) the number of times the child remains seated before reinforcement is given

(D) the passage of time before the child is reinforced

(E) both the passage of time and number of behaviors shown before reinforcement is given

46. Linda (aged 14) views herself as having a very good personality, being able to entertain her female friends by joking, and being well accepted by her female friends. On the other hand, she does not see herself as being a good student or athletically successful. She also sees herself as a "flop" with males. The area in which she is currently most engaged in developing her self-concept is:

(A) academic and verbal

(B) academic mathematics

(C) same-sex relationships

(D) opposite-sex relationships

(E) parent relations

47. All of the following are typical symptoms associated with anxiety EXCEPT:

    (A) upset stomach

    (B) anger and oppositional behavior

    (C) sweaty palms

    (D) increased heart rate

    (E) apprehension and sense of uneasiness

48. Ms. Hollis teaches a tenth-grade course in advanced chemistry. At the end of the course she administers a test to all students. Students who pass the test are able to transfer the course and receive three units of college credit. This test is most likely a(n):

    (A) achievement test   (D) aptitude test

    (B) intelligence test   (E) diagnostic achievement test

    (C) survey questionnaire

49. Ms. Beaman is a first-grade teacher who grades her students according to whether they meet, exceed, or fail to meet expected levels of performance. This type of grading scale is best described as:

    (A) performance based   (D) letter grading

    (B) descriptive   (E) curriculum based

    (C) relative

50. The purpose of a maintenance bilingual education program is to:

    (A) orient non-English-speaking students to English by minimizing their use of their native language

    (B) develop English mastery as quickly as possible

    (C) use students' native language as a transitional means of communication until English is established

    (D) develop competence in both the students' native language and English

    (E) teach the student a basic set of key English vocabulary words and expressions so they can function in American society

51. Most studies conducted in education and psychology use _____
    statistics to determine if significant differences exist between the
    groups.

    (A) nonparametric   (D) t-test

    (B) ratio   (E) inferential

    (C) demographic

52. During the initial stages of new learning it is very important for
    teachers to emphasize:

    (A) structure and routine

    (B) drill and repetition

    (C) problem-solving skills

    (D) vocabulary development and word knowledge

    (E) discovery learning activities

53. According to Skinner, which of the following is a possible side effect
    of punishment?

    (A) the child is not given corrective feedback

    (B) the child's feelings may be hurt

    (C) the child misses out on essential class work

    (D) the child will often feel victimized by their teacher

    (E) the child often will be rejected by classmates because of how
        they see the teacher treating the child

54. "Controversial" adolescents are:

    (A) often socially engaged but sometimes can be aggressive and
        inappropriate

    (B) less social than their peers and often overlooked by them

    (C) socially skilled and well liked by most of their peers, despite
        having clear opinions

    (D) socially unskilled, do not fit in with their peer group, and are
        withdrawn or aggressive

    (E) often socially engaged and highly aware of how their peers are
        responding to them

55. A person with an external locus of control believes that:

    (A) success is the result of hard work and effort

    (B) success is the result of luck

    (C) intrinsic rewards are important motivators for a person

    (D) success is an individual's willingness to practice and grow

    (E) success is an individual matter based on personal values and experiences

56. Mr. O'Hara does not allow his eighth-grade students in computer science and programming to deviate from the specific algorithms used to solve problems. This teaching approach is most likely to negatively affect the students' ability to develop:

    (A) convergent thinking skills

    (B) a sufficient knowledge base to pass the course

    (C) restructuring skills

    (D) creative thinking

    (E) rote thinking strategies

57. Criterion-referenced tests are most often used to evaluate:

    (A) mastery of specific instructional objectives

    (B) a student's achievement as compared with that of others

    (C) completion of broad educational goals

    (D) the level of teacher accountability

    (E) teacher compliance with the standards specified in an individualized education program (IEP)

58. Ms. Greene is a third-grade teacher who experienced significant behavior problems with William. Two years later Ms. Greene has William's brother, John, in her class. On the tenth day of school she speaks privately with John and tells him that she is watching him carefully because she knows he is a troublemaker. She threatens to deal with him severely the first time he misbehaves, even though he

has been well behaved so far. The next day she begins verbally criticizing him in front of the class for minor behaviors. John begins talking back to her and she immediately sends him to time-out. Ms. Greene's behaviors and John's reactions to them reflect the effects of:

(A) a self-fulfilling prophecy

(B) an accurate evaluation of the student

(C) lack of family support for the two boys

(D) Ms. Greene's ability to identify oppositional children quickly

(E) social maladjustment related to the family

59. The role of perception in information processing is to:

(A) sort out relevant from irrelevant information so the person is not overloaded

(B) classify information based on the sensory modality used for learning

(C) assign meaning to new information

(D) keep the person alert and responsive

(E) consolidate new information for storage in the working memory

60. Which of the following statements is true about corporal punishment?

(A) it is considered a form of negative punishment

(B) research has consistently shown it to be effective for aggressive behaviors

(C) it is banned in at least 27 states in the United States

(D) many learning theorists and mental health professionals view it as acceptable and useful

(E) research has consistently shown it to be effective for all types of unacceptable behaviors

61. Mr. Jones is a sixth-grade teacher in a public school. He strongly believes that boys should not be allowed to participate in classes such as home economics and keyboarding. He also believes that boys are behavior problems and need to be punished severely when they misbehave. Mr. Jones's belief system is an example of:

    (A) racial bias

    (B) observational learning experiences

    (C) gender bias

    (D) how teaching experiences influence classroom practices

    (E) self-fulfilling prophecy

62. Maya is in the fourth grade and tries very hard to succeed at everything she does. She is showing:

    (A) a high degree of achievement motivation

    (B) a high level of confidence

    (C) the positive effects of extrinsic motivation in focusing behavior

    (D) focused attention and sustained effort

    (E) strong compensation for feelings of inadequacy and inferiority

63. Juanita is a new third-grade student who has just recently moved to the United States from Mexico. According to research, the best teaching and learning strategies to use with her involve:

    (A) concrete and social learning approaches

    (B) visual and global learning approaches

    (C) a structured and quiet environment with clear learning goals

    (D) a noncompetitive classroom setting that emphasizes group participation

    (E) combining English and Spanish in written and spoken work assignments

64. A psychology instructor administered a group multiple-choice examination to the 80 students in her class. The lowest grade achieved was a 44, and the highest grade achieved was a 91. The following distribution of scores was obtained using letter grades:

Grade	Students
A	2
B	12
C	25
D	31
F	10

For the above distribution of scores, the range is:

(A) 4

(B) 47

(C) 29

(D) 91

(E) unable to be determined from the data provided

65. Albert tried to pass a note to Linda during class while Ms. Taylor was writing on the chalkboard. As Linda took the note and began to read it, Ms. Taylor stopped writing on the board, strolled to Linda's desk, and asked to see the note. Ms. Taylor was showing:

(A) an authoritative disciplinary approach

(B) an Assertive Discipline approach

(C) an authoritarian disciplinary approach

(D) withitness

(E) a dictatorial management approach

66. Philip, a three-year-old child, has learned the word *house* and associates windows, black shutters, a white door, and yellow with it. This is an example of how _____ operate.

    (A) schemata

    (B) concepts

    (C) episodic memories

    (D) algorithms

    (E) language and vocabulary development

67. When a child sees the results of a model's behavior, the effects of the observation can be magnified greatly and motivate the child. This process is called:

    (A) vicarious punishment

    (B) vicarious reinforcement

    (C) synthesized modeling

    (D) vicarious learning

    (E) vicarious imitation

68. Which of the following statements regarding how teachers interact with students in the school is true?

    (A) teachers interact more with girls than boys

    (B) teachers view boys as dependent thinkers who need to be guided by the teacher

    (C) teachers are more detached in how they interact with boys as compared with girls

    (D) teachers reward boys for their creative work more often than they reward girls

    (E) teachers interact with girls and boys at about equal frequencies

69. Which of the following statements is true?

    (A) motivation is stable for most children

    (B) motivation is variable across situations and activities

(C) motivation is best fostered by using extrinsic rewards

(D) motivation is best fostered by using intrinsic rewards

(E) motivation is taught to children by their parents

70. Michael has a great deal of difficulty remaining in his seat during class. His teacher often sees him staring out the window, and he often blurts out answers to questions or makes inappropriate comments. Michael is most likely exhibiting which of the following disorders:

(A) oppositional defiant disorder

(B) conduct disorder

(C) attention-deficit/hyperactivity disorder (ADHD)

(D) ADHD, predominately inattentive type

(E) Asperger's syndrome

71. Which of the following transformed scores has a mean of 100 and standard deviation of 15 points?

(A) grade-level equivalents   (D) T-scores

(B) Z-scores   (E) percentile scores

(C) an intelligence quotient

72. Mr. Ward believes that students should be given at least four warnings for misbehavior before they are actually given consequences. He writes a student's name on the board and puts a checkmark next to the name each time he catches the student misbehaving. Sometimes when a student has accumulated five checkmarks, Mr. Ward will send a note home to the student's parents. This management program does NOT provide:

(A) an operational definition of inappropriate conduct

(B) immediacy of consequences

(C) a strong enough punishment for the students

(D) enough parent contact and feedback

(E) enough primary reinforcers to encourage students to improve behavior

73. Previous learning experiences that affect new learning experiences by making the new learning more difficult or merging it with the previously learned knowledge is:

    (A) retroactive interference   (D) proactive interference

    (B) verbal interference   (E) transfer of learning

    (C) decay interference

74. Observational learning depends on:

    (A) attention, concentration, and intelligence

    (B) attention, retention, physical characteristics, and motivation

    (C) motivation, feedback looping, and information processing

    (D) visual imagery and verbal information

    (E) how much the observer admires or likes the model

75. Frank has just visited a physician who has prescribed Strattera for him. He is to take this medicine before lunch each day during the school year. Frank's physician has most likely diagnosed him as having:

    (A) attention-deficit/hyperactivity disorder (ADHD)

    (B) depression

    (C) anxiety disorder

    (D) suicidal tendencies

    (E) obsessive-compulsive disorder

76. Extrinsic rewards:

    (A) are essential to all forms of school-based learning

    (B) are the least effective way to motivate most younger children

    (C) should include using films and guest speakers to increase their impact on students

    (D) can interfere with the development of intrinsic motivation

    (E) should be paired with verbal support to maximize their positive impact on the child

77. Megan has had a great deal of difficulty getting along with her peers and teachers for the past four years. She often gets into conflicts with them and sometimes behaves very inappropriately toward them. Several times each day she has temper tantrums at school that disrupt the class setting. Megan is most likely showing a(n):

    (A) learning disability

    (B) behavior disorder

    (C) internalizing behavior disorder

    (D) normal reaction to a boring school program because she is gifted

    (E) ADHD pattern

78. A public school has selected a group test to measure students' intelligence levels as part of the admission criteria for participating in a program for gifted children. They give this test to all children during the middle of the third grade and again at the end of the third grade. They have found that many of the third graders have significantly different scores on each test, and teachers are confused about which score to use to make decisions. This test could be criticized for lacking which type of reliability?

    (A) alternate forms   (D) test-retest

    (B) split-half   (E) internal

    (C) Kuder-Richardson

79. Assertive discipline techniques are used appropriately when the teacher:

    (A) uses I-messages to communicate to students how their behavior affects others

    (B) gives clear and firm feedback followed by immediate consequences

    (C) provides a warning statement for the first misbehavior so students have a chance to change and be more personally responsible for their behavior

    (D) uses a written contract with a token economy system to reinforce the terms of the contract

    (E) includes the student's family in the behavior management process

80. A high school student is taking a course in vocational education. In the course the student is required to compute the area of a room to determine the number of tiles needed to replace the floor. This situation is an example of:

    (A) high-road transfer

    (B) metacognition

    (C) general transfer of information

    (D) specific transfer of information

    (E) generalization

81. A child's threats to commit suicide should be interpreted as:

    (A) an attention-seeking behavior by the child

    (B) an attempt by the child to take control of a situation

    (C) an idle comment designed for its shock value

    (D) a cry for help and should be responded to in a professionally urgent manner

    (E) a rather typical characteristic of children and adolescents in dealing with unpleasant tasks

82. Chelsea is in the fourth grade and has performed very well academically. She has recently started to have problems remembering what to do when the teacher gives directions with more than two steps. She sometimes confuses the sequence of the instructions or simply forgets them altogether. Chelsea might be exhibiting which of the following:

    (A) mental retardation

    (B) gifted and talented

    (C) ADHD

    (D) learning disability

    (E) speech and language disorder

83. An acceptable level of test-retest reliability is considered to be at least:

   (A) .70   (D) .95

   (B) .80   (E) .75

   (C) .90

84. A seven-year-old child is taking a science course that discusses plant growth. The teacher explains to the class that seeds are put into the ground and germinate. Through this process the seeds become plants. The child argues with the teacher that it is impossible for a seed to become a plant because the seed does not look at all like a plant. The child's reaction is the result of the child's:

   (A) response set

   (B) functional fixedness

   (C) developmental immaturity

   (D) mental retardation

   (E) lack of parental support in developing the child's basic academic skills

85. All of the following behaviors are characteristic of ADHD EXCEPT:

   (A) increased motor activity

   (B) difficulty with sustained attention

   (C) impulsivity and problems with self-control

   (D) physical and verbal aggression

   (E) difficulty with sustained concentration

86. Joseph is in a special education program where he receives four hours a day of educational and remedial support services as part of his school program. He has been identified as being mentally retarded. At which level of retardation is he probably functioning?

   (A) intermittent   (D) pervasive

   (B) limited   (E) borderline

   (C) extensive

87. Which of the following is NOT required under federal and state statutes when evaluating children?

    (A) the child must be tested in their native language by qualified personnel

    (B) test results should be related to the educational program

    (C) test procedures must be modified for all children considered exceptional

    (D) parents must be involved in the decision to test the child

    (E) each child is entitled to due process

88. Which of the following techniques is NOT a problem-solving strategy?

    (A) IDEAL

    (B) means-ends analysis

    (C) brainstorming

    (D) selective attention

    (E) group discussions

89. A three-year-old child responds to adult questions by making comments such as "go bye bye" and "me eat." This child's communication is described as:

    (A) cooing   (D) telegraphic speech

    (B) babbling   (E) motherese

    (C) holophrastic speech

90. Which of the following statements is true?

    (A) speech disorders are more serious than articulation disorders

    (B) language disorders are more serious than speech disorders

    (C) fluency disorders are similar to articulation difficulties

    (D) speech disorders are more serious than language disorders

    (E) speech and language disorders are easily correctible and usually do not seriously affect school performance

91. Which type of validity measures how well a test correlates with another test?

    (A) face   (D) content

    (B) predictive   (E) concurrent

    (C) construct

92. Most forgetting occurs within _____ after initial learning in school.

    (A) 4 weeks   (D) 48 hours

    (B) 24 hours   (E) 60 minutes

    (C) 1 week

93. Chomsky has proposed the existence of which of the following mechanisms in the development of human speech?

    (A) language acquisition device

    (B) phonological recoding mechanism

    (C) short-term memory storage system

    (D) motherese

    (E) two-store model of memory

94. Sometimes children who have visual or hearing impairments will develop:

    (A) exceptional learning ability in the intact sense organ

    (B) motor coordination difficulties

    (C) learned helplessness

    (D) ADHD

    (E) exceptional written language skills

95. Which type of validity measures how well the test items represent the area or domain measured by a test?

    (A) face   (D) content

    (B) predictive   (E) concurrent

    (C) construct

96. Providing students with clearly expressed objectives and advance organizers will:

    (A) make encoding of information more rapid and accurate

    (B) increase and focus attention

    (C) increase and focus perception

    (D) facilitate retrieval of knowledge from long-term memory

    (E) enhance encoding and decoding of information in the short-term memory system

97. The ultimate goal of development is to:

    (A) reflect the effects of genetics on daily behavior

    (B) allow body structures and physical functions to mature

    (C) lead to better overall adaptation and adjustment

    (D) modify genetically programmed codes to fit the environment where the person lives

    (E) prepare the child for social adaptation as an adult

98. Which of the following is NOT a characteristic of Renzulli's triad model of educating gifted and talented children?

    (A) individual and small-group activities dealing with real problems

    (B) group training experiences to teach problem-solving skills

    (C) general exploration projects and activities to focus interests

    (D) participation in classical studies and the fine arts

    (E) specific individual projects based on a student's expressed interests

99. Ms. Johnson is a second-grade teacher who believes that children will learn to read only when they know the individual sounds represented by each written letter. She spends most of the second-grade year drilling her students in sound–written symbol relationships. Ms. Johnson is teaching her students to read by using a:

   (A) meaning emphasis approach

   (B) whole language approach

   (C) phonics approach

   (D) combined code emphasis and meaning emphasis approach

   (E) language experience approach

100. The IEP for each exceptional child can be considered:

   (A) a legal document that outlines the student's educational objectives and goals

   (B) a set of recommendations to guide teachers in educating an exceptional child

   (C) a summary of the assessment procedures and results used to identify and place a child

   (D) relevant only for children placed into special education programs for more than half the school day

   (E) a set of instructional and curricular guidelines and recommendations that will probably help the child learn better

CLEP INTRODUCTION TO EDUCATIONAL PSYCHOLOGY PRACTICE TEST 2

1.	(B)	26.	(A)	51.	(E)	76.	(D)
2.	(A)	27.	(A)	52.	(B)	77.	(B)
3.	(D)	28.	(C)	53.	(A)	78.	(D)
4.	(D)	29.	(B)	54.	(A)	79.	(B)
5.	(C)	30.	(B)	55.	(B)	80.	(D)
6.	(C)	31.	(D)	56.	(D)	81.	(D)
7.	(A)	32.	(A)	57.	(A)	82.	(B)
8.	(A)	33.	(C)	58.	(A)	83.	(B)
9.	(C)	34.	(C)	59.	(C)	84.	(C)
10.	(A)	35.	(D)	60.	(C)	85.	(D)
11.	(D)	36.	(D)	61.	(C)	86.	(C)
12.	(A)	37.	(A)	62.	(A)	87.	(C)
13.	(B)	38.	(D)	63.	(A)	88.	(D)
14.	(B)	39.	(C)	64.	(B)	89.	(D)
15.	(D)	40.	(A)	65.	(D)	90.	(B)
16.	(C)	41.	(C)	66.	(A)	91.	(E)
17.	(D)	42.	(A)	67.	(D)	92.	(A)
18.	(A)	43.	(D)	68.	(D)	93.	(A)
19.	(C)	44.	(A)	69.	(B)	94.	(C)
20.	(C)	45.	(D)	70.	(C)	95.	(C)
21.	(C)	46.	(C)	71.	(C)	96.	(B)
22.	(A)	47.	(B)	72.	(B)	97.	(C)
23.	(B)	48.	(A)	73.	(D)	98.	(D)
24.	(D)	49.	(B)	74.	(B)	99.	(C)
25.	(A)	50.	(D)	75.	(A)	100.	(A)

DETAILED EXPLANATIONS OF ANSWERS

PRACTICE TEST 2

1.   **(B)**   Character is a dominant set of underlying qualities that a person shows in the general and consistent ways he or she interacts with other people. It is the underlying foundation that directs and governs a person's attitude and approach toward interacting with others.

2.   **(A)**   Acronyms are used to remember lists of items by using the first letter from each word in the list to create one short word that triggers recall of the list. NATO is an acronym for North Atlantic Treaty Organization.

3.   **(D)**   Shaping consists of eight steps that teach a child to behave in a desired way. Shaping is used when the behavior occurs infrequently or not at all. By analyzing the chain of behaviors leading up to the desired behavior, it is possible to gradually change the child's behavior to a more acceptable level.

4.   **(D)**   Object permanence describes a child's capacity to remember objects when they are not visible. According to Piaget it is a characteristic that begins to develop during the latter part of the sensorimotor stage.

5.   **(C)**   Attribution theory emphasizes the belief that people have control over their ability to effect change in their world. With an internal locus of control people believe they are largely in control of whether they succeed or fail.

6.   **(C)**   Dropout rates among high school students are nearly twice as high for children who live in low-SES families. The dropout rates for children living in the poorest families exceeds 50 percent.

7.   **(A)**   It is most likely that much of the content being taught in a course on values clarification deals with a student's attitudes, views, and values about life issues. The purpose of such a course would be to help students clarify their individual perspectives on these issues.

8.   **(A)**   Expository teaching emphasizes the development of abstract thinking patterns that show the underlying common characteristics that link apparently dissimilar concepts and ideas.

9.   **(C)**   In this example only one group is given two independent questionnaires. One way to evaluate the findings from this survey study is to correlate the scores from the depression scale with those from the exercise scale. The researcher has not controlled any variables in the sample.

10.   **(A)**   Research indicates that children learn moral values most effectively by being involved in ongoing and active relationships with adults who guide and support them to make the correct moral responses and choices.

11.   **(D)**   The episodic memory is part of the long-term memory and contains personal and social experiences, events, and activities in which the person has actually participated.

12.   **(A)**   The Premack principle states that a preferred activity is used to strengthen a less preferred behavior so that it will occur more often. In other words, if you do activity A, then you will receive activity B.

13.   **(B)**   According to Piaget, conservation demonstrates a child's ability to see that an amount of matter remains the same regardless of its shape or the number of pieces into which it is divided.

14.   **(B)**   High self-efficacy teachers believe they are able to get most students to learn and be successful in school. They will make the appropriate accommodations to encourage students and motivate them to learn, regardless of how challenging the students are.

15.   **(D)**   Research has shown that the longer children remain in school, the more likely that their scores on intelligence tests will increase (Ceci, 1991). These test score increases probably reflect the effects of mental stimulation and enrichment that are part of continuing education.

16. **(C)** Multiple-choice tests are widely used classroom testing strategy because the questions can be developed in a way that measures rote recall and recognition of specific factual knowledge.

17. **(D)** Research has shown that guided discovery results in more effective transfer of information to new situations and better long-term memory of concepts and facts than does direct instruction (Bay, Staver, Bryan & Hale, 1992).

18. **(A)** The longitudinal design is used to study developmental trends and patterns of growth with measurements taken on the same group of people over several different occasions. This is the most effective way to identify the unique ways in which different mothers form bonds over time with their children.

19. **(C)** If a person believes that the consequences of decisions and behaviors are effective in attaining a goal, that person will view those decisions and behaviors as being morally appropriate and acceptable. Moreover, the person will see her/himself as having character and simply doing what is necessary to avoid failing at a task.

20. **(C)** Maintenance rehearsal occurs when a person repeatedly states, either out loud or mentally, the exact information that is being learned and memorized. It is not a very efficient or effective way to store information in long-term memory, but it can be effective when the person must remember the information for a short time.

21. **(C)** Time-out is a negative punishment because it involves removing the child from a desirable situation (the classroom with peers who give the child attention) and placing him or her into a low-stimulus setting where they are not reinforced for inappropriate behavior. Negative punishment always involves removing something desired by the child contingent upon unacceptable conduct.

22. **(A)** Social interactions provide the child with important information about the world. This information is internalized by the child and related to how he or she sees, perceives, and interprets it. Social interactions and social feedback encourage a child's cognitive and mental structures development.

23. **(B)** Intrinsic motivators are rewards that people experience internally for performing an activity or succeeding at a level they have identified as reflecting success.

24. **(D)** Fluid intelligence reflects a general ability to solve new problems and tasks quickly and effectively. It is one of the two types of intelligence that exist, according to Cattell (1971). The second type of intelligence in this model is crystallized, which reflects the amount of education a person has accumulated over time.

25. **(A)** It is important that the stems for each multiple-choice question are worded clearly to express the intent of the question without confusion or ambiguity.

26. **(A)** Advance organizers are most effective when used to present new and rather complicated information, particularly when this material has a clear organization and structure in which later concepts evolve from concepts and principles taught earlier.

27. **(A)** Reliability describes the consistency of test scores or experimental outcomes across multiple administrations of a test or experiment to the same subject or group of subjects. Unreliable results indicate the presence of random or unsystematic fluctuations in the test instrument.

28. **(C)** An acrostic device uses the first letter from each word in a list to create a sentence in which each word cues the target items in the list. It is a very effective memory strategy to retain lists of information in the proper order.

29. **(B)** An unconditioned stimulus is one in which there is no prior learning necessary for the person to respond in a specific way. Some examples of unconditioned responses include squinting your eyes in reaction to a loud or unpleasant noise, blinking your eyes when someone flicks their fingers at your eyes, or salivating when you eat a preferred food.

30. **(B)** One of the most difficult and challenging tasks for most adolescents is to clarify their personal identity. Adolescents often have an unclear or incomplete sense of who they are and may actually take on different social roles and pretenses to test others' reactions to them.

31. **(D)** Clearly defined and concrete goals help students focus their attention and efforts in a productive way to complete tasks and learn new skills. These goals also help mobilize students and increase persistence and success to achieve a positive outcome.

32. **(A)** The score achieved on an intelligence test simply reflects the ratio between a person's mental age divided by the person's chronological age. This ratio is then multiplied by 100 to eliminate the decimal and make it easier for people to understand the meaning of the score.

33. **(C)** The psychomotor domain presents the sequence of physical abilities and behavioral competence leading to student competence in a subject.

34. **(C)** The teacher's role is that of a consultant and guide to each group. This role requires the teacher to be mobile throughout the classroom and make frequent contacts with each group to keep the momentum moving.

35. **(D)** Internal Review Boards will carefully examine a research study, especially when deception is used. Deception does not mean that the participants will be mistreated or suffer psychological trauma. When done appropriately and judiciously, it can provide the researcher with accurate, important information about real human behaviors and attitudes.

36. **(D)** Cognitive psychology studies how people process and analyze the world. It examines how mental activities such as attention, perception, memory, and problem solving affect the person's interpretation of reality. Each of these cognitive processes occurs within a person's mind and creates an internal view of the external world.

37. **(A)** A secondary reinforcer is any neutral stimulus that is linked with a primary reinforcer. Common secondary reinforcers are money, grades in school, or tokens used in various behavior management programs.

38. **(D)** According to Kohlberg, preconventional moral reasoning is closely linked to compliance with authority because authority gives rewards and punishments to children. This is the first stage of moral reasoning and development and tends to be highly focused on what is in the best interest of the child regardless of how these decisions impact other people.

39. **(C)** As children enter the middle school grades, the effectiveness of most reinforcers that can be used in the schools diminishes greatly. It is not unusual for adult approval to lose much of its influence because peer approval is much more important to children at that age.

40. **(A)** The use of aptitude tests to group students homogeneously has been used with the belief that students with common characteristics or aptitudes will learn more effectively and at higher levels. This practice, called tracking, has been seriously criticized for many reasons.

41. **(C)** Formative evaluation is an ongoing diagnostic process that identifies specifically and clearly areas where the student is having problems and gives corrective intervention directly to correct these problem areas.

42. **(A)** Creating an acronym involves using the first letters of several items that must be remembered to form a familiar word, either real or made up, that triggers recall of the series. FLOPT represents the five lobes in the brain: frontal, limbic, occipital, parietal, and temporal.

43. **(D)** Participation in a study is completely voluntary, even if the person signs an informed consent form initially. The person has the freedom to withdraw from the experiment at any time and for any reason. The researcher cannot seek any kind of legal intervention or threaten to expose the person publicly. The person simply has to refuse to participate without offering any further explanation.

44. **(A)** The long-term memory contains two separate but interrelated files. The first file is called semantic memory because it stores information related to factual knowledge and application of procedures to solve problems or perform skills. The episodic memory contains memories of personal and social experiences or activities that the person has participated in or encountered.

45. **(D)** Interval categories require that a specific period of time passes before the first acceptable behavior shown by the child is reinforced.

46. **(C)** According to Marsh (1993), adolescents develop specific concepts about themselves as people in each of five different areas of life. Self-concept evolves based on the degree of perceived competence and success the adolescent experiences in these areas.

47. **(B)** Anger and oppositional behavior typically reflect some other kind of emotional disorder or problem. The most common symptoms of anxiety are upset stomach and feelings of nausea, sweaty palms, worrying and intrusive thoughts, and an increased heart rate. These symptoms can have a significant and negative effect on the child's ability to function in school.

48. **(A)**   Achievement tests are used to measure the amount of information a student has acquired at the conclusion of a course or program of study.

49. **(B)**   Descriptive grading systems use a variety of terms to describe how the child is performing relative to either teacher expectations or other children in the same class or grade. These grading schemes (usually with only 3 options for evaluation) can be confusing to parents and often fail to provide specifics about the child's actual functional levels.

50. **(D)**   Maintenance bilingual education programs are used mainly during the elementary grades and strive to make students proficient in both English and their native language. These programs retain respect for the child's cultural heritage and traditions.

51. **(E)**   Inferential statistics are widely used in research studies because they allow the researcher to make educated guesses about cause-and-effect relationships when between-group differences are determined. Some of the most commonly used statistics include the t-test and analysis of variance procedures.

52. **(B)**   One of the most important aspects of new learning is the development of automaticity. Automaticity comes about when a child has had sufficient opportunity for drill, practice, and repetition of new skills and concepts that they become automatic when used. This frees the limited attention space in the child's working memory so that more attention and space can be applied to using the information and concepts for problem-solving situations.

53. **(A)**   Skinner argues that punishment approaches never work to change behavior; they merely suppress it. The child is not taught how to behave correctly. Punishment shows the child that if you are more powerful than another person then you can be dominant and in control.

54. **(A)**   Research suggests that adolescents can be categorized into one of four distinct social groups. Controversial adolescents are those who are socially engaged with their peers but also show inappropriate and aggressive behavior at times. Peer reactions to them are mixed, with some peers accepting them and others rejecting them.

55. **(B)**   Persons with an external locus of control attribute success and failure to circumstances that lie outside their control. Sometimes they attribute success or failure to luck, being liked or disliked by a person or teacher, or lack of intelligence or family support. Students with this outlook often do poorly in school because they refuse to put forth the effort necessary to learn.

56. **(D)**   It is important for teachers to stimulate and encourage creative thinking skills by being flexible, being receptive to new perspectives, and allowing a diversity of reasonable solution options to reach the correct solution to a problem.

57. **(A)**   Criterion-referenced tests are used to determine if a child meets a predetermined and specific level of competency following a period of instruction. The testing tells the teacher what level and rate of skill mastery the student has achieved for the objective criteria.

58. **(A)**   The self-fulfilling prophecy, first proposed by Rosenthal and Jacobsen (1968), exists when a teacher's expectations about how a child will either behave or learn come true, even when there were no prior data to support the expectations.

59. **(C)**   Perception occurs in the working memory as new information enters it. Perception analyzes this information, integrates it with past knowledge and experiences, and assigns meaning to it.

60. **(C)**   Corporal punishment is largely viewed as an unacceptable and inappropriate behavior management technique because it has questionable effectiveness and generally does not alter behavior in a positive way. It is banned by at least 27 states in the United States at this time.

61. **(C)**   Gender bias exists when a person has clear-cut and concrete viewpoints about how males and females should behave. These viewpoints reflect biases about how the individual sees each gender according to strengths and weaknesses. The person tends to use these biases in an indiscriminate manner and ignores or distorts an individual's actual strengths and weaknesses.

62. **(A)**   Achievement motivation is a person's desire to do well and perform to the best of his or her ability.

63. **(A)**   Research (Buenning & Tollefson, 1987) has suggested that Mexican American children seem to prefer to learn using approaches that emphasize holistic, concrete, and social learning styles. Approaches that stress abstract or analytical learning experiences are often inappropriate and ineffective and sometimes can create significant learning obstacles for these children.

64. **(B)**   The range is the difference between the highest and lowest scores in a distribution. It is based on the actual test scores, even if these scores are later transformed into letter grades.

65. **(D)**   Withitness describes the teacher being actively involved with and knowledgeable about the classroom dynamics among students and communicating this knowledge to students so they know that the teacher is in control. The concept was proposed by Kounin (1970).

66. **(A)**   Schemata are abstract ideas that reside in the long-term memory. They provide summaries and examples of experiences and knowledge so a person has some expectations about how the world should operate in new experiences. The concepts underlying a schema are called subschemata.

67. **(D)**   Vicarious learning occurs when a child witnesses the effects of a model's behavior in achieving or failing to achieve a desired outcome. This observation helps the child develop a set of expectations about the probability of these same behaviors working well or ineffectively for them.

68. **(D)**   A number of studies have shown that many teachers interact differently with boys and girls. Many teachers view boys as being more independent, less compliant, making more comments and observations during class discussions, and being more conceptual and abstract thinkers. These beliefs affect the quality of interaction between teachers with boys and girls in concrete and significant ways.

69. **(B)**   A person's level of motivation will vary throughout life and be affected by the task in which the person is involved, the people he or she is working with, and personal emotional characteristics at a given time.

70. **(C)**   ADHD is associated with three core symptoms: inattention, where the child is easily distracted; impulsivity, where the child behaves without thinking or evaluating how the behavior might affect others; and hyperactivity, typically shown by a great deal of inappropriate behavioral movements.

71. **(C)**   IQ scores typically have a mean of 100 and standard deviation of 15 points and are based on the normal curve distribution.

72. **(B)**   The children in this class are allowed to misbehave too many times before the possibility of receiving a consequence occurs. Even then, it is not always clear that the misbehaving students will receive the consequence, aside from having checkmarks placed next to their names on the chalkboard.

73. **(D)**   Proactive interference exists when a person learns a set of skills or knowledge and then is presented with a new learning situation in which similar information is taught. The previously learned knowledge can interfere with how easily and accurately the new material is learned.

74. **(B)**   Bandura (1965) proposed that there are four processes essential for observational learning to occur. These are: attention to the model's characteristics, ability to retain what has been seen, having the necessary physical qualities to perform the model's behaviors, and being motivated to behave in that way.

75. **(A)**   Strattera is one of the most commonly used psychotropic medications today to treat ADHD. Some other common medications that are widely used to treat this disorder are Ritalin and Adderall.

76. **(D)**   Relying too much on extrinsic rewards can teach students they should learn only when there is a direct and immediate payoff. Extrinsic rewards discourage children from developing an appreciation of learning as a mechanism to grow and mature.

77. **(B)**   Behavior disorders are characterized by serious and consistent problems in getting along with peers and/or teachers. These children are usually in conflict with others, show inappropriate patterns of social conduct, lack age-appropriate self-control, and sometimes fail school subjects.

78. **(D)**   The test lacks test-retest reliability. Test-retest reliability shows how stable the results are when the same group of children is tested using the same instrument at two different times.

79. **(B)**   Assertive discipline clearly and concretely identifies teacher expectations for conduct and gives students firm and calm verbal feedback, along with the appropriate consequences, for unacceptable behaviors.

80. **(D)** Specific transfer of information occurs when skills or facts learned in one situation are used almost identically to solve a problem in a new and similar situation. In this case the student is using multiplication skills learned in a mathematics class to solve a problem requiring multiplication in a vocational setting.

81. **(D)** Professionals should respond seriously and quickly when a child expresses suicidal ideas or intentions. Typically, these kinds of comments indicate that the child is experiencing levels of stress and emotional pain that are very high and overwhelming. It is a plea for help and should not be minimized or dismissed by the teacher.

82. **(D)** Learning disabilities exist in children who have average or higher intelligence but have difficulty with reading, mathematics, or written language. Many times these disabilities reflect problems with the child's ability to store, access, retrieve, or use information contained in the memory system.

83. **(B)** A minimum correlation of .80 is considered acceptable for tests when their reliability has been established using the test-retest procedure.

84. **(C)** During problem-solving activities it is very important that the teacher understands the child's current cognitive developmental status and functional levels. Trying to present information or knowledge to children who are developmentally unready to understand a concept will simply result in frustration for the teacher and failure for the child.

85. **(D)** ADHD is characterized by three core symptoms: hyperactivity, inattention, and impulsivity. Although some children with ADHD are verbally or physically aggressive, many children with ADHD show no aggression at all.

86. **(C)** Children with extensive mental retardation are likely to spend a large portion of their school day in special education and remedial support services. Most of these subjects will likely be academic in nature. For less-academic subjects (art, music, lunch) these children may be integrated with their regular education peers.

87. **(C)** Standardized tests should be administered in the same manner to all children, unless there is some reason stated in a child's individual educational program that justifies modified test administration procedures.

88. **(D)** Selective attention occurs when people focus on selected aspects of their surroundings so they are not overloaded or overwhelmed by too much stimuli.

89. **(D)** With telegraphic speech a child uses two-word utterances to express their needs or respond to adult input. This stage of speech development eventually leads the child to engage in more sophisticated utterances that become refined and form adult language communications. Most children conclude telegraphic speech utterances by around four years of age.

90. **(B)** In general, language disorders are more serious than speech disorders because a language disorder typically represents difficulty in either understanding spoken language or the ability to express ideas using spoken language.

91. **(E)** Concurrent validity for a test is established by correlating it with a test that is already accepted by the professional community and measures the same traits or characteristics as the first test.

92. **(A)** Research conducted by Semb and Ellis (1994) found that most forgetting in school occurs within the first 4 weeks following initial learning.

93. **(A)** Chomsky argued that humans are born with a mechanism that uniquely predisposes them to learn language. He named this the language acquisition device. Critical periods of time exist in the development of human language. If language development is interfered with during this time, these language skills will be difficult for the child to acquire later in life.

94. **(C)** Children with sensory impairments often have problems with their self-esteem because of the tremendous limitations imposed upon them by the sensory impairment. It is not unusual for these children to develop learned helplessness because of the exceptional challenges they encounter each day in most aspects of their lives.

95. **(C)** Construct validity identifies how well the items making up a test represent the domain or trait that the test claims to measure. This type of validity often relies on the use of factor analysis to demonstrate the existence of factors within the test that are associated with the domain or trait assessed.

96. **(B)**   Explicitly telling students about the specific information they need to learn and remember is an excellent and concrete way to focus their attention and efforts in an efficient manner.

97. **(C)**   Development is the process of changing over time in an orderly, systematic, and adaptive manner. The changes are long-lasting and intended to produce a better overall adaptation and adjustment by the person to the world. It is a highly complex process that is essential to survival.

98. **(D)**   Renzulli's triad model proposes three educational components for all gifted and talented children: general exploratory activities that enable students to learn about topics on their own and begin to focus their interests, group training activities to teach problem-solving skills and develop creative ways of resolving problems, and individual or small-group activities dealing with real-life problems.

99. **(C)**   The phonics approach emphasizes teaching children how to read and spell words by using letters to sound out the word. It is one of the code-emphasis strategies used for basic reading instruction.

100. **(A)**   The individualized educational program, usually referred to as the IEP, is a legal document that outlines specifically and concretely for teachers the child's current level of educational performance, short-term and long-term educational objectives to be achieved, additional support services necessary to help the child, a timeline to complete the plan, and specific evaluation criteria to determine if the educational program is effective for the child.

ANSWER SHEETS

CLEP INTRODUCTION TO EDUCATIONAL PSYCHOLOGY

TEST 1

1. Ⓐ Ⓑ Ⓒ Ⓓ Ⓔ	34. Ⓐ Ⓑ Ⓒ Ⓓ Ⓔ	67. Ⓐ Ⓑ Ⓒ Ⓓ Ⓔ
2. Ⓐ Ⓑ Ⓒ Ⓓ Ⓔ	35. Ⓐ Ⓑ Ⓒ Ⓓ Ⓔ	68. Ⓐ Ⓑ Ⓒ Ⓓ Ⓔ
3. Ⓐ Ⓑ Ⓒ Ⓓ Ⓔ	36. Ⓐ Ⓑ Ⓒ Ⓓ Ⓔ	69. Ⓐ Ⓑ Ⓒ Ⓓ Ⓔ
4. Ⓐ Ⓑ Ⓒ Ⓓ Ⓔ	37. Ⓐ Ⓑ Ⓒ Ⓓ Ⓔ	70. Ⓐ Ⓑ Ⓒ Ⓓ Ⓔ
5. Ⓐ Ⓑ Ⓒ Ⓓ Ⓔ	38. Ⓐ Ⓑ Ⓒ Ⓓ Ⓔ	71. Ⓐ Ⓑ Ⓒ Ⓓ Ⓔ
6. Ⓐ Ⓑ Ⓒ Ⓓ Ⓔ	39. Ⓐ Ⓑ Ⓒ Ⓓ Ⓔ	72. Ⓐ Ⓑ Ⓒ Ⓓ Ⓔ
7. Ⓐ Ⓑ Ⓒ Ⓓ Ⓔ	40. Ⓐ Ⓑ Ⓒ Ⓓ Ⓔ	73. Ⓐ Ⓑ Ⓒ Ⓓ Ⓔ
8. Ⓐ Ⓑ Ⓒ Ⓓ Ⓔ	41. Ⓐ Ⓑ Ⓒ Ⓓ Ⓔ	74. Ⓐ Ⓑ Ⓒ Ⓓ Ⓔ
9. Ⓐ Ⓑ Ⓒ Ⓓ Ⓔ	42. Ⓐ Ⓑ Ⓒ Ⓓ Ⓔ	75. Ⓐ Ⓑ Ⓒ Ⓓ Ⓔ
10. Ⓐ Ⓑ Ⓒ Ⓓ Ⓔ	43. Ⓐ Ⓑ Ⓒ Ⓓ Ⓔ	76. Ⓐ Ⓑ Ⓒ Ⓓ Ⓔ
11. Ⓐ Ⓑ Ⓒ Ⓓ Ⓔ	44. Ⓐ Ⓑ Ⓒ Ⓓ Ⓔ	77. Ⓐ Ⓑ Ⓒ Ⓓ Ⓔ
12. Ⓐ Ⓑ Ⓒ Ⓓ Ⓔ	45. Ⓐ Ⓑ Ⓒ Ⓓ Ⓔ	78. Ⓐ Ⓑ Ⓒ Ⓓ Ⓔ
13. Ⓐ Ⓑ Ⓒ Ⓓ Ⓔ	46. Ⓐ Ⓑ Ⓒ Ⓓ Ⓔ	79. Ⓐ Ⓑ Ⓒ Ⓓ Ⓔ
14. Ⓐ Ⓑ Ⓒ Ⓓ Ⓔ	47. Ⓐ Ⓑ Ⓒ Ⓓ Ⓔ	80. Ⓐ Ⓑ Ⓒ Ⓓ Ⓔ
15. Ⓐ Ⓑ Ⓒ Ⓓ Ⓔ	48. Ⓐ Ⓑ Ⓒ Ⓓ Ⓔ	81. Ⓐ Ⓑ Ⓒ Ⓓ Ⓔ
16. Ⓐ Ⓑ Ⓒ Ⓓ Ⓔ	49. Ⓐ Ⓑ Ⓒ Ⓓ Ⓔ	82. Ⓐ Ⓑ Ⓒ Ⓓ Ⓔ
17. Ⓐ Ⓑ Ⓒ Ⓓ Ⓔ	50. Ⓐ Ⓑ Ⓒ Ⓓ Ⓔ	83. Ⓐ Ⓑ Ⓒ Ⓓ Ⓔ
18. Ⓐ Ⓑ Ⓒ Ⓓ Ⓔ	51. Ⓐ Ⓑ Ⓒ Ⓓ Ⓔ	84. Ⓐ Ⓑ Ⓒ Ⓓ Ⓔ
19. Ⓐ Ⓑ Ⓒ Ⓓ Ⓔ	52. Ⓐ Ⓑ Ⓒ Ⓓ Ⓔ	85. Ⓐ Ⓑ Ⓒ Ⓓ Ⓔ
20. Ⓐ Ⓑ Ⓒ Ⓓ Ⓔ	53. Ⓐ Ⓑ Ⓒ Ⓓ Ⓔ	86. Ⓐ Ⓑ Ⓒ Ⓓ Ⓔ
21. Ⓐ Ⓑ Ⓒ Ⓓ Ⓔ	54. Ⓐ Ⓑ Ⓒ Ⓓ Ⓔ	87. Ⓐ Ⓑ Ⓒ Ⓓ Ⓔ
22. Ⓐ Ⓑ Ⓒ Ⓓ Ⓔ	55. Ⓐ Ⓑ Ⓒ Ⓓ Ⓔ	88. Ⓐ Ⓑ Ⓒ Ⓓ Ⓔ
23. Ⓐ Ⓑ Ⓒ Ⓓ Ⓔ	56. Ⓐ Ⓑ Ⓒ Ⓓ Ⓔ	89. Ⓐ Ⓑ Ⓒ Ⓓ Ⓔ
24. Ⓐ Ⓑ Ⓒ Ⓓ Ⓔ	57. Ⓐ Ⓑ Ⓒ Ⓓ Ⓔ	90. Ⓐ Ⓑ Ⓒ Ⓓ Ⓔ
25. Ⓐ Ⓑ Ⓒ Ⓓ Ⓔ	58. Ⓐ Ⓑ Ⓒ Ⓓ Ⓔ	91. Ⓐ Ⓑ Ⓒ Ⓓ Ⓔ
26. Ⓐ Ⓑ Ⓒ Ⓓ Ⓔ	59. Ⓐ Ⓑ Ⓒ Ⓓ Ⓔ	92. Ⓐ Ⓑ Ⓒ Ⓓ Ⓔ
27. Ⓐ Ⓑ Ⓒ Ⓓ Ⓔ	60. Ⓐ Ⓑ Ⓒ Ⓓ Ⓔ	93. Ⓐ Ⓑ Ⓒ Ⓓ Ⓔ
28. Ⓐ Ⓑ Ⓒ Ⓓ Ⓔ	61. Ⓐ Ⓑ Ⓒ Ⓓ Ⓔ	94. Ⓐ Ⓑ Ⓒ Ⓓ Ⓔ
29. Ⓐ Ⓑ Ⓒ Ⓓ Ⓔ	62. Ⓐ Ⓑ Ⓒ Ⓓ Ⓔ	95. Ⓐ Ⓑ Ⓒ Ⓓ Ⓔ
30. Ⓐ Ⓑ Ⓒ Ⓓ Ⓔ	63. Ⓐ Ⓑ Ⓒ Ⓓ Ⓔ	96. Ⓐ Ⓑ Ⓒ Ⓓ Ⓔ
31. Ⓐ Ⓑ Ⓒ Ⓓ Ⓔ	64. Ⓐ Ⓑ Ⓒ Ⓓ Ⓔ	97. Ⓐ Ⓑ Ⓒ Ⓓ Ⓔ
32. Ⓐ Ⓑ Ⓒ Ⓓ Ⓔ	65. Ⓐ Ⓑ Ⓒ Ⓓ Ⓔ	98. Ⓐ Ⓑ Ⓒ Ⓓ Ⓔ
33. Ⓐ Ⓑ Ⓒ Ⓓ Ⓔ	66. Ⓐ Ⓑ Ⓒ Ⓓ Ⓔ	99. Ⓐ Ⓑ Ⓒ Ⓓ Ⓔ
		100. Ⓐ Ⓑ Ⓒ Ⓓ Ⓔ

CLEP INTRODUCTION TO EDUCATIONAL PSYCHOLOGY

TEST 2

1. Ⓐ Ⓑ Ⓒ Ⓓ Ⓔ
2. Ⓐ Ⓑ Ⓒ Ⓓ Ⓔ
3. Ⓐ Ⓑ Ⓒ Ⓓ Ⓔ
4. Ⓐ Ⓑ Ⓒ Ⓓ Ⓔ
5. Ⓐ Ⓑ Ⓒ Ⓓ Ⓔ
6. Ⓐ Ⓑ Ⓒ Ⓓ Ⓔ
7. Ⓐ Ⓑ Ⓒ Ⓓ Ⓔ
8. Ⓐ Ⓑ Ⓒ Ⓓ Ⓔ
9. Ⓐ Ⓑ Ⓒ Ⓓ Ⓔ
10. Ⓐ Ⓑ Ⓒ Ⓓ Ⓔ
11. Ⓐ Ⓑ Ⓒ Ⓓ Ⓔ
12. Ⓐ Ⓑ Ⓒ Ⓓ Ⓔ
13. Ⓐ Ⓑ Ⓒ Ⓓ Ⓔ
14. Ⓐ Ⓑ Ⓒ Ⓓ Ⓔ
15. Ⓐ Ⓑ Ⓒ Ⓓ Ⓔ
16. Ⓐ Ⓑ Ⓒ Ⓓ Ⓔ
17. Ⓐ Ⓑ Ⓒ Ⓓ Ⓔ
18. Ⓐ Ⓑ Ⓒ Ⓓ Ⓔ
19. Ⓐ Ⓑ Ⓒ Ⓓ Ⓔ
20. Ⓐ Ⓑ Ⓒ Ⓓ Ⓔ
21. Ⓐ Ⓑ Ⓒ Ⓓ Ⓔ
22. Ⓐ Ⓑ Ⓒ Ⓓ Ⓔ
23. Ⓐ Ⓑ Ⓒ Ⓓ Ⓔ
24. Ⓐ Ⓑ Ⓒ Ⓓ Ⓔ
25. Ⓐ Ⓑ Ⓒ Ⓓ Ⓔ
26. Ⓐ Ⓑ Ⓒ Ⓓ Ⓔ
27. Ⓐ Ⓑ Ⓒ Ⓓ Ⓔ
28. Ⓐ Ⓑ Ⓒ Ⓓ Ⓔ
29. Ⓐ Ⓑ Ⓒ Ⓓ Ⓔ
30. Ⓐ Ⓑ Ⓒ Ⓓ Ⓔ
31. Ⓐ Ⓑ Ⓒ Ⓓ Ⓔ
32. Ⓐ Ⓑ Ⓒ Ⓓ Ⓔ
33. Ⓐ Ⓑ Ⓒ Ⓓ Ⓔ
34. Ⓐ Ⓑ Ⓒ Ⓓ Ⓔ
35. Ⓐ Ⓑ Ⓒ Ⓓ Ⓔ
36. Ⓐ Ⓑ Ⓒ Ⓓ Ⓔ
37. Ⓐ Ⓑ Ⓒ Ⓓ Ⓔ
38. Ⓐ Ⓑ Ⓒ Ⓓ Ⓔ
39. Ⓐ Ⓑ Ⓒ Ⓓ Ⓔ
40. Ⓐ Ⓑ Ⓒ Ⓓ Ⓔ
41. Ⓐ Ⓑ Ⓒ Ⓓ Ⓔ
42. Ⓐ Ⓑ Ⓒ Ⓓ Ⓔ
43. Ⓐ Ⓑ Ⓒ Ⓓ Ⓔ
44. Ⓐ Ⓑ Ⓒ Ⓓ Ⓔ
45. Ⓐ Ⓑ Ⓒ Ⓓ Ⓔ
46. Ⓐ Ⓑ Ⓒ Ⓓ Ⓔ
47. Ⓐ Ⓑ Ⓒ Ⓓ Ⓔ
48. Ⓐ Ⓑ Ⓒ Ⓓ Ⓔ
49. Ⓐ Ⓑ Ⓒ Ⓓ Ⓔ
50. Ⓐ Ⓑ Ⓒ Ⓓ Ⓔ
51. Ⓐ Ⓑ Ⓒ Ⓓ Ⓔ
52. Ⓐ Ⓑ Ⓒ Ⓓ Ⓔ
53. Ⓐ Ⓑ Ⓒ Ⓓ Ⓔ
54. Ⓐ Ⓑ Ⓒ Ⓓ Ⓔ
55. Ⓐ Ⓑ Ⓒ Ⓓ Ⓔ
56. Ⓐ Ⓑ Ⓒ Ⓓ Ⓔ
57. Ⓐ Ⓑ Ⓒ Ⓓ Ⓔ
58. Ⓐ Ⓑ Ⓒ Ⓓ Ⓔ
59. Ⓐ Ⓑ Ⓒ Ⓓ Ⓔ
60. Ⓐ Ⓑ Ⓒ Ⓓ Ⓔ
61. Ⓐ Ⓑ Ⓒ Ⓓ Ⓔ
62. Ⓐ Ⓑ Ⓒ Ⓓ Ⓔ
63. Ⓐ Ⓑ Ⓒ Ⓓ Ⓔ
64. Ⓐ Ⓑ Ⓒ Ⓓ Ⓔ
65. Ⓐ Ⓑ Ⓒ Ⓓ Ⓔ
66. Ⓐ Ⓑ Ⓒ Ⓓ Ⓔ
67. Ⓐ Ⓑ Ⓒ Ⓓ Ⓔ
68. Ⓐ Ⓑ Ⓒ Ⓓ Ⓔ
69. Ⓐ Ⓑ Ⓒ Ⓓ Ⓔ
70. Ⓐ Ⓑ Ⓒ Ⓓ Ⓔ
71. Ⓐ Ⓑ Ⓒ Ⓓ Ⓔ
72. Ⓐ Ⓑ Ⓒ Ⓓ Ⓔ
73. Ⓐ Ⓑ Ⓒ Ⓓ Ⓔ
74. Ⓐ Ⓑ Ⓒ Ⓓ Ⓔ
75. Ⓐ Ⓑ Ⓒ Ⓓ Ⓔ
76. Ⓐ Ⓑ Ⓒ Ⓓ Ⓔ
77. Ⓐ Ⓑ Ⓒ Ⓓ Ⓔ
78. Ⓐ Ⓑ Ⓒ Ⓓ Ⓔ
79. Ⓐ Ⓑ Ⓒ Ⓓ Ⓔ
80. Ⓐ Ⓑ Ⓒ Ⓓ Ⓔ
81. Ⓐ Ⓑ Ⓒ Ⓓ Ⓔ
82. Ⓐ Ⓑ Ⓒ Ⓓ Ⓔ
83. Ⓐ Ⓑ Ⓒ Ⓓ Ⓔ
84. Ⓐ Ⓑ Ⓒ Ⓓ Ⓔ
85. Ⓐ Ⓑ Ⓒ Ⓓ Ⓔ
86. Ⓐ Ⓑ Ⓒ Ⓓ Ⓔ
87. Ⓐ Ⓑ Ⓒ Ⓓ Ⓔ
88. Ⓐ Ⓑ Ⓒ Ⓓ Ⓔ
89. Ⓐ Ⓑ Ⓒ Ⓓ Ⓔ
90. Ⓐ Ⓑ Ⓒ Ⓓ Ⓔ
91. Ⓐ Ⓑ Ⓒ Ⓓ Ⓔ
92. Ⓐ Ⓑ Ⓒ Ⓓ Ⓔ
93. Ⓐ Ⓑ Ⓒ Ⓓ Ⓔ
94. Ⓐ Ⓑ Ⓒ Ⓓ Ⓔ
95. Ⓐ Ⓑ Ⓒ Ⓓ Ⓔ
96. Ⓐ Ⓑ Ⓒ Ⓓ Ⓔ
97. Ⓐ Ⓑ Ⓒ Ⓓ Ⓔ
98. Ⓐ Ⓑ Ⓒ Ⓓ Ⓔ
99. Ⓐ Ⓑ Ⓒ Ⓓ Ⓔ
100. Ⓐ Ⓑ Ⓒ Ⓓ Ⓔ

Glossary

Achievement Motivation — the degree to which a person actively strives to excel in life.

Acronym — a mnemonic device that uses the first letter of each item in a list to create a short, easily remembered concept. Acronyms are effective for learning and recalling short lists of items.

Acrostic — a mnemonic device that makes a sentence based on the first letter contained in a list of items to be remembered.

Algorithm — a step-by-step process to achieve a goal or solve a problem.

Analogy — a similarity between a new concept and a previously learned concept.

Attention — a conscious and selective focus on stimuli in the world to determine what is important from what is irrelevant.

Attribution Theory — posits that a person's behavior and motivation are determined by how the person thinks about and views the world.

Automaticity — the ability to perform an operation or task with very little conscious effort.

Brainstorming — two or more people working together to suggest all the ways they can think of to solve a problem. None of the suggestions is evaluated as a possible solution until all suggestions have been made.

Character — a pervasive and dominant set of underlying qualities of a person reflecting a general and consistent tendency to behave in ways that are courageous, honest, responsible, and respectful of the rights of others.

Character Education Program — a program designed to enhance character and moral development in an educational setting and to teach children how to apply this knowledge to real life.

Chunking — a process of combining information into larger sets that are easier to recall.

Classical Conditioning — the association of a neutral stimulus with an automatic response.

Community-Based Education Program — a program that emphasizes democratic decision-making processes in the real world of the community and the larger society, rather than merely in the classroom setting.

Conditioned Response (CR) — a learned response to a previously neutral stimulus.

Conditioned Stimulus (CS) — a previously neutral stimulus that has become repeatedly associated with a learned response.

Contingency Contracting — the teacher and student jointly develop a written contract specifying a set of mutually agreed-on academic and/or social behavioral goals. Rewards or consequences are given based on how well the student meets the contract terms.

Corporal Punishment — a highly controversial behavior management approach that uses physical punishment, such as spanking by using a hand or an object, when the child shows unacceptable behavior.

Culture — the traditions, values, attitudes, and perceptions of reality that guide behavior for a group of people.

Decay — the process of learned information simply fading away from memory.

Dependent Variable — a variable that reflects the effects of the independent variable on the participants in a study.

Development — the process of orderly change occurring over time to improve a person's overall adjustment to the world.

Dual Coding Hypothesis — during initial learning, concrete words and concepts are encoded both as visual images and verbal labels while abstract concepts are encoded only verbally.

Echoic Storage Register — the first stage of auditory information processing with a maximum storage capacity of 4 seconds before information is either transferred to the short-term memory or lost through interference.

Elaborative Encoding — a characteristic of mature learners; the ability to associate new information with information that has already been learned and stored in long-term memory. Also called elaborative rehearsal.

Elective Biography — characterizes a person's life by periods of formal education during childhood and adolescent years that culminate in gaining employment and pursuing additional education as adults. Periods of employment are sometimes interrupted by periods of unemployment because of economic downturns, and the person reenters the formal education system to acquire new skills and reenters the workforce with a more marketable portfolio.

Encoding — the process of forming mental representations of stimuli that have been perceived through the senses, processed in the working memory, and logically organized.

Episodic Memory — a file system in long-term memory that contains personal experiences and activities.

Experiment — a highly controlled study done in a restricted setting with a researcher manipulating several variables or characteristics of the person or situation to determine their impact.

External Locus of Control — a person's belief that regardless of what he or she does, the person has no control over his or her success or failure.

Extinction — the disappearance of a target behavior when the reinforcement is removed.

Extrinsic Motivator — a reward given to a person by someone else.

Extrinsic Reward — an external reward.

Forgetting — loss of the ability to retrieve information from memory due to interference and/or decay.

Formative Evaluation — an ongoing assessment that enables the teacher to determine how well students are learning and comprehending the material being taught.

Functional Fixedness — the inability of a person to use tools or objects creatively to solve problems.

Gender Bias — an individual's belief that because males and females behave differently and have different strengths and weaknesses, one gender is better than the other.

Gender Role Identity — the set of beliefs a person holds about the specific characteristics associated with either feminine or masculine traits.

General Transfer — a concept, skill, or fact learned in one setting is applied to a new problem in a new setting that is not similar to the original.

Grammar — a system of rules that govern how language is expressed.

Graphic Representation — an illustration of a problem, such as a diagram, a flowchart, a brief outline, or a drawing of various parts of the problem using circles or other pictures.

High Road Transfer — applying learned rules, strategies, or algorithms to new tasks and problems intentionally. This type of transfer shows when students know how the principles operate across different contexts and situations and can determine when the rule is relevant to the new task and how to adapt it, if necessary.

Holophrastic Speech — one-word speech that is usually used to express a demand or indicate something that is wanted.

Iconic Storage Register — the first stage of visual information processing with a maximum storage capacity of 1 second before information is either transferred to the short-term memory or lost through interference.

IDEAL Strategy — a five-step sequence to solving a problem consisting of (1) identifying problems and opportunities, (2) defining goals, (3) exploring possible strategies to approach a problem's solution, (4) anticipating outcomes and taking action, and (5) looking back to learn from the strategy used.

Identity — the perceptions and beliefs a person holds about his or her abilities, values, and priorities that motivate and focus that person's efforts and self-perception as a social being.

Ideology of Assimilation — an approach for cultural assimilation and bilingual education that stresses conformity and often causes students to lose their identity with their first culture, language, and ethnic affiliation.

Inclusion — educating exceptional students in a regular educational setting while providing the appropriate supportive and educational services so the students' probability of success is increased.

Independent Variable — a variable that the researcher manipulates carefully to determine how changes affect people's reactions on another variable that is being measured.

Individualized Educational Program (IEP) — a specific curriculum and instructional plan for both regular education and special education teachers and specialists to provide the most appropriate educational experiences in a legally accountable way to help the child reach full intellectual and educational potential.

Internal Locus of Control — a person's belief that success or failure is the direct result of his or her own efforts and capabilities.

Internal Review Board — a board that ensures that the methods used in a study are reasonable and appropriate and will not cause any kind of psychological or physical distress to participants.

Intrinsic Motivator — a reward that a person develops internally for successful performance.

Invincibility Fallacy — a person's belief that he or she is not vulnerable to the kinds of bad things that happen to other people.

Keyword — a mnemonic memory strategy in which a part of a word is isolated, and a visual image is generated to represent the keyword. This technique is useful when trying to remember the meanings of words or learning foreign words.

Law of Effect — *see* Thorndike, Edward Lee.

Long-Term Memory — a cognitive mechanism that has an unlimited storage capacity and creates a permanent record for information that was processed as being significant or important.

Low-Road Transfer — the process of automatically using a previously learned concrete skill or behavior in a new task that is very similar to the one in which the skill was first learned.

Maintenance Rehearsal (Rote Rehearsal) — a short-term memory device in which the person repeats information out loud or mentally in the exact form in which it was processed.

Maturation — the process of physical and biological change that occurs within a child as a result of the interaction between his or her genetic characteristics and the environment.

Mean — the arithmetic average or midpoint of a distribution.

Means-Ends Analysis — a problem-solving strategy in which the goal is defined, the present situation is clarified, an analysis is done to determine the procedures required to reduce the gap between the goal and the situation, and those procedures are implemented and evaluated.

Median — the score at which half the sample falls above and half the sample falls below.

Metacognition — knowing ways to learn, remember, and apply new information efficiently and effectively.

Method of Loci — a mnemonic device that uses visual images associated with a set of well-known locations to recall large quantities of information.

Mnemonic Device — a memory and recall facilitator that enables a person to form associations between knowledge and information that do not naturally exist.

Mode — the score that occurs with greatest frequency in a distribution.

Morpheme — the smallest meaningful unit of language.

Motivation — a set of desires, impulses, or needs that can give a person direction to behave.

Negative Punishment — involves removing something desirable when a person shows an undesired behavior.

Negative Reinforcement — involves removing something undesireable when a person shows a desired behavior.

Negative Transfer — previously learned information interferes with the ability to learn new material.

Neutral Stimulus — a stimulus that is not associated with a response.

Nonroutine Problem (Poorly Defined Problem) — a problem with an unclear goal, so the strategies to reach the goal may be unclear or difficult to identify.

Norm-Referenced Test — a test in which an individual score is interpreted by comparing it to the performance of others on the same test.

Observational Learning — learning to behave by observing the behaviors of others and the results of those behaviors.

Operant Conditioning — a perspective about learning in which all behaviors are seen to be the result of external reinforcement.

Pavlov, Ivan (1849–1936) — the physiologist who won the Nobel Prize in 1904 and believed that emotional disorders in humans were caused by a disturbed nervous system. Most well known for the classical conditioning model.

Perceived Self-Efficacy — a person's beliefs about what he or she is capable and incapable of doing.

Perception — a cognitive process that involves assigning meaning to newly received information based on the past knowledge and experiences of the individual.

Phonemes — the smallest unit of sound that affects the meaning of spoken words.

Phonemic Awareness — the ability to understand that letters and letter combinations create different sounds in spoken language.

Phonology — the process of putting different sounds or phonemes together in a systematic and meaningful way so the sound units express meaning in the form of language.

Piaget, Jean (1896–1990) — one of the most influential contributors to understanding children's intellectual development.

Positive Punishment — the child is given a negative consequence because of showing inappropriate behavior.

Positive Reinforcement — involves the person receiving something he or she desires for behaving in an acceptable way.

Positive Transfer — previously learned information is used in a new situation to solve a new problem.

Premack Principle — teaching a child to learn by using a preferred activity to strengthen a less preferred behavior.

Primary Reinforcer — a reinforcer that is naturally occurring and related to survival (e.g., food, sex).

Proactive Interference — a process in which previously learned information interferes with a person's ability to retrieve information learned later.

Problem Solving — applying knowledge, skills, and information to achieve a desired goal or outcome.

Procedural Memory — one of the storage files of long-term memory that retains knowledge about how to perform the sequence of steps needed to achieve an action or goal.

Productions — the rules and knowledge stored in long-term memory that deal with how to do things and the steps to take for specific problems.

Public Law 94-142 — a federal statute enacted in 1975 to ensure that every exceptional learner receives an appropriate educational program that meets his or her needs and helps the student reach his or her potential as a learner.

Punishment — an outcome or consequence that reduces the probability of an unwanted behavior occurring again in the future.

Range — the difference between the highest score and the lowest score.

Reciprocal Determinism — a model proposed by Bandura that describes the relationships among how children behave, the environments they live in, and how they see and think about their behaviors and their environments.

Rehearsal — retain information in short-term memory at a conscious level through verbal repetition or elaborative encoding.

Reinforcer — anything that increases the probability of a behavior occurring in the future.

Reliability — a measure of the consistency in the scores achieved on the same test for the same people who take the test on two or more different occasions.

Response Cost System — a behavioral management approach in which something desirable is taken away when the child shows an undesirable behavior.

Response Set — the tendency of people to respond to a problem in the way they are most familiar, even though this strategy may not achieve a correct solution.

Retroactive Interference — a process in which newly acquired information interferes with a person's ability to retrieve information that was learned earlier.

Routine Problem (well-defined problem) — a problem with a clear goal so that the possible strategies to reach the goal are either known or easily developed.

Schema (schemata) — stores of information in the mind that describe how a person interprets the world.

Self-Actualization — the desire to become everything that one is capable of becoming.

Self-Efficacy — a person's beliefs about personal competence and skill in a particular situation or area.

Semantic Memory — a file system in long-term memory that involves retention of factual knowledge and information and has little relation to personal experiences.

Sensory Register — a temporary, large-capacity storage mechanism that holds information as it is directly obtained from the outside world through the various senses. Information at this stage of processing is "raw," in that no meaning has been assigned to it and much of it is beyond the person's awareness.

Simple Moral Education Program — a program that usually occurs in a classroom setting and discusses topics such as abstinence-based sex education, abortion, extramarital affairs, cheating, and dishonesty.

Skinner, Burrhus Frederic (1904-1990) — an influential American psychologist who developed a perspective about learning based on reinforcement from the environment.

Socioeconomic Status (SES) — an important variable in performance, reflecting a combination of how much money the student's parents earn annually, their level of education, and the jobs in which they are employed.

Specific Transfer — applying a fact learned in one setting to another setting that is almost identical to solve a new problem.

Standard Biography — a person's biography that at one time in the United States consisted of going to school during childhood and adolescence to learn, become educated, followed by completion of an educational program and entrance into the world of work, and culminating with retirement.

Summative Evaluation — assessment to determine a student's overall level of achievement so a grade can be assigned to reflect level of competence and knowledge.

Syntax — the grammatical structure within a sentence.

Thorndike, Edward Lee (1874–1949) — the first American researcher to develop a theory of human learning based on experimentation. He proposed the law of effect, which predicts that if behavior is followed by a satisfying change in the environment, the probability of that behavior being repeated in similar situations in the future is very high.

Time-Out — a type of negative punishment that requires removing the student from the classroom because the teacher believes that attention from other students is reinforcing the undesirable behavior.

Token Economy (Token Reinforcement Program) — a behavior management approach in which the student earns tokens for acceptable academic performance and/or social behavior. These tokens can be accumulated and exchanged for a reward(s).

Two-Store Model — an information-processing model that describes how information is held in human memory, the various cognitive processes and actions involved in transforming information from the world into a meaningful language system, and how information is transferred from one component to the other. It consists of the sensory register, working (short-term) memory, and the long-term memory.

Unconditioned Response (UCR or UR) — a naturally occurring and uncontrollable response to a stimulus.

Unconditioned Stimulus (UCS or US) — a stimulus that automatically produces a response without the response having to be learned by the organism.

Validity — is a measure of the relationship between test performance and the actual behavior, trait, or construct that the test claims to measure.

Well-Formed Schemata — mental representations that provide the person with clear, useful expectations about and comprehension of situations.

Working Backward Strategy — a problem-solving approach in which a person begins with the goal and works backward to reach the unsolved initial question.

Working Memory (Short-Term Memory) — a limited-capacity cognitive mechanism that can hold about 7 bits of information at a conscious level.

Zero Transfer — skills learned in one setting have no impact on learning new skills in a new setting.

Zone of Proximal Development (zone of potential development) — an element of Lev Vygotsky's socio-cultural theory of cognitive development that represents the difference between the child's abilities a child actually develops and those the child might acquire if living in the appropriate setting.

Selected Online Resources

ADHD

    www.chadd.org

    www.help4adhd.org

    www.ed.gov/teachers/needs/speced/adhd/adhd-resource-pt1.pdf

Asperger's Disorder

    www.udel.edu/bkirby/asperger/aswhatisit.html

Death of a Parent

    www.msue.msu.edu/msue/iac/disasterresp/FamilyIssues/E-1944.pdf

Divorce

    www.divorcereform.org/edu.html

Individualized Educational Plan

    Components: www.ldonline.org/ld_indepth/iep/what_is_iep.html

    Hearing/Mediation: www.ldonline.org/ld_indepth/iep/communication.pdf

    Sample Plan: www.ldonline.org/ld_indepth/iep/success_ieps.html

Learning Disabilities

    Mathematics:

    www.ldinfo.com/dyscalculia.html

    www.ncld.org/LDInfoZone/InfoZone/InfoZoneFact Sheet_Dyscalculia.cfm

Retention in School

    www.ldonline.org/ld_indepth/legal_legislative/retention-in_early_grades.html

    www.ldonline.org/ld_indepth/legal_legislativ/nceo_synthesis_report34.html

    www.nasponline.org/publications/cq315retentionrates.html

    www.nasponline.org/publications/cq28retain.html

INDEX

S